Re-Imagining Supply Chain Management

Supply chain management is a substantially complex area for many businesses due to its diverse set of actions, agents, decisions, risks, and uncertainties. Consequently, supply chains often break up in disarray due to their structural complexity coupled with risks and uncertainties in the absence of clear objectives. Işık Biçer addresses these issues by uncovering the fundamental trade-offs of supply chain management, their economic causes, and strategic implications. He offers a novel framework of supply chain management based on its role in economic systems. The framework shows four effective supply chain strategies according to business models and organizational sensitivity to operational trade-offs. Furthermore, it offers a detailed account of the digital transformation of supply chains, elaborating on crucial aspects of the design and implementation of digitalization. This is an indispensable source for supply chain professionals, consultants, economists, and policymakers with a keen interest in supply chain management.

IŞIK BIÇER is an Associate Professor of Operations Management and Information Systems in the Schulich School of Business at York University in Toronto, Canada. He is also area director of the PhD program and director of an executive certificate program in supply chain management. He teaches graduate-level courses on digital transformation, predictive modeling, and prescriptive analytics in the Tech MBA, MBAN, and MMAI programs at Schulich School of Business, as well as conducting research on uncertainty modeling and convolutional optimization techniques and their applications to supply chains. Işık has worked on several digital transformation projects with various firms, some of which feature in this book. The author of fifteen top research papers, his work has appeared in *Harvard Business Review*, *Journal of Operations Management*, and *Production and Operations Management*. He has also published a graduate-level textbook, *Supply Chain Analytics: Uncertainty Modeling Approach* (2023).

Re-Imagining Supply Chain Management

Uncovering the Hidden Trade-offs in the Digital Age

IŞIK BIÇER
York University, Toronto

Shaftesbury Road, Cambridge CB2 8EA, United Kingdom

One Liberty Plaza, 20th Floor, New York, NY 10006, USA

477 Williamstown Road, Port Melbourne, VIC 3207, Australia

314–321, 3rd Floor, Plot 3, Splendor Forum, Jasola District Centre, New Delhi – 110025, India

103 Penang Road, #05–06/07, Visioncrest Commercial, Singapore 238467

Cambridge University Press is part of Cambridge University Press & Assessment, a department of the University of Cambridge.

We share the University's mission to contribute to society through the pursuit of education, learning and research at the highest international levels of excellence.

www.cambridge.org
Information on this title: www.cambridge.org/9781009619189

DOI: 10.1017/9781009619134

© Işık Biçer 2025

This publication is in copyright. Subject to statutory exception and to the provisions of relevant collective licensing agreements, no reproduction of any part may take place without the written permission of Cambridge University Press & Assessment.

When citing this work, please include a reference to the DOI 10.1017/9781009619134

First published 2025

A catalogue record for this publication is available from the British Library

A Cataloging-in-Publication data record for this book is available from the Library of Congress

ISBN 978-1-009-61918-9 Hardback
ISBN 978-1-009-61916-5 Paperback

Cambridge University Press & Assessment has no responsibility for the persistence or accuracy of URLs for external or third-party internet websites referred to in this publication and does not guarantee that any content on such websites is, or will remain, accurate or appropriate.

For EU product safety concerns, contact us at Calle de José Abascal, 56, 1°, 28003 Madrid, Spain, or email eugpsr@cambridge.org

Contents

List of Figures	*page* viii
Preface	ix
Acknowledgements	xii

I	**Anatomy of Supply Chain Management**	1
1	Economics of Supply Chain Management	3
	1.1 Emergence of Supply Chain Economics	6
	1.1.1 Economies of Scale	9
	1.1.2 Mere Factor of Production?	11
	1.2 Implications of Economic Perspectives for Supply Chain Management	12
	1.2.1 Investment Analysis	13
	1.2.2 Network Externalities	15
	1.2.3 Monetary Policy	17
	1.2.4 Market Analysis	19
	1.3 The Switzerland Example	21
	1.4 Conclusion	23
2	Trade-off Structure of Supply Chain Management	26
	2.1 Trade-offs in Supply Chain Management	27
	2.2 Building Interfaces in Supply Chain Management	32
	2.3 Supply Chain Integration	36
	2.4 Innovative Business Development	40
	2.5 The Premium Business	42
	2.6 Lean Systems	43
	2.7 The Walmart Canada Example	45
	2.8 Conclusion	48
3	Supply Chain Risks and Uncertainties	51
	3.1 Conceptual Sources of Risks and Uncertainties	53
	3.1.1 Operational Risk	55
	3.1.2 Epistemological Uncertainty	56
	3.1.3 Ontological Uncertainty	59

3.2	Practical Sources of Risks and Uncertainties	60
3.3	Operational Risks and Uncertainties in the Service Industry	67
3.4	The Amazon Example	70
3.5	Conclusion	72

II Four Strategies of Supply Chain Management — 75

4 Leading the Operational Edge: Supply Chain Integration — 77
- 4.1 Operational Complexities — 81
  - 4.1.1 Product Variety — 81
  - 4.1.2 Sales Channels and Logistics Networks — 85
- 4.2 Strategies to Integrate Supply Chains — 87
  - 4.2.1 Capacity Management — 87
  - 4.2.2 Lead-Time Reduction — 90
  - 4.2.3 Delayed Differentiation — 93
  - 4.2.4 Operational Excellence — 95
- 4.3 The GlaxoSmithKline (GSK) Vaccines Example — 97
- 4.4 Conclusion — 98

5 Innovative Business Development: Supply Chain Finance — 100
- 5.1 Cash Sources — 102
- 5.2 Supply Chain Finance — 105
  - 5.2.1 Inventory Financing — 106
  - 5.2.2 Reverse Factoring — 108
  - 5.2.3 Securing Payment from Buyers — 110
  - 5.2.4 Other Strategies to Finance Supply Chains — 112
- 5.3 The Starbucks Example — 115
- 5.4 Conclusion — 118

6 The Premium Business: Market-Driven Supply Chain Management — 120
- 6.1 Demand Management — 124
- 6.2 Supply Chain Transparency and Blockchain — 128
- 6.3 Circular Operations Management — 131
- 6.4 Long-Tail Operations Management — 134
- 6.5 The Hugo Boss Example — 137
- 6.6 Conclusion — 140

7 Economic Theory's Sweet Spot: Lean Systems — 142
- 7.1 Designing Lean Systems — 147
- 7.2 Operating Lean Systems — 151
- 7.3 Challenges of Lean Systems — 157
- 7.4 The New York Food Bank Example — 158
- 7.5 Conclusion — 159

III	**Digitizing the Supply Chain**	**163**
8	Design of Digital Transformation	165
	8.1 Operational Due Diligence	165
	8.2 Data Management Strategy	167
	8.2.1 Data Types	168
	8.2.2 Database Architecture	169
	8.2.3 Data Usage	171
	8.3 Understanding Analytical Applications	172
	8.3.1 Descriptive Analytics	174
	8.3.2 Predictive Analytics	177
	8.3.3 Decision (Prescriptive) Analytics	181
	8.4 Boosting the Potential of Digital Solutions	188
	8.5 The Kordsa Example	191
	8.6 Conclusion	193
9	Integrating End-to-End Digital Transformation	194
	9.1 Sales and Operations Planning (S&OP)	195
	9.2 Sales and Operations Execution (S&OE)	197
	9.2.1 Demand Forecasting	198
	9.2.2 Supply Management	200
	9.2.3 Inventory Management	201
	9.2.4 Order Management	204
	9.2.5 Sales and Fulfillment Management	207
	9.3 The Slimstock Example	210
	9.4 Conclusion	212
10	Closing Remarks	214
	10.1 Strategic Implications	216
	10.2 Interactions with Tax Policies	219
	10.3 Corporate Social Responsibility	221
	10.4 Implications for Investment Analysis	224
Glossary		228
References		231
Index		252

Figures

1.1 Economic perspectives of supply chain management and their implications	page 5
1.2 Canada's inflation rate and inventory change (year-over-year) in the manufacturing industry from 2019 to 2023	19
2.1 Five trade-offs of supply chain management	28
2.2 Supply chain strategies based on the mismatch sensitivity and business model	36
3.1 Operational risks and uncertainties	55
3.2 Risk analysis framework in supply chains	62
3.3 Risk analysis framework in the service industry	69
4.1 Scheme of supply chain integration	80
5.1 Objectives and strategies of innovative business development	102
5.2 Dynamic discounting scheme	114
6.1 Challenges and strategies of luxury supply chain management	123
7.1 Establishing lean manufacturing	146
8.1 Data usage in digital systems	171
8.2 Output analysis of analytics and artificial intelligence	173
8.3 Principal component analysis (PCA) and its transformation	175
9.1 Key elements of end-to-end digital transformation	195

Preface

"There is nothing permanent except change." – *Heraclitus*

If Heraclitus were a supply chain thinker in the 2000s, he would have amended his famous quote to state: "Nothing is permanent like the never-changing professional view of supply chain management."

We have experienced massive technological innovations reshaping our lives since 2000. Widespread search engine use (e.g., Google) has reduced search costs for information on the Web. Growth in e-commerce (e.g., Amazon) has altered the purchasing behavior of customers from brick-and-mortar shopping to ordering online. Online purveyors of video streams and shares (e.g., YouTube) have unleashed influencer channel launches on the Internet, cutting our appetite for cable and satellite broadcasts. On-demand video platforms (e.g., Netflix) have upended the Hollywood movie production industry. Ride-hailing platforms (e.g., Uber and Lyft) have shifted the working dynamics of the taxi industry, matching customers with proximate ride-hail drivers. This, in turn, has slashed fares and lured many customers to ride-hailing platforms from cabs. Freelance markets (e.g., Upwork) now access independent talent worldwide to do certain jobs, making recruitment agencies redundant for many professions. Finally, large language models (LLMs, e.g., ChatGPT) have exerted massive impact on businesses and individuals. One year after its launch, ChatGPT started to serve 100 million weekly users and two million developers exploiting tools using artificial intelligence (AI) technology (Porter, 2023).

In markets affected by these technological advances, products and transactions are now vastly different from a few decades ago. For instance, consumers can now order goods tailored to their specific preferences and made by 3D printers. Retailers also tap the omnichannel matrix to fulfill customer demand in alternate ways. Such conveniences were impossible in past markets.

Despite these changes, supply chain management has suffered entrenchment. It has long been cast as the practice of having the right product, at the right time, in the right place to fulfill customer demand without excess inventory. This perception envisions *perfectly matching supply with demand* as the ultimate objective of supply chain management. If supply exceeds demand, firms bear the cost of excess inventory, storage, and handling costs, plus inventory write-downs. When supply falls short of demand, businesses lose product sales in the market. Matching supply with demand perfectly helps abate these costs. One common framework promising effective strategies to match supply with demand (per product and market characteristics) was forged by Fisher (1997). His work still molds supply chain strategies – cited over 1,000 times according to Google Scholar in just the past five years (from 2019 until yearend 2023).

While perception of the role of supply chain management in organizations has stagnated, today's supply chains are vastly different. Perfect match of supply and demand *no longer serves* as constant top priority for supply chain professionals. For instance, "firing customers" is now a popular concept in marketing that makes select demand streams disappear, erasing the need to supply products for them. Likewise, some companies innovate their business models to generate non-operational profits, making supply–demand matching less important. Technological advances have shifted supply chain priorities, thus straying from typical operational objectives. This book re-imagines supply chain management to better align it with business objectives and technological advances.

This book has three parts. Part I introduces the economics of supply chain management (Chapter 1), its trade-off structure (Chapter 2), and supply chain risks and uncertainties (Chapter 3). Part II focuses on four distinct supply chain strategies based on its hallmark trade-off structure: supply chain integration (Chapter 4), its finance (Chapter 5), the premium business (Chapter 6), and lean systems (Chapter 7). Part III features the digital transformation of supply chain management discussing its design (Chapter 8) and implementation (Chapter 9) processes. Finally, we present closing remarks in Chapter 10.

This book aims to spark critical views about how to reposition and transform supply chain management in today's world. To this end, we begin with the economics of supply chain management, as it is exceedingly difficult to understand and improve supply chains without knowing its evolution in economics. Initial economic ideas of capitalism, dating back to Adam Smith in 1776, deemed supply chain management as *part of markets* where the pricing mechanism in efficient markets coordinates product flows. Since markets have proven inefficient in practice, subsequent economic thought began isolating supply chain management from markets – a view still shaping supply chain practices and leading to economists' perception of supply chain management as a *factor of production*. When goods are made available in the market efficiently for customer purchase, the way supply chains are managed becomes unimportant for economists. Indeed, economists often suggest that improvements to supply chains must focus on lowering operational, logistical, and supply–demand-mismatch costs.

Yet supply chain management is not a mere factor of production. We cannot simply detach markets from supply chains. The way supply chain activities are enacted exerts a strong impact on market demand. For example, online retailers improve their supply chain management by cutting delivery lead times, which then boosts market demand. The prompt delivery of online orders also justifies premium pricing paid by customers. Therefore, supply chain management directly influences market demand and prices, elevating from its perceived role as a factor of production. Meanwhile, supply chain management has not fully escaped its being a factor of production as cast by Adam Smith because markets are not efficient enough for such liberation. Indeed, supply chain management straddles both markets and factors of production, being overly sensitive to business models and operational trade-offs.

This brings us to the trade-off structure of supply chain management. Under this anatomy, we identify four distinct supply chain strategies. Each has unique traits and different priorities within the broad scope of supply chain activities. Supply chain executives must have a clear understanding of these strategies. Otherwise, any attempt to transform supply chains physically or digitally may fail or underperform aimed benefits of transformation projects. In this book, we fill this gap to help decision-makers achieve supply chain excellence. We hope that the methods and insights discussed in this book will help decision-makers improve their knowledge and leadership skills in supply chain endeavors and practice.

Acknowledgements

First, I would like to thank my institution (Schulich, School of Business, York University), my doctoral and post-doctoral supervisors (Suzanne de Treville and Ralf Seifert), colleagues, research partners, and Cambridge University Press editor Valerie Appleby for inspiring me to write this book. This book would not have been possible without their support. I have greatly benefited from my collaborations and research discussions with (*alphabetically* sorted) Taner Bilgic, Vibhuti Dhingra, Adam Diamant, Ioannis Fragkos, Mustafa Hekimoglu, Raha Imanirad, David Johnston, Yara Kayyali-Elalem, Merve Kirci, Murat Kristal, Dhrun Lauwers, Feng Lin, Junyu Liu, Dimitrios Logothetis, Florian Lucker, Divinus Oppong-Tawiah, Morteza Pourakbar, Lauri Saarinen, Philipp Schneider, Ata Senkon, and Murat Tarakci. I hope to continue to work closely with them on future research projects. I am also extremely grateful to Huseyin Ates, Danny Bloem, Leonardo Meira, Sean Militello, Onur Gur, Carolina Pimentel, and Jose Urdaneta for sharing their precious industry experience with me. Finally, I would like to thank Paula Gowdie Rose for her administrative support and Brad Miller for copy-editing. I appreciate very much their efforts and acknowledge that all errors and omissions are naturally my responsibility.

Anatomy of Supply Chain Management

1 Economics of Supply Chain Management

In an economic system, manufacturers procure raw materials from suppliers and transform them into finished goods. Next, the finished goods are traded in markets to fulfill various consumer needs. Supply chain management is at the center of both production and fulfillment activities. Therefore, it is often considered the backbone of global economy and economic growth (Bhatia et al., 2013). Companies that excel in supply chain management can enhance revenues while reducing costs. Thus, they achieve a competitive edge and sustainable profits even during turbulent times.

For example, electronics giant Samsung has a well-connected, resilient supply chain network including strategic production locations close to their suppliers (Wong, 2023). Unlike its competitors, Samsung increased profits in 2020 owing to its excellent supply chain practice despite the COVID pandemic (Byford, 2021). Shipping company FedEx also has a long-standing reputation for supply chain excellence such that the delivery giant manages a complex supply chain network to deliver both personal and business parcels (e.g., online orders for many ecommerce retailers). FedEx's supply chain performance helped improve its financials in 2024 despite the deteriorating market for parcel deliveries (Fung, 2023; Fung, 2024). Excellence in supply chain management helps companies like Samsung and FedEx fulfill market demand efficiently, which in turn helps cut both production and logistics costs.

Supply chain excellence is important not only for manufacturers, retailers or logistics companies but also for most service companies (e.g., airlines, hotels, and restaurants). Service companies transform select resources into a service. Acquisition and conversion of resources into a service may enlist several supply chain activities. Thus, excellence in supply chain management helps increase profits while reducing the waste of resources. Fast-food chain Wendy's, for instance, partnered with big-data platform provider Palantir Technologies to connect a large network of suppliers, distributors, and restaurants, which helped improve Wendy's profits while eliminating food waste (Stroh, 2024).

At the macro level, a nation with robust infrastructure and strong supply chain networks can facilitate supply chain flows, improving its overall productivity. Nations also benefit from supply chain excellence by reducing waste of Earth's limited resources. When most companies wield supply chain excellence in an economic system, limited resources are utilized efficiently, creating more wealth for individuals while lowering the carbon footprint of operational activities. For example, Switzerland's many corporations that excel in supply chain management also enjoy the support of healthy economic policies and robust infrastructure. As a result, this country preserves natural resources at the highest quality and offers a wealthy life to its citizens (the Switzerland case is discussed later in this chapter). This poses an important question: How can organizations achieve supply chain excellence?

Excellence in supply chain management is highly challenging, with no one simple formula or method. One prerequisite is having a strong understanding of the *economics* of supply chain management. In this chapter, we will survey economic perspectives and relate them to supply chains as shown in Figure 1.1. We will focus on two economic views for understanding the dynamics of supply chains – namely, Ronald Coase and Adam Smith. Supply chain management has been heavily influenced by Coase's approach, leading to the perception of being a factor of production. Because supply chain management straddles production and markets in practice, this singular view causes some serious problems: (1) misguided investments, (2) network externalities, (3) myopic monetary policies, and (4) incomplete market analysis. This chapter examines all these problems in detail.

Economists study market dynamics to secure price stability, income equality, and sustainable growth of societies. Several branches of economics now scrutinize how our society is shaped by the dynamics of economic systems. For example, central banks peg the interest rate and transact securities in efforts to manage inflation and price stability. Microeconomics looks at how firms use resources to create value for society via their constructed networks that shape the structure of supply chains. Surely, economists working as experts in central banks, government organizations (e.g., Department of Commerce), international agencies (e.g., the World Trade Organization), for-profit companies, and

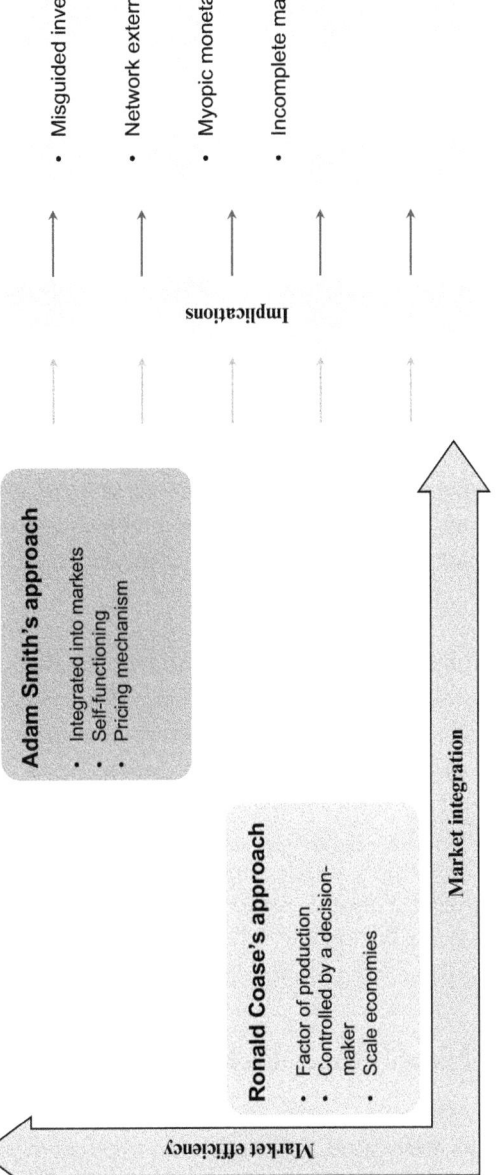

Figure 1.1 Economic perspectives of supply chain management and their implications

nonprofit organizations exert strong influence, either positively or negatively, in our lives.

The development of liberal economic models dates back to the eighteenth century. Adam Smith then positioned economics as the "science of wealth" (Aspromourgos, 2008). Smith asserted that wealth is created by *division of labor and free markets*. Division of labor prods individuals to specialize in specific tasks. This type of specialization helps people improve productivity by focusing on certain skills. Individuals then exchange goods and services in free markets. An economic system thrives when markets function efficiently with talented people being employed to do certain tasks that are aligned with their expertise.

Creating sustainable economic wealth is in some way analogous to winning the UEFA Champions League trophy. A football team is composed of eleven players, each specializing in distinct aspects of the game. Expectations from a goalkeeper and a striker are very much different, promoting division of labor in a team. Having all top players for each area is not enough to win a game. The players must also control the ball and move it efficiently between different zones of the pitch, resembling free markets in an economic system. Despite all efforts, the best team in the tournament may still lose a game due to *external factors*, such as rivals, weather, and spectators. Eventually, they can still win the trophy after losing a game.

In economic systems, there are also such factors as supply and demand having an impact on the welfare of individuals. When product supply falls short of demand, for example, price bids upward. In free markets, such a price increase only causes short-term inconvenience, like the football team losing a game but winning the trophy in the end. Rising prices encourage other suppliers to make the product, hence increasing the supply. The rise in supply lowers the price, pushing it to equilibrium value. The supply and demand levels at equilibrium pricing determine the long-term economic activities in the system. The flow of goods and services is always improved by an efficient pricing mechanism in free markets, promoting economic welfare.

1.1 Emergence of Supply Chain Economics

When markets are efficient as envisioned by Adam Smith, the price of a product reflects its true value, and people trade goods without any friction. Here, supply chain management is considered *a part of markets* because flows of goods are controlled by the pricing mechanism of markets. In other words, there is no need for decision-makers to manage the supply chain, since its management would simply comprise smoothly performing, self-functioning tasks.

For example, Uber Eats owes its success to integrating supply chain management into markets. In the past, restaurants had been offering home delivery services by using their own resources. When they received orders, their employees were tasked to deliver them to customers' homes. Restaurant managers had to manage those logistics activities. Now, restaurants opt out of managing home delivery (except pizzerias) and employing any fleet for that. Instead, the platform coordinates those activities by collecting orders from platform users and inducing platform drivers to do deliveries through an effective pricing mechanism.[1]

Unfortunately, platforms at Uber's scale and efficiency are scarce, and markets are often inefficient in practice. This causes (1) *search* and (2) *contracting costs* (Coase, 1937). First, people incur search costs to discover fair prices of products in markets. Second, contracting costs accrue for transactions because trade must be organized according to a contract. In a trading relationship without any contract, each party may behave opportunistically and harm the other. To avoid such mischief, parties enact a contract listing responsibilities and rights. Therefore, individuals incur search and contracting costs to trade a good or service, which is referred to as "the cost of market inefficiencies."

The cost of market inefficiencies can be eliminated when certain supply chain activities are controlled by a central decision-maker. When the cost of controlling the activity matrix is less than the cost of market inefficiencies, a firm arises to manage activities in-house. For example, an individual may need to buy a specific service from another person *repeatedly* to produce a good. Contracts written *per service* will create inefficiency for the individual. When a firm is established and the person providing the service is hired as an employee, high contracting costs can be eliminated. Here, a decision-maker in the firm becomes

---

[1] Uber's pricing strategy resembles the pricing mechanism in an efficient market. It is known as surge pricing, where prices change immediately depending on the demand. Uber does not force drivers to make deliveries. They just offer higher rates when there is more demand. This pricing strategy coordinates the supply chain. Visit the following for more information about Uber's surge pricing policy: https://uber.com/ca/en/drive/driver-app/how-surge-works/.

responsible for controlling the activities of the employee. However, managing activities in-house may become costlier than dealing with market inefficiencies depending on the complexity of activities, firm size, and alternative solutions offered in the market. Therefore, any advantage of carrying out activities in-house may vanish in future depending on these factors.

The cost of market inefficiencies affects the scope of supply chain activities, which in turn determines a firm's size. Ronald Coase asserted in his seminal work that firms grow under three circumstances (Coase, 1937). *First*, the cost of controlling new activities in-house should not exceed the cost of market inefficiencies. Here, decision-makers may face more challenges in managing complex activities in-house as their firms grow. It is rational to stop growing a firm when the cost of controlling new activities exceeds the cost of market inefficiencies.

For example, pizzerias (e.g., Domino's and Pizza Hut) often have their own fleet for home delivery because they can keep the cost of home delivery lower than the charges paid to the platforms such as Uber Eats.[2] Nevertheless, the platforms offer immense potential for reaching new customers. Therefore, it would be more appealing for pizza chains to use the platforms for increasing sales while managing delivery service in-house. Domino's Canada started to follow this strategy in 2024 by forming a partnership with Uber Eats such that customers can place their orders via the app, but deliveries are done by Domino's employees as usual (Harrison, 2024).

Second, decision-making *quality* must be preserved when controlling more activities. Decision-makers carry out multiple duties as their companies grow. Therefore, the quality of their decisions would erode because human attention is limited, and decision quality is affected by the level of workload. The growth of firms must be limited to where the quality of the decision-making process is preserved. *Finally*, the growth of firms must offer the benefits of scale economies. Producing goods in large volume allows companies to better utilize resources, thereby reducing production costs. This phenomenon is referred to as

---

[2] Although Uber Eats cut search and contracting costs, leading to an improvement in market efficiency, they charge disproportionately high fees. In efficient markets, however, prices must reflect the true value of products and services. There is a direct conflict between high platform fees and efficient pricing mechanism, which causes the cost of market inefficiencies (Rana & Haddon, 2023).

1: Economics of Supply Chain Management

"economies of scale," which helps manufacturers reduce costs while expanding their businesses.

The economic tenets of Coase are still at work in structuring supply chain networks toward two important outcomes, the first being economies of scale tending to spawn centralized supply chain networks. The second is viewing supply chain management as a factor of production, thus placing cost efficiency at the center of supply chain strategies.

1.1.1 Economies of Scale

Manufacturers must make fixed investments to secure the resources necessary to carry out production activities. They must build plants, buy machines and trucks, construct offices, and so on. Regardless of firm size, such investments must be made to start production. Next, manufacturers operate those resources to produce some goods for sale in markets. They must pay salaries, utility bills, and other operating expenses. Unlike investment costs, operating expenses increase linearly with firm size and the production level. When mass production is enacted in mega plants, the proportion of fixed investment costs to operating expenses shrinks, which helps boost return on investment. Such a strategy also makes it possible to repeat specific activities over time. This helps workers learn how to use resources (e.g., machines and trucks) in ways that maximize efficiency. Therefore, carrying out production in mega factories also helps manufacturers increase efficiency.

In short, economies of scale may benefit organizations in two ways: (1) increased return on investment, and (2) increased efficiency. Hence, it helps lower per-unit product costs. The cost advantage from economies of scale, for instance, shaped the automotive industry in the prior century. In 1913, Ford started the mass production of automobiles in the Highland Park assembly plant to reduce market price via economies of scale. Henry Ford designed and built his assembly lines to improve efficiency (Ford Motor Company, n.d.). At that time, other automakers enlisted skilled craftsmen who did all the assembling and molding of cars at one station. Ford's assembly line used conveyor belts to move automobiles to workers where each handled a *single* task. Instead of one craftsman building the entire car, Ford assigned only one task to each worker who acted in repetition. Although a single-task assignment had a negative impact on the motivation of employees, assembly lines did help Ford boost output. Thus, the price for a Ford Model T fell to $260 in 1925 from $825 in 1908. This price drop led to a surge in demand for Ford cars. Next, Henry Ford attempted to control sourcing activities and shrink the cost of raw materials by acquiring his vendors (Gelderman, n.d.). Highland Park facilities later moved to a newly built River Rouge site. Ford further acquired railways, coal mines, timberland, and so on. Such control of various activities along different segments of the supply chain proved to be a viable strategy given the surge in demand for Ford cars and well-known benefits of economies of scale. Henry Ford successfully implemented this strategy and built his conglomerate.

More than a century after Ford pioneered mass production, manufacturers still explore the opportunities from economies of scale in their supply chains. However, supply chains are now much more complex than in 1920. Therefore, the projected costs and benefits calculated before production-related investments may not materialize, often forcing producers to reverse investment decisions or change plant locations over time. For instance, production activities in many industries had been outsourced to China between 1980 and 2010 to exploit economies of scale coupled with low production costs. When both the labor and real-estate costs in China reached the level of Western economies, many firms relocated production from China to the United States, India, and Mexico. As a result, field investments in manufacturing have increased in the United States from $41 billion in 2010 up to $108 billion in 2022 (Keilman, 2023). Even Apple, which heavily relies on Chinese production, opted to move some of its production of iPhones from China to India in 2023 (Roy et al., 2023).

Economies of scale tend to favor centralized supply chain networks. Here, production activities of a manufacturer are carried out in a single or a limited number of mega facilities to serve markets dispersed worldwide. Despite the decrease in production costs, centralized networks incur high logistics costs, elevated inventory in transit, extended shipping times, and massive vessel traffic in main ports. Such negative consequences of scale economies may exceed any benefits, potentially rendering this strategy counterproductive in the design of supply chains. Thus, this strategy can no longer be affordable because rapidly changing market dynamics are making centralized production infeasible in the long term.

1.1.2 Mere Factor of Production?

The term "factor of production" is used in economics to describe inputs needed to make products available in the market. There are four main factors of production: (1) capital, (2) land, (3) labor, and (4) organization. Entrepreneurs make *capital* investments to build factories that transform select natural resources extracted from *land* to products with the effort of *workers*. Then, decision-makers *organize* supply chain activities to make products available in the market for consumption. Here, supply chain management is cast as organizational effort, thus deemed a factor of production.

Factors of production describe four important input types isolated from markets and *not* included in influential economic models. Although supply chain management involves complex activities in practice, it finds simplistic treatment in economics. Indeed, economists see supply chain management as a set of activities confined within the boundaries of firms where central decision-makers organize those activities in-house. Inter-firm supply chain transactions are ignored by economists. This view conflicts with real-world supply chain practices. For example, supply chain management involves coordinating flows of goods, information, and capital among supply chain (both internal and external) parties. There are many actors in supply chains who do specific tasks, and companies put much effort synchronizing all actors. Cisco, a US-based electronics company, has been investing heavily to integrate supply chain activities that *take place in other companies* (Cisco Systems, 2014), suppliers and contact manufacturers that merit discussion later in this book.

There are more examples of firms that invest in the integration of inter-firm supply chains. Economists, however, ignore such integration efforts, since they believe that the inter-firm transactions occur naturally in markets by virtue of the pricing mechanism. As Coase said in his seminal work (Coase, 1937): "The integrating force ... already exists in the form of price mechanism. It is perhaps the main achievement of economic science that it has shown there is no reason to suppose that specialization must lead to chaos."

This economic ideology says that supply chain management *must* focus on micro activities executed *within* organizational boundaries because the flow of goods to outside entities is assumed to occur efficiently without any control by decision-makers. Such a view contradicts current supply chain practices. Both practitioners and scholars of supply chain management work on the development of systems and methods for *integrating* supply chains among *different* firms.

Another important aspect related to this economic ideology is that decision-makers are encouraged to fixate on the *cost efficiency* of supply chains. After all, supply chain costs must be kept below the cost of market inefficiencies to grow the firm. While salient for supply chains, cost efficiency is not always the top priority. Supply chain professionals often prioritize the *resilience* and *responsiveness* of supply chains over cost efficiency.

1.2 Implications of Economic Perspectives for Supply Chain Management

Supply chain executives ought to revise their economic perspectives to better design and operate supply chains effectively in our current economic systems. Such a revision of economic ideology is not easy, yet possible. For example, information technology attained revised thinking that embraced Internet technologies during the last three decades. Google's launch in 1998 by Larry Page and Sergei Brin awed investors with its technological innovation. Google's search engine successfully listed the most relevant web pages, impossible by other search engines such as Yahoo or Excite. Yet it was not then clear to investors how this would generate revenues (Carlson, 2009).

As the founders mused different revenue models (e.g., charging user fee for site services), a famous economist from the University of California-Berkeley, Hal Varian, coauthored a book with Carl Shapiro on information economics. The book perfectly conceptualized information as a product wielding trade value in the market (Shapiro & Varian, 1999). Varian later became the chief economist at Google. With this revised economic thinking, tech firms developed effective business models. Now, we use a variety of Google's products without cost! In other words, Google pays us (not cash, but free access to its services) to collect data useful in its Ads program. Without Varian's economic thinking, it might not have been possible for untold millions of people to benefit from such services.

This case shows how important economists are to society, where even re-imagination of economic systems could change our lives significantly. Unfortunately, the extensive understanding of supply chain economics suffers from two shortcomings. First, the negative aspects of economies of scale are not well known, with implications for *investment analysis* and *network externalities*. Second, supply chain management is not merely a factor of production as it exerts powerful influence in shaping markets. This second shortcoming impacts both *monetary policy* efforts in stabilizing prices and *market analysis*.

1.2.1 Investment Analysis

Some companies invest heavily to forge their supply chains. For example, Henry Ford bought railroads and mines to build his network igniting the mass production of Ford autos. Tesla spent $5.5 billion to build its Berlin giga factory in 2022 (Sozzi, 2022). While companies like Tesla and Ford invest in building production *and* supply chain networks, others hesitate to make supply chain investments. For example, Apple does not own facilities that produce iPhones. Instead, it partners with the Taiwanese contract manufacturer Foxconn. In 2022, Apple sold 232 million iPhones mostly assembled in Foxconn facilities (Perrigo, 2023). Apple's decision of not investing in production facilities would be unrelated to high *fixed* investment costs given its status as one of the most valuable companies in the world. Indeed, the company does not need to make such an investment in supply chains.

Strategic decisions as to a company owning its production sites versus outsourcing it to a contract manufacturer require a detailed investment analysis. Two cost elements play a vital role in these investment decisions. The first is total product cost covering raw material, production, warehousing, and shipping costs that accrue until the product reaches the customer. Economies of scale help reduce this first cost element. The second is the *hidden cost of mismatches* between supply and demand – that is, cost of product shortages when demand exceeds supply, or cost of excess inventory when demand falls short of demand. To reduce this hidden cost, firms often improve the responsiveness of their supply chains. They integrate supply chain operations (from procurement of raw materials to fulfillment of customer orders), which in turn helps them react quickly to sudden fluctuations in customer demand. When demand plummets unexpectedly, integrated supply chains reduce the supply and avoid excess inventory. When demand escalates, integrated supply chains ramp up the supply to meet demand. In the end, integrated supply chains ought to successfully reduce the mismatch costs. However, supply chain integration often leads to decentralized supply chains, conflicting with economies of scale. Thus, operational expenses run high for integrated supply chains, leading to higher total product costs.

Suppose a manufacturer procures goods from an offshore production facility where operations and labor would be cheaper than at home. However, long lead times linked to offshore facilities expose supply chains to serious mismatches. Offshore production would offer a cost edge over domestic production – for example, 5 percent, 10 percent, or 15 percent cheaper than the domestic alternative. Key question: Is the reduction in total product costs high enough to offset the increase in supply–demand mismatches? The answer to this question shapes not only a firm's investment strategies but also its supply chain networks.

Having collaborated with different companies and US Department of Commerce, we quantified the impact of long lead times on the mismatch cost and developed a cost-differential frontier as a function of lead time (De Treville et al., 2014). For firms facing volatile market demand, an offshore production decision that looks *only* at total product cost may cause a huge loss due to supply–demand mismatches. Despite high total product cost, reshoring production near markets would help businesses increase profits by reducing mismatches. K'NEX Brands, a family-owned toys company, reduced costs by 20 percent after reshoring its production to the United States, even though total product cost was cheaper in China.[3]

Hewlett Packard (HP) followed a similar strategy to improve the bottom line of its notebook division. In 1997, HP was a top player in the notebook computer market. Yet HP's notebook division was losing money. Its supply chain network was misaligned with the market (Slagmulder & Van Wassenhove, 2004). HP had traditionally focused on *total* product cost and attempted to reduce it. Mismatch costs had not been explicitly observed in its accounting. To fathom the level of mismatch costs, HP first formed a team of experts from different departments and academia. In electronics, obsolescence cost is high because consumers shun products using old technology. Thus, products have short lifecycles with average prices declining over time. After weighing these aspects, the team's analysis revealed that the mismatch costs

---

[3] Visit the following link for more information about the K'NEX reshoring case: https://acetool.commerce.gov/cost-risk-topic/inventory.

account for around 50 percent of total inventory value. Following this analysis, HP restructured its supply chain and improved *responsiveness*. As a result, they reduced inventory by 50 percent and reversed the notebook division from money-losing to profit-making in just two years.

Unfortunately, not all manufacturers are as successful as HP in turning around operations. We would often see such problems in firms strongly influenced by the CFO because finance professionals are mostly influenced by Coase's view of supply chain management by their education. To understand the influence of executive members in an organization, the best approach is to look at compensation. Kimberly-Clark, a US-based consumer goods and personal care company, paid its second highest compensation, after the CEO, to its CFO in 2022.[4] On August 25, 2023, the company announced its decision to stop selling Kleenex facial tissues in Canada due to high operating costs and the supply constraints (Evans, 2023). This scuttled 15 percent of the market share. Executives and investors often cite the importance and challenges of growth. Kimberly-Clark must have invested much time and capital growing the business to reach its 15 percent market share in Canada. Then the sudden decision to exit the market! What seemed impossible for Kimberly-Clark proved profitable for other companies (e.g., Kruger) remaining in the Canadian market. Cost calculations that justify economies of scale often fail to incorporate the *hidden* costs of supply–demand mismatches. The cheapest supply chain structure can prove so *fragile* that the operating system unravels when demand and the input prices fluctuate.

1.2.2 Network Externalities

The utility of a product for consumers grows with the crowd of people using it. This phenomenon is referred to as "network externalities" in economics. Products and services here become more convenient in a market with more users (Katz & Shapiro, 1985). There are two factors influencing network externalities. First, people share their experiences about products with others. If a product is useful for a group of people, it is recommended to other people quickly where they can use it to their increased utility. Second, the cost of a product

---

[4] The company's executive compensation values are available via https://ca.finance.yahoo.com/quote/KMB/profile.

falls as more people consume it. When the number of customers using Uber rises, for example, the platform attracts more ride-hail drivers. The increased availability of drivers trims ride-hailing charges, which in turn lures more customers. In the end, the platform becomes highly convenient for both drivers and customers.

Unfortunately, network externalities do not often benefit supply chains. As supply chain networks expand, serious problems can emerge due to capacity limits. When companies stop investing in supply chains, they land in a vicious cycle. Those with a high operational capacity can fulfill customer demand rapidly. Fast service then brings new customers and more demand for the products. As demand increases under limited capacity, customers start facing delays where operational success stories are replaced by customer complaints or other issues. Here, one widespread problem is losing customers to rivals. Another is the outsourcing of some activities to contract manufacturers to overcome capacity shortages where the outsiders could learn the technology and become competitors in the long term.

In the aerospace industry, big players like Boeing and Airbus had been manufacturing most aircraft components in-house pre-1950 (Rossetti & Choi, 2005). With demand burgeoning after World War II, both decided to outsource the production of most components to select suppliers. Outsourcing does not cause any problem if the strategic objectives of suppliers and manufacturers are well aligned. However, aircraft manufacturers made a big mistake at one point when they forced suppliers to expand capacities and cut prices in the 1990s. This made suppliers with excess capacity incur large losses. They reacted to the excess capacity problem in an unforeseen way. They disintermediated the supply chain and started selling spare parts *directly* to airline companies. Aerospace manufacturers generate substantial profits from service contracts with airline companies, and much here was lost to the suppliers. Failure to manage network externalities had shackled these manufacturers with hefty losses.

Like aircraft manufacturers, network externalities brought challenges to Apple that led to Samsung becoming a key player in the smartphone industry. Samsung entered the smartphone industry as one of the largest suppliers to Apple, supplying displays and chips for iPhones and iPads (Jackson, 2011). After Samsung's operational capability to produce the displays and chips yielded a close collaboration with Apple, the former evolved into one of the biggest smartphone manufacturers in the world.

1: Economics of Supply Chain Management   17

Given Samsung's ability to produce advanced technology products, Apple could not replace Samsung after becoming principal foes in the smartphone market.

As exemplified in these cases, network externalities pose supply chain issues to firms. Nevertheless, some companies take the challenges seriously and react by building an effective supply chain network instead of ignoring or sugarcoating them. For example, Amazon developed from scratch a fulfillment network as the company grew its sales volume. Amazon had initially outsourced its express delivery services to FedEx. Until 2019, these two worked together delivering orders to Amazon's customers promptly. When Amazon ably built its *own* network of logistics fleet, this deal ended (Kim, 2019). In sum, Amazon vertically integrated the logistics services when network externalities made such a move feasible. Though several hardships from network externalities persist for supply chains, executives can make strategic investments that turn challenges into opportunities à la Amazon.

1.2.3 Monetary Policy

Supply chain professionals often face challenging uncertainties when making critical decisions. For example, we have cited the role of total product and the mismatch costs in choosing *where* to produce goods. The mismatch costs may lie hidden to decision-makers, as in the HP case, with important decisions being made in the dark. Despite these challenges, executives tend to carefully enlist detailed risk analyses before drafting final decisions that appear optimal given current pricing and cost parameters. Facing high inflation, though, optimal decisions might soon prove suboptimal in the wake of price volatility, leaving huge sunk investment costs.

Economic policies tend to establish price stability in markets, offering a positive impact on supply chains. In some cases, however, policies are too lax in keeping prices highly stable. Supply chains are far more vulnerable to price instability than markets. Therefore, failure to achieve price stability may wield a devastating impact on supply chains while market prices proceed unscathed. Given that economic models consider supply chain management a factor of production, economic policies ignore the impact of price stability on supply chains while fixated on market dynamics.

Central banks are duty-bound to ensure price stability of economic systems. Bank of Canada's website, for example, states, "We are Canada's central bank. We work to preserve the value of money by keeping inflation low and stable." When inflation is high, they increase the interest rates to induce savings and curb demand, which tames inflation. However, central banks often hesitate to raise interest rates in deference to corporate financial stability, while incurring a hefty cost: destabilized supply chains. On September 6, 2023, Bank of Canada announced its decision to hold the interest rate steady at 5 percent (Evans, 2023b). The bank had increased the interest rate from 0.25 percent to 5 percent gradually to reduce inflation in 2022 and 2023. Inflation abated from a reported 8 percent in 2022 to 2.8 percent in June 2023, next rebounding to 4.0 percent in August 2023. Though violating the targeted 2 percent, Bank of Canada stopped increasing the interest rate. This decision can be attributed to the Bank's tendency to favor leveraged individuals and firms. We see here a trade-off between inflation and interest rates. On the one hand, leveraged companies (having high debt) suffer under high interest rates as the cost of borrowing escalates. For a company with $10 million in debt, the interest rate hike from 0.25 percent to 5 percent amplifies its annual interest expense twentyfold from $25K to $500K! On the other hand, inflation escalates both wages and the cost of materials in classic fashion. Still, what about the *hidden* costs that accumulate along supply chains?

Figure 1.2 plots the inflation rate and manufacturers' total inventory change in Canada from March 2019 to July 2023.[5] The solid line shows the inflation rate measured as consumer price index, whereas the dashed curve represents the inventory change, adjusted for seasonal fluctuations (e.g., firms often keep seasonal inventory for salient reasons such as Christmas shopping). When the inflation rate is under control (i.e., less than the targeted 2 percent level), manufacturers can better anticipate future prices and consumers' purchasing preferences. This helps them make inventories leaner as observed by the declining trend in the inventory change before 2021. High inflation after 2021 causes a tight correlation between inflation and inventory changes.

---

[5] Data courtesy of Statistics Canada and Bank of Canada. The inventory data was extracted from Statistics Canada: https://www150.statcan.gc.ca/t1/tbl1/en/tv.action?pid=1610004701 for the manufacturing industry that has the classification code of NAICS:31-33. The consumer price index was extracted from Bank of Canada: https://bankofcanada.ca/rates/price-indexes/cpi/.

1: Economics of Supply Chain Management

Figure 1.2 Canada's inflation rate and inventory change (year-over-year) in the manufacturing industry from 2019 to 2023

However, the magnitude of change in the inventory is much higher than that of inflation. Inflation rates neared 8 percent in July 2022, but inventory change reached 30 percent! Under high inflation, it becomes tougher to match supply with demand due to price fluctuations coupled with ever-present supply chain uncertainties. Thus, high inflation spawns inventory risk. Supply chain executives need stable pricing to manage inventories and make their systems as lean as possible. Otherwise, keeping interest rates low while the inflation being high would cause cheap debt-financing to promote supply chain inefficiencies. Yet economists often overlook the impact of their decisions on supply chain management while ably addressing other economic and market issues.

1.2.4 Market Analysis

Despite economic thinking that casts supply chain management as a factor of production, many real-world examples have shown supply chain management to influence market dynamics. For example, evolution of ecommerce can be attributed to supply chain innovations. Amazon has long invested in supply chain management to raise its market share. To convince traditional shoppers to buy online, Amazon has regularly reduced delivery times (Goode & Calore, 2023). Without same-day or next-day delivery, it would not have been possible to lure impatient customers to shop online. Amazon's success in shrinking lead times has obviously helped the retailer increase its customer count and revenues. Copying its success, many other retailers have invested in building operational capabilities that offer a seamless ecommerce experience to their customers. E-tailers have injected supply chain management *into* the markets (contrary to the view of supply chain management being just a factor of production), thus altering the economic system. Ecommerce is now an integral component of our economic system shaping global markets. It accounted for 17 percent of total 2020 retail sales, with more than 1.5 million workers employed by Amazon alone (Ikenson, 2022; Novet, 2023). This could have been impossible without supply chain management innovations targeting markets.

Integrating supply chain management with markets also helps companies identify wide-ranging business opportunities. Amazon also invested in technology to control and monitor supply chain activities. Instead of relying on software services offered by other companies, it developed its own Amazon Web Services (AWS). Having arisen as a supply chain management byproduct, AWS later turned into a software business serving other firms. AWS' 2020 annual sales exceeded $80 billion contesting software giants Microsoft and Google in cloud systems. Therefore, Amazon's supply chain success fertilized new opportunities in the market meriting a business valuation in the hundreds of billions of dollars.

Amazon is not the only company that has reshaped its market and elevated profits, flexing its muscle in supply chain management. Nestlé too operates a robust supply chain network with different parties: coffee bean farmers, production sites, and retailers. As part of a research project in collaboration with Nestlé Switzerland, I was awed by the robustness and responsiveness of this company's supply chain (De Treville et al., 2014). Owing to its strong supply chain management practice, Nestlé successfully allied with Starbucks to bring Starbucks' coffee to regional markets (Weissman, 2018). This helped Nestlé strengthen market power in the coffee industry.

Typecasting supply chain management as a factor of production reinforces an economic system that operates in the sequence

1: Economics of Supply Chain Management

"manufacture-sell-consume." For example, Adidas has long been making and selling shoes. Before the widespread adoption of the Internet, customers were aware of new models after being displayed in retail stores. In other words, customers were not involved in the production decision as markets were isolated from the job floor. Today's firms are trying to change this model for select products, especially those with high margins. Adidas now offers customized shoes such that customers can design shoes on the company website per their preferences and submit purchase orders (Seifert, 2002). After receiving the purchase orders, Adidas initiates production. Therefore, the "manufacture-sell-consume" practice has radically remapped into "sell-manufacture-consume." Many brands from watchmaker Rolex to bag-maker Timbuk2 now offer customized products to customers. Because companies make products in response to customer orders in this setting, supply chain management can no longer be dismissed as just a factor of production. It is now a vital hand in trade shaping market forces.

1.3 The Switzerland Example

Switzerland is a great case of what a nation can achieve when economic policies center on supply chain management. Swiss corporations and government have a keen sense as to the economics of supply chain management, which has strongly contributed to the Swiss economy. Switzerland is a small European country located between Germany, France, and Italy with a population of 8.7 million as of 2021. It is the most innovative, one of the wealthiest lands in the world.[6] Some argue that the wealth of the Swiss economy can be attributed to the banking system in which the Swiss government offers protection to foreign accounts. However, the truth is that the wealth of the Swiss economy is due to its strong economic system emphasizing supply chain management that makes manufacturing in Switzerland viable despite its high wages. One firm, Rotho Group, makes basic plastic items such as file boxes and bins in the country.[7] How can a company stay competitive in

---

[6] Switzerland is the top innovative country according to World Intellectual Property Organization's (WIPO) ranking: https://wipo.int/global_innovation_index/en/2022/.

[7] The company website is https://rotho.com/. Rotho's products are described as "made in Switzerland" on Amazon (e.g., https://amazon.ca/Rotho-Organizing-System-23-Transparent/dp/B000MWTJQ2).

the production of such basic office supplies, while other developed nations have been importing such items from offshore countries? Switzerland has a strong supply chain network, one very well integrated into markets. Although the labor cost is remarkably high, Swiss manufacturers can minimize other cost elements, such as inventory and overhead – allowing to the country's robust and integrated supply chains. This makes Swiss manufacturing competitive in the European markets.

Two key factors have helped Switzerland excel in supply chain management: (1) price stability and (2) robust infrastructure. Swiss governments have always managed to keep inflation exceptionally low. The inflation rate has ducked 3.5 percent, even during the COVID pandemic when other developed nations suffered near 10 percent rates. Such price stability helps Swiss companies make supply chain decisions weighing only inherent supply chain uncertainties without much exposure to price volatility. Switzerland also enjoys one of the most robust infrastructures in the world. From a supply chain perspective, the most important part of the infrastructure is the rail system operated by the Swiss Federal Railways (SBB), which also offers frequent cargo services to businesses at fair prices. This equips Swiss producers to stay competitive, although this strategy forfeits some of SBB's profits (Briginshaw, 2022). However, any loss at SBB is not a problem for the Swiss government-owned SBB Cargo as long as Swiss companies can still generate high revenues (Raimondi, 2023).

Coupling its success in supply chain management with its innovation culture, there are strong production bases in Switzerland. The watch industry is in the Geneva area, which includes its most famous brands (e.g., Rolex, Patek Philippe, the Swatch Group) and the local suppliers. The food industry is based in the Lausanne-Fribourg area, with Swiss giant Nestlé headquartered in Lausanne. There are also many dairy farms, plus chocolate and cheese factories in the Fribourg footprint. This same Fribourg exports tons of Gruyère cheese all around the world (Moses, 2023). Zurich's tech industry is home to giant ABB's headquarters. Owing to its popularity as Europe's techno-hub, Zurich attracts plenty of global tech companies such as Google, IBM, and Microsoft. Finally, the pharmaceutical industry based in the Basel area is home to drug giant Roche.

The separation of industries into distinct geographical areas forces firms to keep suppliers close as part of integrated supply chains. Supply chain integration helps address any negative aspects of network externalities as companies can ramp up production quickly to meet increasing demand from network externalities. For example, Rolex launched temporary production sites to meet increasing watch demand in 2023 (Hoffman, 2023). While some companies in other nations take on excess inventory risk to handle rising demand, Rolex tackles the production issues of network externalities without taking such a risk, benefiting from a strong watchmaking network in the Geneva area of Switzerland. The Swiss example shows that manufacturing in high-cost economies is feasible, but a systematic approach must begin with updated economic thinking.

1.4 Conclusion

Supply chain management is arguably the most crucial factor shaping the development of corporations and economies. Companies must excel in supply chain management to generate sustainable profits in the long term. Many real-world examples have shown that even highly innovative companies can suffer financial hardships under a fragile supply chain presence. For example, Dutch electronics company Philips had been Europe's most innovative company in the 2000s. Yet its inability to manage its complex supply chain incurred serious financial problems. The firm scored an operational turnaround by selling off business units to gain better control over its supply chains (Mocker & Ross, 2017).

To thrive in global markets, companies must innovate to deliver more value for customers at a lower cost. Innovation often takes place in two forms: (1) product and (2) process innovation. *Product innovation* targets development of niche products or salient upgrades to existing products so that market demand is fulfilled. *Process innovation* mostly relates to supply chain activities. It aims to enhance technological systems toward excellence in supply chain management. For Apple, *product innovation* is more important than process innovation as it sells hundreds of millions of iPhones and iPads to customers worldwide. Product innovation obviously dominates any process innovation in sparking peak demand. For many other businesses (probably 95 percent of all established firms in the maturity stage), however, *process innovation* holds much more salience. Despite its success in product innovation, for example, Philips faced financial plagues that were solved by prioritizing supply chain management (Mocker & Ross, 2017).

The four stages of the corporate business cycle well clarify the innovation trajectory (Seifert et al., 2016). The first one is the *birth stage*, where entrepreneurs develop a product and launch the start-up business. Here, product innovation is critical because start-up founders often work solely on improving the *product* to attract more customers. Profitability is not a main concern at this stage. Start-ups often consume cash and demand capital from investors to innovate products and sustain the business. The second is the *growth* stage, which begins after start-ups achieve a successful product-market fit. At the growth stage, supply chain management becomes important to make products available in different markets. After marketing, supply chain management here truly becomes the second-top priority. The third stage is *maturity*, where companies reach peak potential markets and generate high revenues. Here, supply chain management occupies *priority one* to transform high revenues into worthwhile profits. Any failure to excel in supply chain management puts companies in risky situations reminiscent of Philips. Excluding Apple-esque design and sales of products that feature continuous upgrades, most decision-makers must emphasize innovation as to supply chain management in the maturity stage. The final stage is *decline*, where companies downsize operations and divest assets to trim the cost of ongoing businesses.

Considering the entire business lifecycle, companies generate most profits during the *maturity* stage. Effective supply chain practices help firms increase profits. Start-ups able to delineate the long-term supply chain plan and convince investors of its viability would merit dedicated support with greater seed capital. Therefore, start-up founders must develop a supply chain plan early even while focusing on product innovation during the birth stage.

Finally, excellence in supply chain management makes companies highly competitive. Product innovation can be easily copied by rivals. For example, Amazon launched cloud services with AWS in 2006. Google and Microsoft followed Amazon by launching cloud services in 2008 and 2009, respectively.[8] Cloud service providers have proliferated in the market, offering customized services to many corporations. Though service providers may secure various patents and intellectual

---

[8] The reader is referred to the *Wall Street Journal*'s documentary for more information about the big tech competition over cloud computing: https://bicersupplychain.short.gy/Y7015d.

property, such efforts may not defend market share because technology can be developed in alternative ways to serve market demand. Supply chain management differs from product development in its level of duplication difficulty. Design and development of highly effective supply chain systems can sometimes be copied, but the *implementation* is much tougher. Therefore, a firm that excels in supply chain management cannot be easily imitated by rivals execution-wise. This bestows a competitive advantage to those with superior supply chain practices. To attain such excellence, decision-makers must start by revising the traditional economic template we have just outlined.

2 Trade-off Structure of Supply Chain Management

Supply chains often have a complex structure that involves several activities carried out by different supply chain partners. The movement of goods from suppliers to retailers and consumers can be done in alternative ways such as cross docking, direct shipping, omnichannel retailing, vendor-managed or consignment inventory, and so on. The abundance of the alternatives indeed contributes to the complexity of supply chains such that even for standard items shelved in a drugstore or a convenience shop, supply chains can be perplexing.

Imagine a toothpaste supply chain that involves suppliers, a manufacturer, and retailers where the product moves from upstream suppliers to downstream retailers (Kell, 2024).[1] Supply chain activities are initiated via information exchange when the manufacturer places an order to procure raw materials from suppliers. After receiving the procurement order, suppliers prepare the requested raw materials for shipment. Next, logistics companies transport them from suppliers to the manufacturer. Raw materials are next processed into tubes of toothpaste at the manufacturer's facility. Suppose that the manufacturer does not directly serve consumers, which is quite common in practice. Therefore, the goods are sold to retailers to reach consumers.

Retailers often want their orders shipped to distribution centers for *storage until delivery* to retail stores. Alternatively, retailers can receive shipment to a *cross-docking* area of distribution centers where products park for a limited time (e.g., couple hours) before being transported to the retailing sites. Cross docking allows retailers to allocate bulky shipments from manufacturers to assigned trucks routed to various stores. Here, products in cross docking do not occupy actual storage spaces in fulfillment centers. In some cases, manufacturers ship

---

[1] Upstream activities take place earlier in supply chains. For example, the procurement of raw materials from a supplier is an upstream activity, while the delivery of an order to a customer is a downstream activity.

the goods directly to retail sites without going through any distribution center, known as *direct shipping*. Retailers finally sell products in store or online. Online orders are often packed and delivered to customers from fulfillment centers. Some retailers also utilize their stores for online orders such that nearby customers can pick up online purchases within some store radius. This practice is also known as *omnichannel retailing*.

These are just a fraction of activities that supply chain executives must synchronize to keep costs from mounting along the chain. Supply chains complicate further when control of certain activities is transferred from one party to another. For example, retailers may hold the manufacturer responsible for managing inventory where the latter monitors stock levels in retailer distribution centers for automatic replenishment as needed. This practice is known as *vendor-managed inventory*. Manufacturers can also be held financially liable for products located on the retail premises. Inventory here is recorded on the *manufacturer's* balance sheet although it is physically stored at retailer locations – an approach called *consignment inventory*.

Decision-makers can utilize a combination of these practices to architect supply chain networks. To this end, they must conduct detailed analyses for the planning and execution of resources in an economic way, where the viability of each practice depends on the fundamental trade-offs of supply chain management.

2.1 Trade-offs in Supply Chain Management

There are five fundamental trade-offs of supply chain management. These trade-offs are summarized in Figure 2.1. The first one is related to the acquisition of resources in that decision-makers are exposed to the trade-off between in-house production and outsourcing costs. In-house production costs include capital expenditures to acquire production resources (e.g., machine and equipment) and operational expenses to utilize these resources. Outsourcing costs involve search, contracting and coordination costs to utilize the assets of a contract manufacturer. The comparison between in-house production and outsourcing costs helps decision-makers identify whether they need additional resources or supply chain partners to execute some operations. For instance, McDonald's has been outsourcing supply chain planning and logistics activities to Martin-Brower to benefit from the latter's logistics network

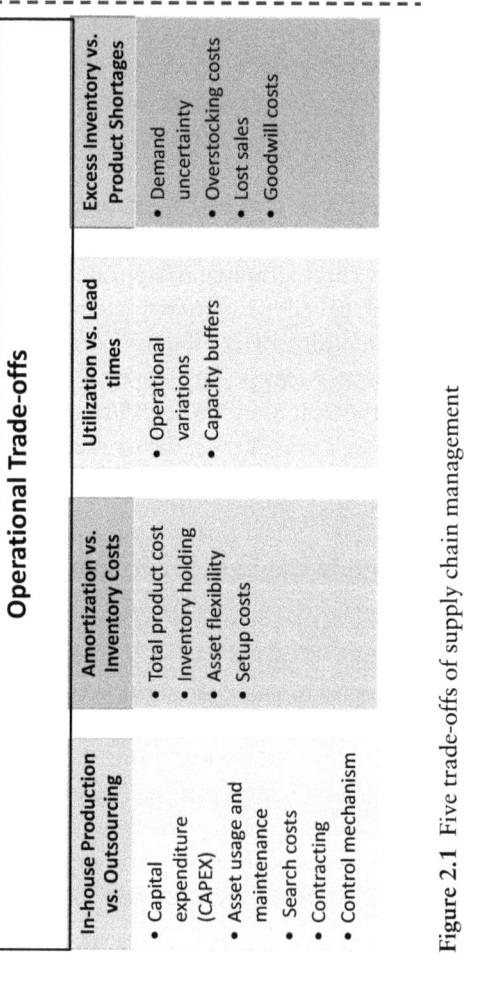

Figure 2.1 Five trade-offs of supply chain management

and efficiency. Owing to its effective franchising system, McDonald's also managed to expand their restaurant footprint with little investment. Thus, the restaurant chain capitalizes on the benefits of outsourcing to grow the business and profits. In contrast, Walmart owns its warehouses, distribution and fulfillment centers, as well as stores to fulfill diverse needs of consumers. The retail giant maintains supply chain activities in-house to keep operational costs under control.

Second, supply chain executives are exposed to the trade-off between amortization versus inventory costs. Resources that are utilized to execute supply chain activities have limited lifetimes. In some industries, companies are even forced by regulators to replace machines or their parts periodically (i.e., fleets of airline companies), further reducing product lifetimes. Having a limited lifetime for an asset causes its value to depreciate over time. The *amortization cost* is indeed the depreciation loss of an asset. When a machine or equipment has a high price tag but a short lifetime, its amortization cost will be relatively high. Then, the high amortization cost induces decision-makers to utilize the asset at a high rate so that the fixed cost per product can be minimized. However, this leads to the accumulation of inventory in supply chains, resulting in high inventory holding costs. If demand for the product slows down, the high utilization will further cause costly inventory write-offs. Decision-makers ought to set utilization rates of their assets depending on these cost parameters.

The trade-off between amortization versus inventory costs can be moderated by utilizing resources for multiple purposes and shortening setup times. Multi-purpose machines are used to produce several items. If demand for a product slows down, machines will be switched to produce other products. This helps eliminate unnecessary inventory holding and write-off costs while keeping utilization of resources at high rates. However, switching production requires subsequent setups. When the item being produced by the machine is replaced by another, employees would need to change the specifications and carry out some tests. This changeover period is referred to as *setup time* of the machine. Long setups would be costly for manufacturers. Nevertheless, they can cut setup times and truly benefit from multi-purpose resources by making some investments in automated, quick changeover systems.

Setup-time reduction may be impossible in certain cases. Then, decision-makers tend to increase the order quantity for each product to reduce the number of setups. However, large order quantities cause long production cycles and inventory accumulated along the supply chain. In the operations management literature, economic order quantity optimizes the trade-off between amortization and inventory holding costs depending on the setup times (Erlenkotter, 1990).

The third trade-off is between high utilization of resources and production lead times. Manufacturers may not be able to employ their resources fully in the presence of operational variations. For example, machine breakdowns, employee absenteeism, and the halt of logistics activities cause operational variations, which in turn lead to uncertainties about the production lead time. Such uncertainties can be absorbed by a production system if decision-makers reserve capacity buffers – for example, the resources are not utilized more than 80 percent so that 20 percent capacity buffer is always reserved. Otherwise, operational variations coupled with high utilization (e.g., more than 95 percent) result in long lead times. Here, the planning horizon of supply chain activities increases due to extended production lead times, which causes higher inventory levels accumulated along the supply chain. When the utilization rate of resources is kept at a moderate level, operational variations can be absorbed by increasing the utilization if needed. Such a strategy helps reduce production lead times. But the production cost increases given that the capacity of resources is not utilized fully.

Fourth, the demand for products is mostly uncertain in the market such that companies are exposed to (1) *excess* inventory and (2) product *shortage* risks. If firms stock more than what is demanded by customers, they incur excess inventory costs. Excess inventory is often liquidated in discount stores at prices below cost, leading to a net loss. Even worse, excess inventory may not sell even at discount stores; hence, companies write off inventory from their accounts. Canadian electronics company BlackBerry once made the most popular smartphones with a near 40 percent market share in 2010. After a 2013 product launch failure, the company ended up with many unsold smartphones. BlackBerry wrote off inventory of $1 billion in 2013. Following the inventory write-off announcement, the company laid off thousands of employees, and its stock price plummeted (Connors & Terlep, 2013; Miller, 2022; Silcoff et al., 2013).

When demand exceeds available stock, companies suffer an opportunity cost of lost sales. Shoppers seeing empty shelves at the retail stores might exit without buying anything, causing an opportunity cost for the retailers. Even worse, customers may switch to a rival and never return in the long-term (Anderson et al., 2006). Stock-outs thus imperil profitability for organizations.

The final trade-off is between revenue growth and supply–demand mismatches. Supply–demand mismatches are described as the monetary loss of companies due to excess inventory and stock-out costs. When decision-makers determine stock levels of their products in the face of demand uncertainty, companies would incur excess inventory costs for some items and stockout losses for others at the same time. Global research and market analysis company IHL Group has been studying the cost of supply–demand mismatches in the retail industry for the past seventeen years (Blair, 2023). Collaborating with several retailers and information technology companies, IHL amassed data from different resources and estimated the total cost of the mismatches. In 2023, the group reported the estimate of annual mismatch costs near $1.77 trillion in the retail segment. The mismatch costs would be even higher in other industries. For example, it is well known in supply chain management literature that manufacturers and suppliers face demand uncertainty worse than even for retail, which is a phenomenon known as "the Bullwhip effect" (Lee et al., 1997). As the mismatches increase with demand uncertainty, their costs for suppliers and manufacturers likely outrun that for retailers. Such a mismatch peril looms critical for several industries although nonretail research is sparse.

Although eliminating the mismatches between supply and demand is critically important for businesses, decision-makers occasionally accept the mismatch risk to grow revenues. For example, Starbucks has lost operational focus in the last five years and concentrated on increasing the usage of its mobile payment app. As a result, the coffeehouse chain increased income from nonoperational activities while suffering from excess inventory charges (the Starbucks case will be discussed in detail in Chapter 5). Supply–demand mismatches may occur in companies under strategic shifts, but senior executives weigh those risks when they set business objectives to grow revenues. If companies achieve business objectives and supply chains are aligned with those objectives, we must deem supply chain management to be effective.

The last trade-off shapes the business model of companies. When companies advance in digital technologies and build interfaces between supply chain management and other areas (e.g., finance, information technology, and marketing), they are likely to manage the last trade-off effectively. This also helps them innovate their business model and increase bottomline.

2.2 Building Interfaces in Supply Chain Management

Supply chain management is often described as the practice of having the right product, at the right time, in the right place to fulfill customer demand without keeping excess inventory. Such a description makes the ultimate objective of supply chain management perfect matching of supply with demand. Narrowly, this viewpoint reflects only the *operational* aspect of supply chain management, neglecting both finances and technology. Supply chain management reaches way beyond matching supply and demand. It is indeed the practice of coordinating operational, information, and capital flows within and across firms to achieve business targets. No one disagrees that supply–demand mismatches erode profitability. Likewise, there is no disagreement that perfectly serving customer demand helps companies increase sales. But business goals can conflict with common supply chain objectives. Here, supply chains should adjust to align with overall business objectives.

For example, Amazon struggled with supply–demand mismatches when they were promoting their marketplace innovation known as fulfillment by Amazon (Pallot, 2021). Nevertheless, the company accepted the mismatch risk to innovate business model and increase revenues. Luxury brands also target business goals that trigger high supply–demand mismatches. They introduce limited-edition versions of new styles where the quantity and price are set at the very beginning. When sold out, such firms do not produce another batch to fulfill extra demand. Therefore, they often face stock-outs. From the supply chain management perspective, stock-outs are seen as a profit forfeiture that must be averted. However, luxury brands treat limited-edition products as their business legacies. Hence, they do not pay much attention to supply–demand mismatches resulting from limited-edition offerings.

When business objectives deviate from the ultimate objective of supply chain management (i.e., perfect matching of supply with demand), organizations incur the cost of supply–demand mismatches. Nevertheless, they can offset high mismatch costs by shrewdly managing cash flows with their supply chain partners. Firms generating outsized profits from financial operations should be willing to lose a fraction of it under a tiny rise in supply–demand mismatches. The apparel maker Kontoor Brands, the umbrella parent for brands Wrangler and Lee, has reframed its supply chain to improve cash flow (Broughton, 2022). It refuses to sell clothes through some channels and to specific customers if the management team believes that fulfilling such a demand would impair its cash management practice. Per supply chain ideology, this is considered a loss of profit due to unfilled demand. However, business objectives set by senior executives prevail over supply–demand mismatches. For that reason, supply chain leaders must concentrate on aligning not only the operational but also information and capital flows among supply chain partners. They must also build interfaces between supply chain management and other departments, such as finance, information technology, and marketing, so that coordination along the supply chain can be performed smoothly.

Bridging interfaces with other departments is important for supply chain management. First, the interface between operations and marketing is crucial to allocate supply chain resources to specific channels that are strategically important. It is the responsibility of marketing to go to market, understand customer dynamics, and share insights with operations and finance teams. Based on these insights, companies sometimes "fire" customers to boost the bottom line (Shin et al., 2012).

Customers who inform sales representatives about their future orders well in advance of the delivery dates and pay the invoices immediately are more attractive than others who place urgent orders and delay payments. Marketing analysts must weigh both the short- and long-term feasibility of serving specific customers or sales channels. In the light of their evaluations, supply chain professionals may need to stock more Stock Keeping Units (SKU) at specific sites for high service levels, while customers in other regions would face stock-outs. For example, Primark (an Irish fast-fashion retailer) does not sell products online, but only in store. The company refused to open an online store (not even in a single country) during the COVID pandemic (Jack & Frei, 2021). Recall the pandemic forcing the retail closures. At that time, Primark had inventory on site even while in-store demand was zero! Meanwhile, online demand peaked during the lockdowns; still, no resource or inventory was reallocated to the online channel by Primark management. This result is clearly inefficient from the supply chain management perspective; however, it was a company decision, and supply chain managers could not easily change that.[2] Still, they could have improved profits within such boundaries. When stores reopened, for example, Primark could have liquidated inventory and cut buffer stock levels to minimize inventory cost. Likewise, the company could have negotiated consignment terms with suppliers where the suppliers are paid *after* products are sold.

The interface between operations and finance is critical to develop supply chain strategies that enhance cash flow. Companies could prioritize channels where customers prepay for services they receive. Firms can expand product portfolios, offer different promotions, and guarantee high service levels for such channels. They can also develop advertising campaigns to divert customers to those channels. Other strategies may defer payment on the supply side, which will later be discussed in detail. Supply chain performance is highly affected by all such strategies. Supply chain management thus should focus on keeping the chain performance at an elevated level while aligning decisions according to specified cash improvement objectives.

Building an interface between operations and finance also allows supply chain executives to educate the finance staff as to cost-accounting practices. Finance departments in companies use either traditional or activity-based cost (ABC) accounting principles. The former allocates overall operating expenses equally to each product. The latter analyzes the activities in detail and allocates overall operating expenses to different activities (Kaplan & Anderson, 2004). These accounting practices must be improved to granularize the impacts of supply chain inefficiencies on product costs. For instance, online sales cause product returns and subsequent operational costs for handling them. How can these costs be allocated to each product? Manufacturers keep capacity buffers to deal with operational variations. Having capacity buffers may benefit some products (i.e., those with high demand uncertainty) than others. How can the cost of reserving capacity buffers be allocated to products? The extant accounting practices do not address these questions effectively. To this end, finance professionals need the expertise of supply chain executives to develop an effective accounting practice. Such an accounting practice, in turn, helps supply chain executives grasp the

---

[2] Primark's rationale for not selling goods online will be discussed in Section 4.1.

actual cost of serving a customer concisely. Hence, they can manage operations for different channels more effectively.

Finally, the interface between operations and information technology is necessary to digitize the supply chain. Organizations use information technology to render supply chains transparent so that decision-makers can monitor supply chain activities in real time. Blockchain and RFID are two cases of tech applications that improve supply chain transparency. These technologies provide supply chain professionals with accurate data so they can react to issues in supply chains promptly. Information technology can also support supply chain professionals by offering decision support tools and predictive models. Demand planners use analytics dashboards to predict future demand and observe sales trends. They need this information in optimization tools to determine production quantities. Overall, there are three dimensions of the interface between information technology and operations. The first one is *descriptive* applications that make supply chains transparent. The second is *predictive* applications that resolve uncertainty in supply chains. The last one is *prescriptive* applications that allow decision-makers to optimize their actions. All improve supply chain performance and reduce the cost of mismatches.

In supply chain management, elimination of the mismatch risk is just one dimension. Not all companies are sensitive to this risk. For these types of companies, it is not necessary to overinvest in reducing the mismatches. Primark need not build an integrated supply chain that can be highly effective in handling online orders. Primark does not have an online channel! Instead, decision-makers must build interfaces in supply chain management to maximize performance while avoiding needless investments. If companies want to manage *cash flow* effectively and generate nonoperational profits, they must focus on the interface between operations and *finance*. When the objective is to increase sales in a certain market or segment, decision-makers must emphasize the interface between operations and *marketing*. When they aim to retain market share and alleviate operational inefficiencies due to the mismatches, they must focus on the interface between operations and *information technology*. This would allow a better match of supply with demand while helping integrate the supply chain.

Building interfaces of supply chain management with other departments helps managers develop an effective business model and

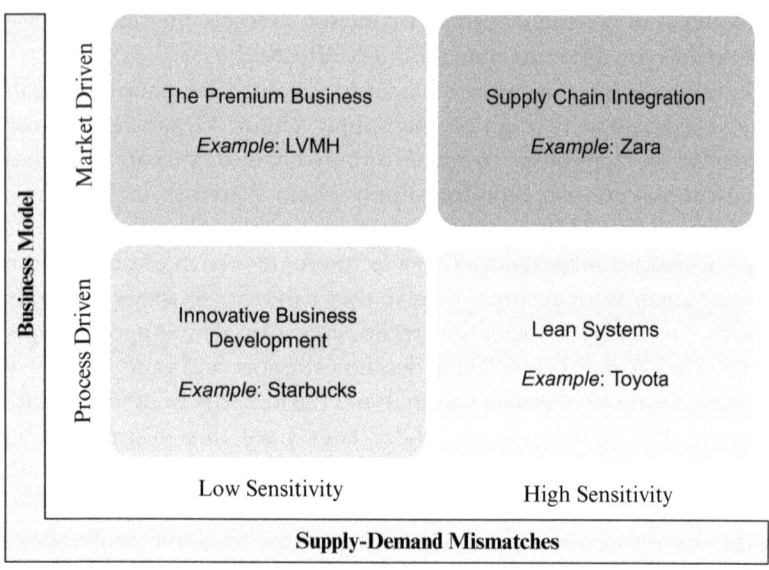

Figure 2.2 Supply chain strategies based on the mismatch sensitivity and business model

manage operational trade-offs. Hence, they can correctly identify supply chain priorities. Focusing on the relationship among the interfaces, business models, and the five fundamental trade-offs, Figure 2.2 presents effective supply chain strategies. We classify companies by their sensitivity to supply–demand mismatches on the horizontal axis. When a company has a high sensitivity, averting supply–demand mismatches emerges as top priority for decision-makers. Otherwise, managers would pay attention to other supply chain priorities such as improving cash flow or customer experience for premium segments. We also group firms by their business model on the vertical axis. A business model may be *market-driven*, gravitating to market integration and the fulfillment of diverse customer needs. Or a business model could be *process-driven* – that is, focusing on extracting maximum value from business processes.

2.3 Supply Chain Integration

Firms that fall into the upper-right quadrant of Figure 2.2 are sensitive to mismatch risk. Their business models are driven by the market where they excel in introducing new products frequently according to changing trends and customer preferences. For that reason, demand uncertainty elevates for these types of companies. However, this does not mean that they face a high mismatch risk. If their supply chains are responsive enough to fulfill customer demand, supply–demand mismatches can be minimized without keeping much inventory. Fast-fashion retailers, for example, keep production near markets to react quickly to sudden fluctuations in demand. Fashion brands like Zara and Uniqlo follow this approach of not stocking too much inventory in retail stores and warehouses. This helps cut excess inventory when demand for a product becomes lower than expected. When demand turns out to be high, the stores expedite orders from the nearby production facility. Thus, stores are quickly replenished with inventory for peak demand (Monroe, 2021).

Supply chain integration makes possible the fulfillment of fluctuating market demand without bearing high mismatch costs. To achieve this, companies must:

1. locate manufacturing near markets,
2. keep enough capacity in supply chains, and
3. reduce setup times and costs.

For fast-fashion retailers, having production sites near markets yields a sizeable drop in the mismatches. Indeed, fast-fashion retailers are among the most successful companies in abating the mismatch risk even though product lifecycles are much shorter than other retailers such as department stores (Hausman & Thorbeck, 2010). This results from fast-fashion efforts to decentralize supply chains with manufacturing facilities close to markets. A decentralized production network makes it possible to meet customer demand from a nearby plant, thus trimming shipment time between production and markets. However, a decentralized network may not suffice to establish a responsive, rapid reaction to uncertain demand. An offshore facility with excess capacity may be more responsive than a domestic, highly utilized facility. Thus, domestic manufacturers must reserve enough capacity to compete with offshore manufacturers in terms of supply chain responsiveness.

Capacity is always limited in organizations. A limited number of Uber drivers means that Uber riders must wait for service during rush hour. Shipping companies mobilize a fixed number of vessels such that procurement orders from Asia to the United States often delay during

Christmas seasons due to capacity limits (Toh, 2021). Manufacturers have machine and workforce constraints that cap the production rate (John, 2023). Such limitations delay order fulfillment of customers who may even abandon their orders after protracted waiting. To avoid these circumstances, companies must invest in capacity expansion.

Suppose a restaurant can prepare sixty meals per hour, and average hourly demand is fifty. Here, the chef is busy 83.3 percent of the time – a utilization rate of 50/60. Nearly 17 percent (1–0.833) of customers are served instantly without delay because the chef idly waits for a new customer 17 percent of the time. If kitchen capacity expands to 120 meals per hour, 58 percent of customers will be served at once. Thus, higher capacity shortens wait time and boosts customer satisfaction.

When operational capacity is high, resource utilization rates decline. Here, new customer demand can be met on the spot. Otherwise, new customer demand is fulfilled after a long delay. We would experience these dynamics when we visit a cafe or restaurant. If there were only one barista serving all customers, we would wait. If the café owner hires another barista to double capacity, our wait time shrinks. In practice, few customers tolerate a long waiting time to receive goods or services. If the wait time for Uber exceeds ten minutes, ride seekers tend to walk or use public transport. Likewise, if customers see a long queue at a shop, they go elsewhere. To avoid losing customers to a rival provider, companies operating a high-utilization system often offset their lack of capacity by having additional inventory.

Suppose a manufacturer with a utilization rate of 70 percent begins production in April to meet the demand that will be realized in May. Given the one-month period between the start of production and fulfillment of demand, the manufacturer keeps thirty days of stock. If utilization rises to 80 percent, the manufacturer would start production in March and keep sixty days of inventory. If it soars to 90 percent, production would start in February and the manufacturer would keep a three-month stock. Thus, inventory costs escalate as capacity becomes more restricted.

Capacity limits will exert severe impact on operations if production is maintained with setups. Companies often have multi-use resources where the same machine can produce different items. The automobile assembly line can make different models. Soft drink producers use the same tank to make different flavors. When switching production from one item to another, employees must set up resources. Setups can take different forms. For an automobile assembly line, workers change the tool specifications and carry out tests before starting production of another model. For a soda maker, tanks must be carefully cleaned according to their industry's standards of good manufacturing practices (FDA, 2024). It takes time to enact setups, and firms may incur additional costs during any setup. In addition to cost and time consumption, setups occupy operational capacity. If setups take long, it is more appealing for a manufacturer to set a minimum production quantity (batch size) for each product to reduce the frequency of setups.

Imagine a soda company offering two flavors: orange and strawberry. The company has a single tank producing 100 gallons daily. Setup takes two days. If the production volume for each flavor is set at 100 gallons, the tank makes 100 gallons of one flavor (e.g., orange) in one day and next undergoes a two-day setup. Then, the tank yields 100 gallons of the strawberry on the fourth day and faces another setup for the fifth and sixth days. Here, the tank is utilized only *one-third* of the time to make soft drinks. During the month, the company effectively uses the tank only ten days to yield 1,000 gallons of soft drink. If the production volume is set at 1400 gallons, the tank makes orange flavor for fourteen days. Setup occurs during the fifteenth and sixteenth days. The next fourteen days, it produces the strawberry flavor. Here, production capacity nearly triples to 2800 gallons per month!

In the presence of setups, manufacturers face capacity and inventory risks resulting from the trade-off between amortization and inventory costs. On the one hand, fewer setups mean more production capacity and lower amortization cost allocated to each product. On the other hand, inventory risk increases with fewer setups. When production volume is 1400 gallons, the company cannot change the flavor for fourteen days. Once a production run for the orange drink begins, no strawberry can be scheduled for fourteen days. Thus, the company must stock enough strawberry soda to serve this demand for the next two weeks! The capacity and inventory risks are alleviated when the setup time is minimized. If the setup time is reduced to less than an hour, for instance, the company can change the flavor every day while keeping the production volume at almost full capacity. Therefore, the capacity is maximized while inventory risk is kept at the minimum level.

Companies achieve supply chain integration by locating production close to markets, keeping enough operational capacity, and reducing setup times and batch sizes simultaneously. They can thereby fulfill fluctuating customer demand in the market without keeping too much inventory. Otherwise, inventory accumulates in various stages along the supply chain. Here, we introduce three components of supply chain integration. Achieving them helps companies squeeze supply, production, and delivery lead times. However, operational costs may increase due to integration efforts. In Chapter 4, we will investigate effective capacity management, lead-time reduction, process redesign (i.e., delayed differentiation), and cost-reduction strategies to operationalize supply chain integration in an economical way. Organizations that encounter operational complexities, such as product variety or a large supply chain network, especially need integrated supply chains.

2.4 Innovative Business Development

Companies that fall into the bottom-left quadrant of Figure 2.2 are not sensitive to the mismatch risk. These types of companies develop impactful business processes where they can generate nonoperational profits. If their business models allow them to receive payments from customers in advance of the delivery of the product or service, the collected amount can be used in financial markets to generate additional profits. When receipt of advance payment is not possible, companies can defer payments to suppliers and retain extra capital that can be invested in financial markets yielding nonoperational income.

In the retail industry, net profit margins of big players (e.g., Walmart, Costco, and Target) run a thin 2–3 percent of their revenues. To ensure profitability, retailers collect revenues at purchase from shoppers. But they pay days later their suppliers of goods. This capital invested in financial markets will generate additional profits. Here, large retailers sustain operations because extending the payment terms with their vendors helps offset the costs of supply–demand mismatches, thus making them less sensitive to the mismatch risk. Canadian retail giant Loblaws, for example, announced revenue of $13.7 billion for the fourth quarter of 2022 from retail operations (Loblaw Companies Limited, 2023). In the same quarter, it also scored revenue of $417 million from financial activities – a major share of adjusted net earnings of $575 million. Financial activities are thus vital for Loblaws and other retailers.

This business model works well for retailers that can liquidate inventory in a short time. If demand proves low and inventory stays in store a long time, however, retailers often tend to squeeze their suppliers into extending payment terms. According to a Wall Street Journal article, a partner at Ernst & Young said "retailers ... often look to push out the payment terms on their suppliers if they have a lot of goods sitting on the shelf" (Broughton, 2022b). Retailers are often duly criticized for exploiting vendors when they have excess inventory. One chief executive of a nonprofit organization (i.e., Food and Consumer Products of Canada) stated in 2020: "They [retailers] are just using the manufacturers as a bank" (Financial Post Staff, 2020).

Implementing innovative business models like Loblaws' can be challenging because executives have complex supply chain priorities beyond a perfect match of supply and demand. Central to such a business model lies delayed payment terms with suppliers. This can be detrimental for suppliers' financials. For that reason, companies must find another way to fund suppliers as they wait for payment. In supply chain finance, instruments such as reverse factoring and dynamic discounting help finance the suppliers. For example, Procter & Gamble (P&G) uses reverse factoring in collaboration with Citibank to finance P&G's suppliers while they await payment from P&G (Citibank, 2019). Another risk of extended payment terms for suppliers is default of their invoices. When suppliers offer long payment terms to retailers suffering low credibility, they bear the invoice-default risk. To hedge this risk, suppliers can buy vendor-put insurance where an insurer pays the invoice amount in case of buyer default. Vendor-put insurance was launched for suppliers in the initial phase of the COVID pandemic, first by J.P. Morgan and later by other financial institutions (Wallace & Steinberg, 2020). Though a promising hedge for invoice default risk, vendor-put policies can be extremely expensive. Here again, supply chain executives must develop an effective strategy to improve supply chain performance while minimizing costs and financial risks.

To benefit from supply chain finance, companies should "turn" inventory at a high rate where inventory does not loiter on shelf. Inventory turnover is a widely used productivity metric calculated as the yearly cost of goods sold (COGS) divided by average inventory. It tracks how often inventory is replenished per annum. If the value of inventory turnover is twelve, then a *monthly* inventory on average meets customer demand. With twenty-five turns, the firm wisely maintains a two-week stock. Companies with high inventory turnover generate more with less unsold stock and lower cash. They collect revenues from customers quickly and use this capital in financial markets to yield additional income until paying their suppliers. If companies establish an effective supply chain finance mechanism and achieve high inventory turnover, they can effectively generate greater *nonoperational* profits in financial markets without impairing suppliers. Therefore, supply chain finance is crucial for process-driven companies in the bottom-left quadrant. We will discuss in detail alternative supply chain finance strategies in Chapter 5 of this book.

2.5 The Premium Business

Companies residing in the top-left quadrant of Figure 2.2 can markup their products at ultra-high margins. Their business models are market-driven because they cater to wealthy customers' aesthetic needs. Extremely high margins make such companies less sensitive to the mismatch risk. Supply chain management is seen as a practice to facilitate marketing and sales activities. For example, the French company LVMH owns luxury brands such as Louis Vuitton, Dior, and Hennessy. The marketing team managing each brand often launches campaigns to promote their brand for specific occasions, such as the Chinese New Year celebration, where Hennessy offers some limited-edition spirits each year to Chinese customers (Parkes, 2021).

Supply chain excellence is not a major concern for such brands because the agenda of top executives is centered on the sales and marketing campaigns. They target a sales trajectory for each brand, designing each marketing and promotion activity to reach assigned milestones along the trajectory. Marketing professionals set volume and pricing of limited-edition products per their judgments. When products sell out rapidly, excess demand goes unserved, and the firm loses the opportunity to earn further profits. Yet no one questions such missed opportunity, and the campaign appears a success for the marketing team. If products do not sell well, an expeditious campaign emerges to reach the sales goals. Supply chain management plays only a supporting role here such that supply chain professionals are tasked to make products available in the market within a reasonable time as requested by the marketing department. Here, serious supply chain issues often remain unresolved.

Supply chain priorities of luxury brands are more related to quality assurance, supply chain transparency, and circular economy than perfectly matching supply with demand. Given blockchain technology's high potential to improve supply chains along these dimensions, it has merited strong interest from luxury brands. In 2021, for instance, three prominent luxury groups formed the Aura Blockchain Consortium to tap blockchain potential (Paton, 2021). In Chapter 6, we will discuss the implications of the premium business for supply chain management in detail.

2.6 Lean Systems

Companies that fall into the bottom-right quadrant of Figure 2.2 are sensitive to the mismatch risk because they sell products at low margins and cannot earn profits from nonoperational activities. When demand is low, excess inventory risk severely impacts profits. While the mismatch risk is very real to them, supply chain integration is not viable because low margins cannot justify the high operational costs of integrated supply chains. In the automotive industry, margins suffer fierce price wars in this contested market. Auto manufacturers do not have innovative business models (except Tesla), so they rarely generate profits from the nonoperational side. Here, the industry is cost-driven and sensitive to the mismatch risk.

To operate in such an environment, companies need stable demand to make supply chain decisions well ahead of actual order inflows. From a practical angle, near-term predictions are expected to be more accurate than those for the long term. For example, if a person is asked after lunch how much money is needed for that evening, the answer is easy. If the question is how much money is needed for an evening three months from now, the answer would be wrong. It is difficult for us to know where to be and what to do three months from now. For an academic soldiering on the same things for the last two years (only talking about myself), it is possible to answer the question for any day three months ahead. Stable demand is analogous to a boring academic in the sense that it can be predicted long before the observed reality.

Companies with a stable demand can focus on cost efficiency such that production and procurement decisions are made in a way that minimizes the total cost. They tighten inventory at resourceful levels. They streamline operations and procurement activities to minimize cost. They eliminate idleness of staff and machinery to optimize productivity. But such benefits accrue only for stable demand. Firms delivering such improvements exploit *lean systems*. Principles of lean systems originated from lean manufacturing that was first developed by Toyota. To better understand these principles and how lean manufacturing differs from other production systems, we wisely look at the history of automobile manufacturing.

As discussed in the first chapter, Henry Ford pioneered the auto industry assembly line, building the first massive assembly plant in Highland Park, Michigan. The key feature? Conveyor belts moved automobiles to different stations where workers at each station repeated a specific task. Division of labor drove workers to specialize in assigned jobs, leading to marked productivity improvement. Hence, Ford achieved a near 60 percent price cut in seventeen years (1908–1925). To retain price leadership, Ford enacted a vertical acquisition strategy to control all production, assembly, and transport of cars. While Ford was building his empire, General Motors (GM) developed a different strategy to compete. Alfred Sloan joined GM in 1918, later rising to president in 1923 (Gartman, n.d.; Sloan, 1964). Sloan avoided a price war with Ford. Instead, GM offered high-quality and luxury cars at premium prices. Unlike Ford, GM declined the vertical acquisition strategy. Instead, it eyed *customer satisfaction* and introduced a more diverse portfolio of cars to the market. Contrasting Henry Ford's product portfolio strategy summarized by his quip "any customer can have a car painted any color that he wants so long as it is black," Sloan wanted to manufacture cars "for every purse and purpose" (Neil, 2000; Sloan, 1964).

The 1960s saw soaring fuel costs, which induced US customers to buy compact, efficient Japanese cars. Toyota had engaged its own Toyota Production System to minimize its production costs while offering customers a menu of high-quality cars. The Toyota Production System was later dubbed "lean manufacturing" (Womack et al., 2007). Lean manufacturing focuses on eliminating wasteful activities along production without jeopardizing the quality and value of cars. It emphasizes the *just-in-time* production model where production schedules can be placed only after receiving a customer order. Hence, lean manufacturing helps cut auto prices owing to waste elimination and the just-in-time model's strict inventory control.

Despite its well-known advantages, lean manufacturing fails when demand is volatile. During the COVID pandemic, for example, many companies that had been implementing lean principles saw their inventories swell. One *Financial Times* article described this as a shift from just-in-time to just-in-case (Khalaf, 2020). Supply disruptions and product shortages during lockdowns forced most firms toward high buffer inventory to reduce the risk of product shortages. After the disruption risk subsided, lean companies resumed just-in-time.

Lean manufacturers push "aggressive selling" to reduce demand fluctuations and smooth production. When demand is low, they encourage sales representatives to offer loyal customers new car deals. Their low production costs (reflecting eliminated waste) enable retail price cuts to spur market demand. When demand overshoots, customers are convinced to wait. One can argue that the most critical point of lean manufacturing is production smoothing by "aggressive selling." When the sales push fails to smooth production, lean manufacturing incurs waste in supply chains such as occurs during the lockdowns. Is it not fascinating how a lean-*pull* system aimed at removing waste morphs into a *push* program having the mismatches?

Chapter 7 will systematically survey lean manufacturing and classify the operational tools and methods used to establish lean manufacturing. To this end, we will focus on the *design* of lean systems that help eliminate wasteful activities. We will later discuss how lean manufacturing can be *implemented*.

2.7 The Walmart Canada Example

Walmart Canada exemplifies how organizations can effectively address the fundamental trade-offs given in Figure 2.1 to manage supply chains. The retailer operates in a market with high concentration such that the Canadian retail market is dominated by the Loblaw Group.[3] Walmart Canada is the main competitor of the Loblaw Group although its total revenue is around $6 billion in 2023, which is lower than that of Loblaw. Given the retail footprint and large supply chain network of the leader, Walmart Canada faces many challenges in competing with the Loblaw Group. Nevertheless, they have successfully managed the supply chain trade-offs to stay competitive and serve Canadian consumers since 1994 (Souza, 2024).

---

[3] Many well-known Canadian retail chains (e.g., Loblaws, Fortinos, T&T, NoFrills, and Shoppers Drug Mart) are Loblaw subsidiaries, and the Group generated more than $50 billion in revenue in 2023. Visit the following link for Loblaw's financial reports: https://bicersupplychain.short.gy/G6FI9W.

Walmart Canada operates more than 400 stores and 17 distribution centers. The retailer employs more than 100,000 people (Toneguzzi, 2022). All operations in stores and distribution centers and the logistics activities between them are managed and controlled by Walmart (Hack, 2024). It has a large fleet of trucks moving goods from distribution centers to stores frequently. Focusing on the first trade-off (i.e., in-house operational vs. outsourcing costs), Walmart keeps critical operations in-house to fulfill customer demand timely and economically. Outsourcing logistics activities fully is not feasible for the retailer due to a high product variety, which would negatively impact service levels in stores. Nevertheless, Walmart Canada outsources only the shipping of online orders to select couriers such as Freightcom (Khurana, 2020). Here, the destination for online orders changes dynamically every day because the customers who place orders online differ over time. The planning and management of online orders can be costly for the retailer if they utilize their own fleet. Thus, outsourcing the delivery for online orders helps the retailer fulfill customer demand while keeping costs at a low level.

Walmart Canada determines the assortment in stores according to the second trade-off (i.e., amortization vs. inventory holding costs). In the retail setting, the amortization cost is equivalent to the fixed cost of shelf space. Retailers tend to reserve more space for popular products when the cost of shelf space is high. Then, the shelves are emptied quickly. *If it takes a long time to replenish the empty shelves*, keeping popular items would not be feasible. Instead, niche items with remarkably high margins would be more profitable because they stay on shelves for a long time, without any need for replenishment, and generate high profits. Here, the replenishment time can be considered the setup time. To cut the setup time, Walmart associates are tasked to replenish the shelves quickly. Thus, Walmart can reserve more space for popular items, generate high revenues, and turn inventory quickly.

Walmart Canada capitalizes on the third trade-off (i.e., high utilization vs long lead times) to increase the inventory turnover for a wide variety of items. When the shelf space is limited, items must be kept in storage areas before being exhibited to customers. This leads to an increase in days of inventory (analogous to production lead time in the manufacturing setting) and operational inefficiencies. Walmart Canada addresses this issue by operating large mega stores where the shelf space is not highly limited. Thus, products reach shelves quickly, increasing the inventory turnover of the retailer.

The fourth trade-off (excess inventory vs. product shortages) shapes Walmart Canada's inventory management and demand forecasting practices. The retailer coordinates inventory management, promotion, and demand forecasting practices to determine the ideal stock level of each SKU that optimizes the trade-off between excess inventory costs and product shortages. For durable goods, retailers like Walmart Canada – that is, having many megastores with enough shelf space – target high service levels. For that reason, managing the trade-off is not challenging for durable goods. For perishable items and food products, however, the cost of excess inventory is high. Walmart invests in automated replenishment and demand analytics to reduce the ordering cycle and forecasting horizon. This helps the retailer match supply with demand and minimize the mismatch costs for the perishable items (Nassauer, 2023).

Finally, Walmart Canada is also exposed to the last trade-off (i.e., revenue growth vs. supply–demand mismatches) to grow its business sustainably. The retailer built micro-fulfillment centers in the storage area of their megastores to implement omnichannel retailing, so they can sell products from megastores to customers online and grow revenues. Omnichannel retailing allows customers to pick up their orders from stores or get them delivered to their homes. Micro-fulfillment centers are considered a retail innovation that rely on automated systems. They are in mega stores where traditional warehousing equipment and machines do not fit. They are connected to the storage rooms of mega stores through conveyor belts. When an order is received from a customer, the products constituting the order are carried from storage rooms to the order preparation area by conveyor belts. Next, the order is prepared and transferred to the dispatching area. If the customer prefers to pick up their order from the store, it waits in the dispatching area for the customer's arrival. Otherwise, it is given to a courier to be delivered to the customer's home.

There are two operational risks of omnichannel retailing. First, it consumes the products in the storage area so that Walmart would need to replenish inventory more frequently. Second, associates need to go inside the store and pick up products from shelves in some cases. This eventually leads to a decrease in service levels for in-store customers. Therefore, omnichannel retailing makes Walmart Canada exposed to a higher risk of supply–demand mismatches. Nevertheless, its revenue growth will likely offset the increased risk of the mismatches, making omnichannel retailing more appealing to elevate profits.

In summary, Walmart Canada scrutinizes all five trade-offs to build their supply chain structure. The retailer uses supply chain integration and innovative business development practices to grow the business and increase revenues. It has a large amount of free cash flow in its accounts because revenues are collected immediately from customers, while the payments to suppliers are deferred according to payment terms. The excess cash can later be used in financial markets to generate nonoperational profits. The omnichannel practice also helps Walmart Canada increase sales. While capitalizing on the benefits of nonoperational profits and elevated sales owing to the omnichannel practice, the retailer integrates the supply chain to keep the mismatches at a certain level. To this end, Walmart Canada maintains most supply chain operations in-house and replenishes inventory frequently to cut lead times.

2.8 Conclusion

There is a common misperception that supply chain management is often regarded as the practice of delivering the right product, at the right time, in the right place to fulfill customer demand without keeping excess inventory. This definition reflects only the *operational* perspective and does not apply to companies with little sensitivity to supply–demand mismatches. Supply chain management is much more complex than this definition because modern supply chains also involve the coordination of information and capital flows. It is not possible to optimize operational decisions without weighing the information technology and financial dynamics of supply chains. Supply chain executives must therefore master a keen awareness of all interfaces among operations, finance, marketing, and information technology. This will help them align supply chains with business models and achieve supply chain excellence.

Focusing on the interfaces, we categorize supply chain strategies into four depending on companies' sensitivity to supply–demand mismatches and their business model. These four categories are not mutually exclusive as firms can often straddle more than two categories. Walmart Canada operates in the middle of supply chain integration and innovative business development. Another example is Seven Eleven Japan that operates in the middle of supply chain integration and premium business strategies. Originally founded in the United States as a convenience store chain, Seven Eleven's Japanese operations were later launched in 1973 under its licensing agreement with a Japanese retail chain. Having expanded exponentially, Seven Eleven Japan now operates 40 percent of all convenience stores in that country (Dooley & Ueno, 2019). The company had also acquired the *global* Seven Eleven in 1991, owning the brand worldwide ever since.

Convenience stores typically see high supply–demand mismatches due to low inventory turnover and infrequent replenishment. Because their prices are substantially higher than those of mega stores, they share some of the characteristics of premium business strategies. To cushion the negative aspects of mismatches, they shelve a limited selection of items. In contrast, Seven Eleven Japan has integrated its supply chain to *widen* product variety and services (Chopra, 2005). Seven Eleven has long invested in information technology to achieve supply chain transparency and real-time data transfer linking suppliers, distribution centers, stores, and the headquarters. Store owners have direct access to key analytical tools that help them determine what to order at a specific time on a specific day. Stores are replenished several times daily. Seven Eleven Japan offers thousands of different SKUs in each convenience store along with many other services such as home delivery, locker storage, insurance brokerage, ATM, photo, printing, bike sharing, laundry, and so on.[4] Owing to its supply chain integration strategy and premium pricing, Seven Eleven Japan is one of most important companies in Japan. Its umbrella firm, Seven & i Holdings, generated sales of $88 billion in 2023 served by 125,701 employees.[5]

Given that some firms like Walmart Canada and Seven Eleven overlap different categories, our identification of four supply chain strategies is diverse enough to cover a complete spectrum of supply chain practices in the real world. At the center of our identification lies the alignment of supply chains with business objectives. To achieve such alignment, executives must fully grasp the main goal, the reason for

---

[4] Visit the company website for a detailed list of store services: www.sej.co.jp/services/.
[5] Seven & i Holdings' financials are available via: www.fortune.com/company/seven-i-holdings/global500/.

existence, of their firms. Next, they must frame supply chains where the flows of operations, information, and capital can move smoothly along the chain. Such a supply chain framework allows decision-makers to quantify both its risks and uncertainties. The ensuing Chapter 3 further details the framework, risks, and uncertainties of supply chains.

3 | *Supply Chain Risks and Uncertainties*

Supply chains are exposed to various risks spawned by sourcing and production issues, plus high uncertainty in demand. Supply chain risks distinctly foil perfectly matching supply with demand. Supply-side disruptions and delays impact the availability of products. Firms affected by these risks face product shortage and lost demand. In 2000, two major players vied in the cellular phone market: (1) Nokia and (2) Ericsson. Both were sourcing radio frequency chips from the Philips chip plant in Mexico. When a fire struck the Philips plant in March 2000, Nokia engineers quickly retooled production to use other chip plants run by Philips. Nokia also changed the chip design for procurement from other chipmakers. However, Ericsson did not promptly react to the chip crisis. In the fire's wake, Ericsson forfeited potential sales of $400 million (Latour, 2001; Tomlin, 2006). Nokia's agile management of the crisis helped boost market share by 5 percent to a 36 percent level (Pringle, 2002).

In March 2011, Japan saw its strongest earthquake ever, born in the Pacific 132 km (or 82 mi) off the main island and causing massive tsunamis around 40 meters high. Sadly, it killed over 15,000 and displaced thousands (National Geographic Society, 2011). Japan, as the world's fourth largest economy with GDP standing at $4.29 trillion in 2023, has long had a strong production network in the electronics, computer, and automotive industries.[1] Following the tragic quake, most plants were closed in Japan, exerting a negative ripple effect on global supply chains from automotive to electronics and computer industries (Lohr, 2011). At the time of the earthquake, for example, Japanese electronics manufacturer Toshiba was making nearly one-third of memory chips. Many worldwide purchasers of chips and flash memories from Toshiba faced product shortages due to the

---

[1] Japan's macroeconomic indicators as of 1980 are available on the International Monetary Fund's website: www.imf.org/external/datamapper/profile/JPN.

plant closures in Japan. This spiked spot prices of chips 10–27 percent (Helft & Bunkley, 2011). The global automotive industry also suffered supply disruptions of Japanese-made auto parts. For example, GM closed its Louisiana plant (Lohr, 2011). On a macro scale, Japan's economy shrank 3.7 percent in the first quarter of 2011 due to quake-disrupted supply chains (Tabuchi & Wassener, 2011).[2]

Despite the devastating impact on the global economy, such supply disruptions were considered rare before 2020. It was not until the beginning of the COVID pandemic that we observed such frequent disruptions. In the second half of 2020, many manufacturers cut production outputs due to global chip shortages resulting from the virus lockdowns, the labor strikes near French sites of global chipmakers, and the factory fires in Japan (Boston, 2020). In 2021, the Suez Canal was blocked by a massive ship for six days. It was estimated that the entire value of daily product flow through the Canal totaled around $9 billion. Accumulated cost of delivery delays due to the blockage was estimated to be $900 million (Guardian Cairo Staff, 2021; Stevens, 2021). In 2022, many manufacturers in China stopped their operations under the lockdowns such that total volume of products passing through the Shanghai Port decreased around 40 percent (Jie, 2022). The war between Russia and Ukraine that started in February 2022 unleashed soaring food prices and global grain shortages, a situation described as the "global food crisis" (Hayashi, 2022). In 2023, political tension in the Red Sea caused more delays and disruptions in global trade. Transit companies rerouted containerships to avoid attacks; this, in turn, elevated China-to-Europe shipping costs 115 percent in a few weeks (Berger & Paris, 2024). Due to escalating supply disruptions, supply chain resilience became the hottest agenda topic of senior executives from COOs to CFOs (Williams-Alvarez, 2023).

Even when manufacturers mitigate disruptions and delays on the supply side, they yet struggle to make products available in the market due to production problems in their facilities. Quality problems, poor design of components, and machine failure trigger halts in production. For example, Ford stopped production of electric trucks after one vehicle fire ignited during a quality check (Eckert & Felton, 2023).

---

[2] The increasing trend in Japan's GDP stopped in 2011 due to the earthquake. The country's GDP also declined between 2012 and 2015, indicating that it took four years for Japan to complete economic recovery.

3: Supply Chain Risks and Uncertainties 53

This resulted in a truck shortage and long wait times for customers seeking to buy Ford trucks. Fortunately, Ford's quality engineers detected the problem during the production stage before vehicles hit the market. This helped the carmaker avoid costly recalls.

Samsung and Philips both suffered quality and production problems leading to colossal recall costs. In 2017, Samsung produced and marketed faulty Galaxy Note 7 smartphones where the model's battery could overheat and burn. The cause? Ambitious design objectives and poor manufacturing practices. The company recalled this smartphone at a total cost of $6 billion (Mozur, 2017). Poor production and quality assurance practices at Philips led to serious health problems for patients using its sleep apnea and ventilator products in 2021. Philips recalled almost three million machines and agreed to pay hefty lawsuit compensation. In the aftermath of the product recalls, Philips appointed a new CEO, underwent an organizational overhaul, and laid off nearly 10,000 employees (Meijer, 2023; Roland, 2021).

Manufacturers able to mitigate disruption and production risks can better source raw materials and produce final products. They can further stock inventory at planned levels to fulfill customer demand. However, firms cannot completely avoid supply–demand mismatches due to demand uncertainty. As discussed above, mismatch costs are colossal for many industries such as retail, manufacturing, and more. To match supply with demand, supply chain professionals must tackle not only supply risks and production problems but also *demand uncertainty*. Imagine a producer that ably manages all risks and uncertainties that, in turn, helps attain the perfect match between supply and demand. This manufacturer could still face cash-flow problems that occur when their buyers fail to pay invoices. Supply chain professionals must also have a strong understanding of cash-flow uncertainties to translate operational success into financial results. To this end, they must fully grasp both conceptual and practical sources of supply chain risks and uncertainties.

3.1 Conceptual Sources of Risks and Uncertainties

Frank Knight, a prominent economist and the founder of the Chicago School of Economics, distinguished risk from uncertainty such that risks can be measured and quantified, while uncertainty may yield unprecedented outcomes we never observed before (Knight, 1921).

As for demand, we often invoke "demand uncertainty" because it would turn out to be unexpectedly high or low, beyond our expectations. For example, toilet paper demand during the COVID pandemic was unprecedented to where retailers stocked out. When people speak of indicators directly influenced by markets, they often use the term "uncertainty" – for example, demand uncertainty or price uncertainty. Because market dynamics are often unpredictable, unprecedented outcomes often manifest in markets due to irrational or unexpected behavior of people – a phenomenon known as "irrational exuberance" (Shiller, 2016).

When people speak about technology and operations, they often use the term "risk" – for example, technology risk, process risk, and operational risk. Companies having proprietary information as to their technology and operations rely on in-house experts who can lay out potential outcomes from a range of actions. However, they cannot specify *which* outcome would be realized per action. While ambiguity in a system may end up with harmful outcomes, the risk of running the system can still be quantified by experts. Therefore, companies face various risks on the operational side, whereas they are exposed to demand and price uncertainties on the market side because transactions in the marketplace are uncontrollable compared to production activities.

From a conceptual point of view, both risks and uncertainties emerge from the tension between knowledge and truth. Figure 3.1 maps knowledge versus truth and the resulting risk and uncertainties.[3] First, organizations exposed to *operational risks* cannot always predict accurately the precise outcome of certain acts. However, an in-depth knowledge of operational dynamics helps the organization weigh the benefits versus costs of specific actions. This is considered *operational risk* because agents can lay out potential outcomes here. Here, employees' knowledge correctly reflects the truth about operational dynamics. However, the organization is still exposed to operational risks due to some variations in work processes. For example, a production engineer

---

[3] *The Cambridge Dictionary* defines knowledge as "understanding of or information about a subject." Given that individuals' understanding of and information about subjects may be misleading, knowledge may fail to reflect the truth in systems. Considering the possibility of false knowledge, our classification differs from other approaches that implicitly consider knowledge an accumulated set of true information (Bohn, 1994).

3: Supply Chain Risks and Uncertainties

Figure 3.1 Operational risks and uncertainties

may predict that shutting down a machine for half an hour would cause delivery lags in customer orders between one and three days. Although the engineer knows the process and potential implications of shutting down machines very well, it would not be possible to pinpoint the exact impact of breakdown on deliveries.

Uncertainty emerges in two different forms. The first occurs when our knowledge is so distorted that people are duped into believing fake information, which is referred to as *epistemological* uncertainty. This type of uncertainty stems from our own ignorance that occludes rational analyses of others' actions and incentives. The second form of uncertainty arises when the state of knowledge is not enough to characterize the dynamics of systems. This is called "*ontological* uncertainty" – also referred to as "unknown unknowns" or "deep uncertainty" such that the truth about the dynamics of systems remains unidentified (Roberts, 2020). When a firm introduces a niche product to the market, its demand is ontologically uncertain. In other words, decision-makers cannot predict accurately the demand nor specify its range because such a product has never sold before.

3.1.1 Operational Risk

Organizations create value where they excel in certain operational activities over time. While they can control such operations along several dimensions, some variations may still exist. Organizational knowledge might correctly identify the truth about an object or a working system. However, extensive knowledge may not suffice to eliminate process variations, thus incurring operational risks.

There is no strategic value in carrying operational risks. Eliminating them helps organizations boost profits and solve product quality issues. To this end, firms can develop in-house capabilities through digital transformation and advanced analytics to mitigate operational risks.

For instance, PepsiCo and Colgate invest in advanced preventive-maintenance technologies to detect irregular machinery sounds in their factories, which in turn helps avoid quality problems and machine breakdowns (Loten, 2022). Automakers also benefit from such technologies to detect defective parts before they are assembled into cars (Uberti, 2020). These efforts indeed lead to minimizing operational risks.

If eliminating operational risks internally is not viable, firms may *transfer* them to other supply chain parties. In the semiconductor industry, it is common to see manufacturers attempting to transfer operational risks because they would cause serious yield problems. In 2024, for example, new-generation wafers (i.e., discs ranging from one to twelve inches in diameter on which chips are printed) fabricated by Intel failed to pass quality tests to start large-scale production (Cherney, 2024). To transfer operational risks, Intel buys select types of wafers from Taiwanese manufacturer TMSC although the former has six wafer fabrication sites (Intel Corporation, n.d.; Norem, 2023).

When elimination and transfer of operational risks are both infeasible, organizations suffer from them and lose profits. In the end, companies have three options in dealing with operational risks: (1) control it in-house, (2) transfer it to other supply chain parties, or (3) suffer and lose profits.

3.1.2 Epistemological Uncertainty

One of the biggest rivalries in men's tennis featured Andre Agassi versus Boris Becker. These two stars faced each other fourteen times. After losing the first three matches in 1988 and 1989, Agassi won the next eight in a row. He lost only once more to Becker after 1989. Agassi's dominance on the court was due to Becker's facial "tell" that Agassi described after retiring (Davis, 2021). In a conversation with journalists in 2017, Agassi disclosed: "if … he put his tongue in the middle of his lip, he was either serving up the middle or the body. But if he put it to the side, he was going to serve out wide." When he eventually admitted this to Becker, Boris nearly fell off his chair: "I used to go home all the time and just tell my wife: it is like he reads my mind." In sports, players create uncertainty to trick their foes, and no one expects, for example, Becker to outright signal where he intends to serve! Those working to resolve such competitive uncertainties attain

3: Supply Chain Risks and Uncertainties

more career titles and reputation, just as Andre Agassi won eight grand slams versus only six for Boris Becker.

Decision-makers' knowledge that suffers distortion from information inaccuracy or agency conflict means exposure to epistemological uncertainty. In the case of a tennis match, each player faces epistemological uncertainty created by his opponent. To manage this uncertainty, each player must first rationalize the rival's behavior and then optimize one's decision. This is exactly what Agassi did in his matches against Becker.

Organizations have incentives to create epistemological uncertainty. Still, it is not a sustainable strategy to keep epistemological uncertainty at a high level. Imagine a farmer aiming to sell ten watermelons always at the best price in the farmers' market. However, less than half the ten watermelons are expected to be ripe. Suppose a restauranteur has learned over weeks that only 40 percent of the farmer's watermelons are ripe. Whenever the restauranteur attempts to buy watermelons from the farmer, he first asks which ones are ripe. If the farmer does not disclose any information, then the buyer opts out. If the farmer designates five watermelons of the ten, then the odds of selecting a ripe one improve. Here, the restauranteur would buy all five.

In practice, an organization is free to determine how much to disclose (or not disclose) of its proprietary information with outside parties. They may create epistemological uncertainty that would, in turn, yield increasing profits *in the short term*. However, too much epistemological uncertainty might repel partners or incur retaliatory actions. Thus, epistemological uncertainty must be kept at low or moderate levels in practice.

Epistemological uncertainty can be dangerous if one party (e.g., supplier) in a supply chain makes specific investments for the other party (e.g., buyer). As discussed in Section 1.2.2, large manufacturers in the aerospace industry (e.g., Boeing and Airbus) had induced their suppliers to expand their capacities in the past so that manufacturers could have a high service level without bearing the inventory risk. Suppose that an airplane manufacturer procures raw material facing uncertain demand that varies between 200 and 500 units. To ensure stock from the supplier, the manufacturer spreads the story that its demand always exceeds 500 units. Here, the supplier is exposed to epistemological uncertainty distorted by the manufacturer. If the supplier invests according to such distorted information, it would be exposed to losses, if not outright bankruptcy risk. In the 1990s, some suppliers in the aerospace industry made such unwise investments due to the epistemological uncertainty (Rossetti & Choi, 2005). The victims next retaliated by selling their products to airline companies in the aftersales service market. In other words, they disintermediated the aerospace supply chain and started selling their goods directly to customers of the manufacturers. Given that manufacturers earn substantial profits from aftersales service contracts, their earnings were negatively affected by this disintermediation. Therefore, the manufacturers lost profits due to the epistemological uncertainty they themselves created!

Decision-makers must rationalize the behavior of other supply chain parties to manage epistemological uncertainty. To this end, expert knowledge is especially important to minimize the negative aspects of epistemological uncertainty because experienced supply chain executives can effectively interpret the signals conveyed by others. Under a contractual relationship among supply chain parties, epistemological uncertainty would fade away because the contracts are binding by their nature. Therefore, the specified terms and purchase quantities in contracts can be regarded accurate without any distorted information. If buyers in supply chains inform their suppliers using *non-binding* communication channels (e.g., telephone conversations or vague emails), such information must be treated with caution and production schedules should not be purely based on it. While collecting data from different channels, Statistics Canada evaluates quality of the data and marks them such as "very good," "good," and so on to advise readers as to the quality and accuracy of data. Such an approach can be used in supply chains to minimize any negative impact of epistemological uncertainty on production levels.

Epistemological uncertainty may affect companies in distinct ways. For example, firms often survey social media to anticipate potential product sales or to understand customer trends. However, fake news and disinformation saturate social media. Recent advances in generative artificial intelligence (AI) have enabled the creation of phony videos and photos that look genuine. Fraud artists may fabricate news and use AI technology to support their false claims. Supply chain professionals who rely on social media for demand forecasting or other planning must be aware of the negative aspects of epistemological uncertainty due to the availability of fake information in social media. To this end, managers must check the credibility of news resources and corroborate them by using alternative sources. Otherwise, they risk making ill-founded decisions that destroy value.

3.1.3 Ontological Uncertainty

When the knowledge of employees in an organization *lacks the truth* as to the dynamics of their business, the organization is exposed to *ontological* uncertainty. Ontological uncertainty occurs when a new product is launched, a fresh business model is developed, or a disruptive innovation arises. Here, it is difficult to predict how the business will evolve in the future. For that reason, ontological uncertainty poses both threats and *opportunities* for organizations.

When Microsoft launched the portable media player Zune in 2006, they expected to steal market share from Apple's iPod. Zune had some interesting features at that time such as an effective subscription service that allows users to listen to shared songs. Microsoft also pursued an effective and artistic marketing strategy that looked appealing to music and technology enthusiasts. Despite all these efforts, the expectations from Zune never materialized (Rosoff, 2012).

Companies launch new products in anticipation of generating long-term profits. However, decision-makers often lack enough experience about the market dynamics of *new* products. Therefore, new product launches often end up with failure for several reasons such as poor product-market fit, insufficient capital, tough competition, poor timing, and so on (Cohen, 2024). For instance, the failure of Zune can be attributed to tough competition and Apple's strong dominance in the market. Nevertheless, product failures can be replaced by success stories when decision-makers manage ontological uncertainty effectively.

If decision-makers secure sufficient capital, test the product in different settings to collect customer feedback, and exhaustively improve the product to address customers' concerns, they can manage the ontological uncertainty effectively and help generate positive returns in the long term. The strategic importance of ontological uncertainty for organizations might be aptly expressed in a Chinese proverb: "There [are] no fish in clear water." If there is no ontological uncertainty in a business ecosystem, all wealthy investors invest in high-return projects and entrepreneurs cannot grow their startups. Amazon's evolution from an online book seller to e-commerce giant and technology company is a success story of managing the ontological uncertainty, which will be discussed later in this chapter. Another example is Facebook's transition from a social networking platform to an AI company.

Facebook started to invest in AI in 2014 when the company acquired virtual reality firm Oculus for $2 billion. Later in 2021, the company changed its name to Meta, reflecting the growing interest in metaverse. Owing to these efforts and continuous investments, the company has recently developed the Meta AI assistant and launched Meta-Ray-Ban smart glasses that can identify objects. At the time of this writing, it was already announced that the smart glasses would have the ability to translate conversations between different languages in real time (Gallagher, 2024). The virtual reality and AI solutions will later be integrated to Meta's platforms such as Facebook and WhatsApp.

Although Meta achieved an increase in the market value in the end, the journey of Facebook toward Meta was incredibly challenging such that the company suffered from some unforeseen risks. The magnitude of virtual reality expenses caused a lack of investors' confidence in the past, and the company lost 78 percent of its market value in around one year after the name change. Such a loss is part of the business because expectations may not be realized necessarily in the presence of ontological uncertainty. Nevertheless, Meta developed an effective contingency plan and found out a way to generate revenues from AI solutions. This also helped the company rebuild investors' confidence. Eventually, Meta increased its market value more than six-fold in less than two years (from November 2022 to September 2024).

In summary, organizations must be aware of the conceptual sources of operational risks and uncertainties. They wisely strive to eliminate *operational* risks, rationalize *epistemological* uncertainty to protect themselves from distorted information in supply chains, and invest toward resolving the *ontological* uncertainty to sustain long-term profitability.

3.2 Practical Sources of Risks and Uncertainties

A company's business model wields direct impact on its profitability, operational risks, and uncertainties. Decision-makers would be willing to take some risks of losing revenues if the upside potential of uncertainties outweighs the cost of potential losses. For this reason, dispelling every type of risk and uncertainty is not viable for any organization. Instead, decision-makers must focus on eliminating all types of *unnecessary* and *economically infeasible* risks or uncertainties. To this end, it is essential to identify key risk indicators and operational parameters that highly correlate with uncertainties in the supply chain. This can be achieved by laying out operational activities and their links to flows of information, operations, and capital (Biçer, 2022).

Figure 3.2 below presents the risk analysis framework that relates operational activities to risk indicators. Its concepts originate from Biçer (2022), and it extends the basic form of Biçer (2023, Figure 1.2). In the top tier, the impact of key lead times and customer-vendor accounts on the flows of information, goods, and capital is illustrated. Manufacturers purchase raw materials from suppliers and convert them into finished goods. Procurement activities start with searching for a supplier who can deliver raw materials at a reasonable price. Manufacturers contact their existing suppliers and negotiate terms for potential orders. They may also shop for new suppliers and assess their capabilities to fulfill the raw material demand. After analyzing all the options, manufacturers select a supplier and place a procurement order from that supplier. The time elapsing from when a procurement search starts until the delivery of the raw materials to the manufacturer is referred to as *procurement lead time*. This time window covers search activities, negotiation, assessment of suppliers, contracting, and the final physical delivery of ordered raw materials.

The time elapsing from when a procurement order is placed until its delivery to the manufacturer's side is referred to as *supply lead time*. Manufacturers sourcing raw materials from offshore suppliers via ocean transshipment have longer supply lead times than those sourcing from domestic providers. The longer the supply lead time, the higher the risks of supply disruptions and delivery delays. When the supply lead time increases, the ordered raw materials pass through more stages along the shipment from the supplier to the manufacturer. Those stages can be the Suez Canal or the Port of Los Angeles, where glitches incur supply disruptions or delivery delays.

During May–June 2023, some labor issues emerged at the ports of both Los Angeles and Long Beach. The Port of Los Angeles is the busiest port in the United States, processing over $400 billion in cargo per year (LaRocco, 2023). When the union representing port workers opted to slow down operations on May 30, the median

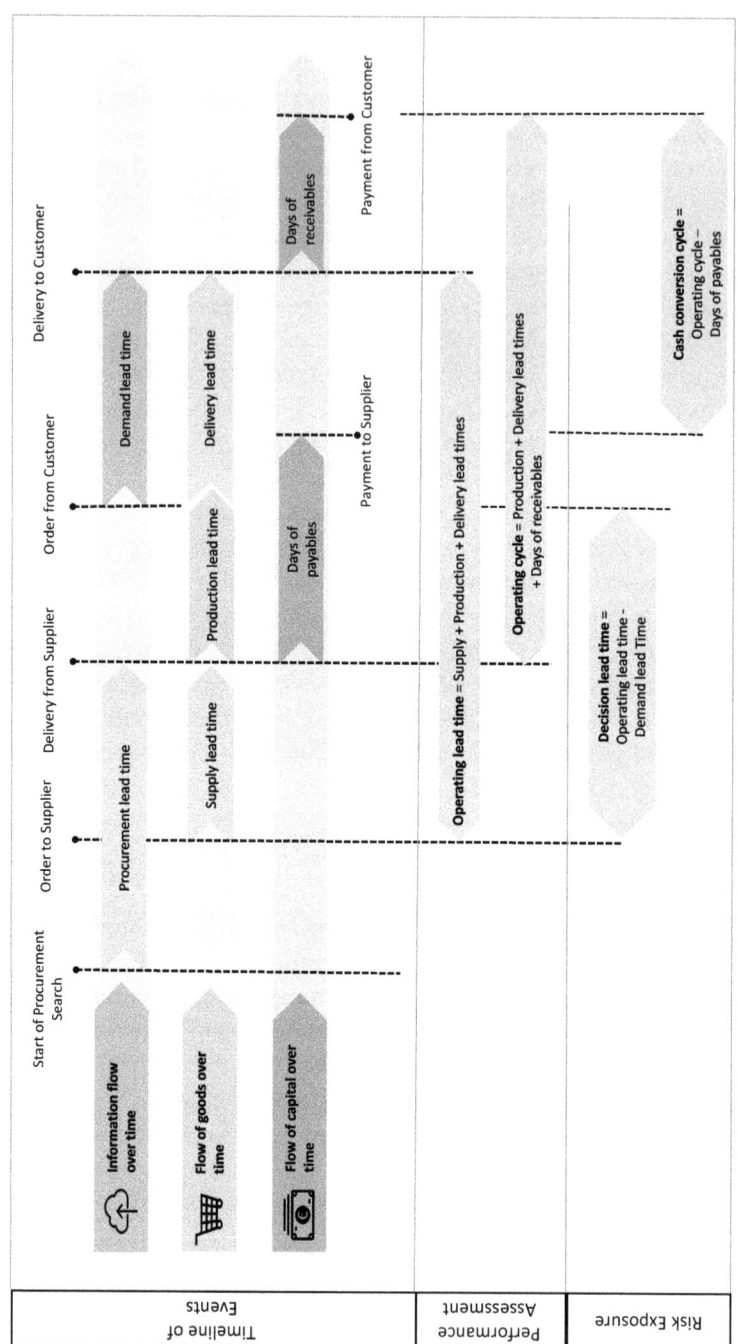

Figure 3.2 Risk analysis framework in supply chains

3: Supply Chain Risks and Uncertainties

waiting time for vessels to be processed at the LA Port swelled from 7.9 hours to 16.3 hours in just one day (LaRocco, 2023b). Manufacturers and retailers buying goods and raw materials from offshore suppliers remain vulnerable to such glitches due to long supply lead time and distance.

Manufacturers able to procure diligently can expedite the supply lead time significantly. They may have arrangements with suppliers where the yearly total volume of orders must be more than the minimum guaranteed order quantity. This type of deal induces the supplier to reserve capacity for the manufacturer. When a purchase order is placed for a specific item, the supplier can deliver it promptly. Here, supply lead time can be shortened per purchase order. Yet procurement lead time can be exceptionally long as negotiating terms of trade, setting a guaranteed order quantity, and writing the contract all take a long time.

For example, Li & Fung, a trading company based in Hong Kong, reduced the supply lead time from several months to five weeks for its customers. Li & Fung specializes in supply chain coordination for the apparel industry (Magretta, 1998). The company receives orders from apparel brands to fabricate a menu of new styles each season. To this end, Li & Fung collaborates with many textile and apparel producers in different footprints such as China, India, Bangladesh, Taiwan, and Sri Lanka. They develop a production plan to fulfill customer demand. They also reserve at least 30 percent of producers' capacity to gain flexibility. After they set up the production plan, apparel brands next can place purchase orders for each style a mere five weeks before the season. Therefore, the supply lead time for apparel brands is five weeks. Still, *procurement* lead time exceeds nine months because it involves all the contracting and supply chain coordination activities that Li & Fung enact before apparel brands place their purchase orders.

After receiving the raw materials from suppliers, manufacturers fabricate these into finished goods and deliver them to customers. The time that elapses from when the raw materials are received until the completion of production is referred to as *production lead time*. When the production is completed, the finished goods are delivered to customers. The time window for the delivery of goods to customers is called *delivery lead time*. The sum of production and delivery lead times in Figure 3.2 yields the total time duration in which inventory is kept in financial accounts. For that reason, total length of production and delivery lead times is also referred to as *days of inventory*, which is an inventory-productivity metric for producers. In the electronics industry, days of inventory may vary from two months to as much as two years (Manners, 2023). In apparel, it swings from two to eight months (Anzolin & Aloisi, 2021). Manufacturers with high capacity and operational flexibility where setup times are extremely low enjoy a short production lead time, thus helping them curb their days of inventory. However, reducing the production lead time alone is not always enough to cut days of inventory sharply if *delivery* lead times for outbound logistics are exceptionally long. This happens when a manufacturer is located far away from its customers.

The total lead time of supply plus production plus delivery equals *operating lead time* that starts with the purchasing order of raw materials and ends with the delivery of final goods to customers. Operating lead time defines how long it takes for a manufacturer to create value for customers. Manufacturers with short operating lead times are highly effective in managing their supplier relations, producing finished goods, and delivering items to customers. Therefore, they quickly create value for customers without bearing the risk of supply–demand mismatches.

When the operating lead time is protracted, manufacturers are considered ineffective in creating value for customers. In such cases, they are exposed to high supply–demand mismatches because critical decisions such as procurement of raw materials and production scheduling are made well before customer demand is known. If the operating lead time is four months, for example, the inventory decisions that would impact the fulfillment of customer demand must be made four months in advance of the realization of demand. Therefore, the manufacturer must rely on demand forecasts in a horizon of four months. If the manufacturer cuts the operating lead time to two weeks, the inventory decisions must be made only two weeks in advance of realization of demand. It is much easier to predict accurately the demand two weeks ahead than four months in advance. The resulting supply–demand mismatches due to long operating lead times will impose operational inefficiencies in organizations.

Some operational inefficiencies due to long operating lead times can be offset by making customers wait for their orders. The *demand lead time* is a time window that starts with receiving a customer order and ends with its final delivery. Customers are occasionally willing to wait for shipment of their orders. For example, Adidas customers are willing to wait four to six weeks to buy custom shoes that are designed by themselves. The bag designer Timbuk2 delivers standard bags within two days, whereas it takes two to three weeks to deliver customized bags (Timbuk2 Company, n.d.).

A manufacturer knows the demand at the instant when a customer order is received, which starts the clock for the demand lead time. Therefore, operations during the demand lead time are carried out with known demand information. Suppose a manufacturer has a supply lead time of 1.5 weeks and days of inventory of 2.5 weeks, thus totaling four weeks of operating lead time. The demand lead time is three weeks. In this case, the *procurement* order must be placed four weeks in advance of the fulfillment of customer demand. Thus, the procurement decision is made with demand *uncertainty*. Yet demand lead time exceeds the days of inventory, and here all *production* and *outbound logistics* decisions are made while knowing the demand perfectly. Hence, the mismatch risk for this manufacturer is limited only to the raw materials, and it can erase all the mismatch and capacity overutilization risks for the production stage and outbound logistics.

To measure the exposure to the mismatch risk, manufacturers scrutinize *decision lead time*, which is the *difference* between operating and demand lead times. The decision lead time rises with supply, production, and delivery lead times, but truncates as the demand lead time grows. Extended decision lead time means higher risk of mismatches between supply and demand. When manufacturers have a high demand uncertainty for their products, they are expected to be exposed to high mismatch risk. These manufacturers must cut the *decision* lead time to curtail the mismatch risk. This can be attained in two ways: (1) reduce the operating lead time and (2) expand the demand lead time. For example, Zara and Uniqlo have targeted a lower operating lead time to minimize the decision lead time. To this end, the focus has been on strengthening supplier relationships and accelerating its fabrication practices (Monroe, 2021). Other firms, such as Timbuk2, convince their customers to wait for their orders. Here, businesses extend the demand lead time to reduce the decision lead time that, in turn, helps reduce the mismatch risk.

Supply chain practices also impact corporate *financial risk*. Our framework in Figure 3.2 features metrics that capture a company's exposure to cash-flow uncertainty. Manufacturers have payment terms with both suppliers and customers. The payment term with suppliers is known as *days of payables*. This time window enjoins when a producer must remit invoices to its suppliers. Manufacturers that delay payables to suppliers are well-positioned to manage their working capital. However, this would hurt the suppliers' cash flow. For example, the suppliers of Giant Bicycles were affected negatively in 2023, when Giant declared its decision to delay payments due to deteriorating market conditions (Mallon, 2022).

The payment term with customers is referred to as *days of receivables*. It is the time window during which manufacturers collect revenues from customers. Producers able to expedite their receivables manage working capital effectively by collecting revenues from customers quickly. The time length that covers the sum of days of inventory plus days of receivables is the *operating cycle*. This is the time length that elapses from the instant when a manufacturer starts operational activities until revenues are collected from customers. In other words, it covers the period during which the manufacturer spends cash to sustain operations. Therefore, the operating cycle defines how long it takes to generate revenues. A prolonged operating cycle signals financial inefficiencies, some of which are transferrable to suppliers by extending the days of payables.

This brings us to another important metric – that is, the *cash conversion cycle*: the difference between the operating cycle and days of payables. Cash conversion cycle equals the time length to finance operations. Suppose the daily operating expense of a manufacturer is $10 K. If the manufacturer has 100 days of cash conversion cycle, it should hold a working capital of $1 million (i.e., $10 K*100) to sustain operations. Reducing the cash conversion cycle by fifty days, for example, would permit the release of $500 K, half the former working capital. This would, in turn, strengthen the financial position of the manufacturer.

Decision lead time and cash conversion cycle have ramifications for the business model of manufacturers. When decision lead time is negative, the manufacturer first receives orders from customers. Only after collecting demand data, the manufacturer carries out all operational activities such as placing purchase orders with suppliers and producing goods. No mismatch between supply and demand arises here because customers simply wait for the products. When the decision lead time is positive, the manufacturer carries out some or all operational activities *before* knowing customer demand. In this case, manufacturers stock raw materials and/or finished goods before knowing the demand. Therefore, manufacturers are exposed to supply–demand mismatches when the decision lead time is positive. With a positive cash conversion cycle, manufacturers should keep working capital to finance operations. If the cash conversion cycle is negative, spare capital can be used in financial markets to yield more profits.

3.3 Operational Risks and Uncertainties in the Service Industry

The framework given in Figure 3.2 applies to manufacturers or retailers where the firm sources materials from suppliers and delivers goods to customers, comprising a *physical* flow of goods. In supply chains, manufacturers or retailers also work with *service* providers such as logistics firms and maintenance service companies. Dynamics in the service industry are distinct from those in retail or manufacturing: a service provider offers a service, not physical product, to their customers. Despite this structural difference, service management is a part of supply chain management because some activities along supply chains are dependent on service providers. Risks and uncertainties in the service industry logically exert a cascading effect on supply chains. For example, the way logistics companies manage their risks would impact ocean shipment time, which directly affects supply lead time. Therefore, supply chain executives must have a clear understanding as to the risk framework of their service providers.

Service firms mobilize their resources to fulfill customer demand. For example, logistics companies deploy trucks and offer transport services to producers. Banks and insurers employ clerks that financially serve their customers. To acquire and utilize select resources, they incur fixed and variable costs. Logistics companies make huge investments in their vehicle fleet, such investments exemplifying fixed costs in the service industry. Tapping their resources incurs operational costs such as fuel and driver payroll that comprise variable costs. Under high fixed and operational costs for their resources, service providers aim to utilize resources at remarkably high rates to make profits. Yet high resource utilization causes long waiting and service times for customers, having a negative impact on the speed and quality of services. At the center of service operations management lies the trade-off between the utilization of resources versus lead times (i.e., waiting times for customers).

To alleviate this trade-off, companies try to match customers with resources effectively. For example, Uber is the most popular ride-hailing platform in the world, which is used by many drivers and customers. Because it achieves the matching of customers with drivers very effectively, Uber can increase the utilization of drivers while reducing the waiting time for riders. This, in turn, helps the platform lower the riding costs and attract more drivers and customers to use the platform. To manage the trade-off and identify such business opportunities in the service industry (e.g., Uber's business model), decision-makers must outline the flows of information, services, and capital. To this end, Figure 3.3 presents an updated version of the risk framework configured for the service industry.

Service operations start when resources are assigned to serve customers. For example, most banks open their doors at 9:00 AM on weekdays to serve customers. One may be unable to find an Uber driver after midnight as drivers are mostly available from morning to late evening. Having resources available to serve customers does not mean that a resource is actively utilized. The time elapsing from the instant when a resource is available until it starts to serve a customer is *resource acquisition time*, as shown in Figure 3.3. Long resource acquisition time indicates operational inefficiency. It is the sum of the *idle time* of the resource plus *customer waiting time*.

Uber utilizes a geospatial matching algorithm to minimize resource acquisition time to make the platform attractive for both drivers and ride-hailers (i.e., using the Ringpop technology that forwards requests to correct node (Lozinski, 2016)). When a customer calls for an Uber ride, the app matches the customer with a nearby driver to reduce the customer waiting time. This helps Uber reduce the resource acquisition time and lure more customers to the platform owing to fast service. As the customer count grows, idle time for drivers shrinks and the resource acquisition time is reduced additionally. Thus, the mechanism of the platform is designed to cut the resource acquisition time.

The time that elapses from when a customer requests a service until its completion is called *demand lead time*. It has two components. The first one is the *customer waiting time* (also part of resource acquisition time). Uber makes this information available to customers so that they can monitor the waiting time for a ride after submitting a request on the

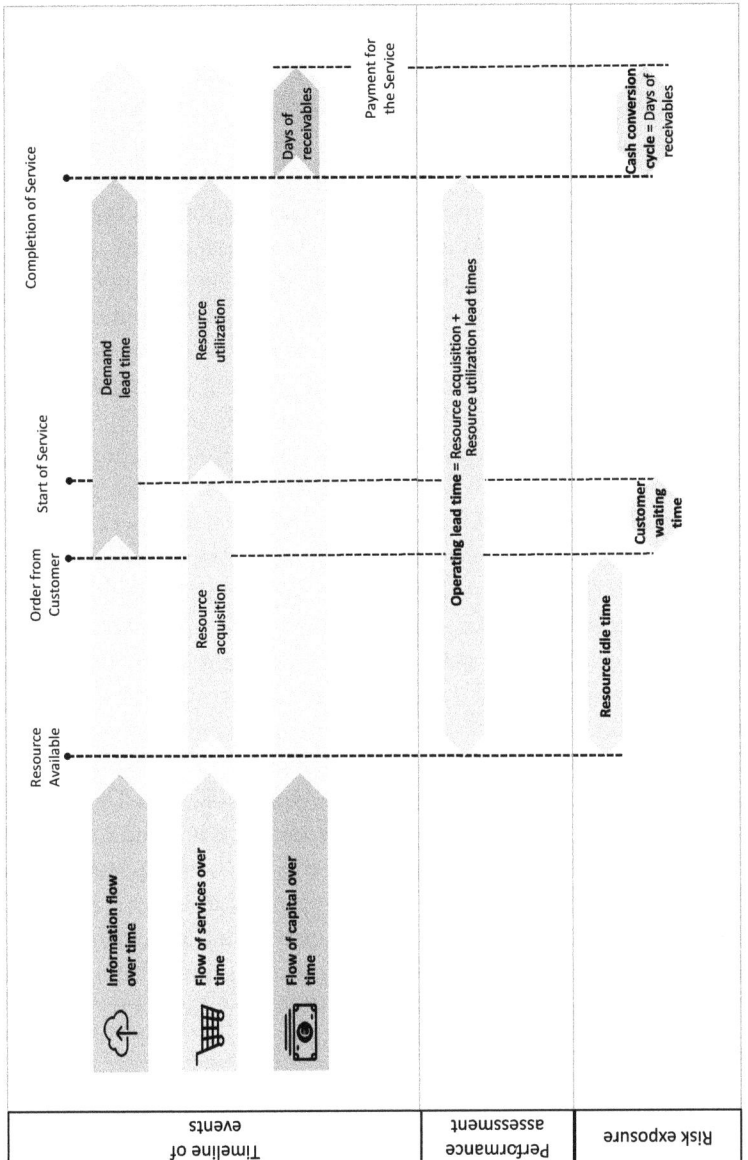

Figure 3.3 Risk analysis framework in the service industry

platform. The second is *resource utilization time*, which is the time length from the instant when the service starts until its completion. Service firms can reduce the demand lead time by increasing resource levels, which helps trim customer wait times during rush hour. They can also pursue process improvements that expedite operations to cut *resource utilization time*, which in turn leads to a reduction of the demand lead time.

The sum of resource acquisition plus utilization times is the operating lead time. It is the total duration for a resource to complete a customer service. This parameter is a key indicator of operational and financial efficiencies for the capital-intensive service industry. For example, logistics firms own expensive trucks providing transport services. These trucks incur ongoing costs covering maintenance and depreciation. Suppose a new truck depreciates $1,000 monthly plus a yearly cost of maintenance and repairs nearing $5,000. Labor cost for a truck driver can total $200 daily. Hence, the daily fixed cost per truck is around $246 (200+1000/30+5000/365 = $246). If the operating lead time is one day per service priced at $230, this business will not prove profitable. If average operating lead time can shrink to half a day by optimizing workload and scheduling, then business would earn profits.

In the service industry, providers have payment terms only with customers, not suppliers. Though most service providers (e.g., Uber, logistics companies) are paid instantly by their customers, there may be cases where a customer would delay payment. The *cash conversion cycle* protracts positive with any lag in revenue collection. This would hurt the financials of service providers, especially when capital investments are large. Here, the cash conversion cycle is an important indicator of the financial risk in the service industry, which correlates with the cash-flow uncertainty. One more important risk indicator is *operating lead time*, which correlates with operating costs. Decision-makers and finance professionals must focus on these two metrics to stabilize the finances of capital-intensive service models.

3.4 The Amazon Example

In the first quarter of 2024, Amazon reported total revenue of $143.3 billion with a profit margin of 7.25 percent. The revenue breakdown of its financials shows that only 38.2 percent of total revenue came from online stores. The remaining part came from the

3: Supply Chain Risks and Uncertainties

marketplace (24.1 percent), Amazon Web Services (17.4 percent), Ads (8.2 percent), Prime subscriptions (7.5 percent), and other business units (Richter, 2024). This diversity of revenue streams indicates that Amazon is not a typical e-commerce retailer but a tech giant. However, the current outlook of the company is very much different from how it started the business.

Amazon was founded in 1994 as an online bookstore (Popomaronis, 2020). At that time, Amazon was competing with other bookstores such as Barnes & Noble. It gradually expanded product offerings such that Amazon started to sell CDs and DVDs and launched electronics and toys categories before 2000. In the 2000s, Amazon established itself as the biggest online retailer in the world. Then, it increased technology investments in cloud computing (i.e., Amazon Web Services) and other innovations such as the marketplace allowing third-party sellers to sell their products on Amazon. The technology giant also launched Echo and Alexa products and started to offer digital content and prime subscriptions. Such an evolution of the company was unforeseen in the 1990s.

Amazon was born amid ontological uncertainty. At the online retail giant's founding, Jeff Bezos contacted investors to raise capital. However, investors asked what the Internet was, and they were very skeptical of Amazon's future (Kadakia, 2020). At that time, the future of online retail was highly exposed to ontological uncertainty. Amazon would not have attained high growth over the years if the future of e-commerce had been clear in the 1990s. Otherwise, big players (e.g., Walmart) would have invested in developing a supreme online platform and have prevented Amazon's evolution from an online bookstore into a retail giant. In other words, Amazon owes its success to the ontological uncertainty about customer trends and technology innovations so that the company's efforts came to fruition in the long term.

When it comes to the risk management framework given in Figure 3.2, Amazon has performed well given some limitations. We must recognize that Amazon has long been a growth-oriented company that aims to sell everything online. The procurement and supply lead times cannot be controlled easily given diverse product variety. For that reason, Amazon must have central warehouses and hold inventory sufficiently to fulfill the customer demand in a timely manner. Because demand from different regions is fulfilled from one warehouse, Amazon can offer a large product variety beyond the capabilities of other retailers. Amazon has also cut the delivery time over the years. The company can deliver orders for prime customers in the same day owing to its strong supply chain footprint. This helps Amazon spur sales by attracting customers with short demand lead times.

Regarding cash-flow management, Amazon offers efficient payment services to their customers. The customers can own a digital wallet from Amazon – that is, Amazon Pay – to pay their bills and benefit from some deals. The number of Amazon Pay account owners reached 180 million in 2023 (Batra et al., 2024). The digital wallet makes it possible for customers to reload money to their accounts. This, in turn, leads to a reduction of the cash conversion cycle such that Amazon has enjoyed negative cash conversion cycle for a long time.

Overall, Amazon has long managed supply chain risks and uncertainties very effectively from both conceptual and practical points of view. It evolved from an online bookstore to a tech giant by carefully investing in ontological uncertainty, designing supply chain network according to lead times and customer expectations, and developing digital solutions to improve cash management.

3.5 Conclusion

Supply chain networks are exposed to various risks and uncertainties. To manage them, supply chain professionals must have a strong understanding of both the conceptual and practical sources of risks and uncertainties inherent to supply chains.

We began this chapter with the *conceptual* sources such that there are three types of risks and uncertainties based on the mapping between the knowledge of organizations and the truth about operational systems. The first is measurable process variation that leads to *operational risks*. Decision-makers can outline the outcomes of such variations. However, they cannot fully keep them under control. Operational risks negatively affect the bottomline of companies, and they must be eliminated. The second conceptual source is the *epistemological uncertainty*, which arises from distorted information in supply chains. Suppliers and customers may be less than transparent to gain operational flexibility and to increase their advantages. Writing contracts with them is the safest way to avoid epistemological uncertainty. If this is not possible, decision-makers must rationalize the actions of supply chain partners to mitigate the epistemological uncertainty. The third

3: *Supply Chain Risks and Uncertainties*   73

conceptual source is *ontological uncertainty*, where the reality about operational systems remains unknown. This type of uncertainty is also described as "unknown unknowns" or even "deep uncertainty." Ontological uncertainty brings challenges but also worthwhile *opportunities* to organizations. Therefore, firms must invest in the ontological uncertainty to realize its upside potential.

To identify the practical sources of risks and uncertainties, we have mapped a risk analysis framework depicting the flows of information, goods (or services), and capital in supply chains. In practice, supply chains can be more complex than what we have depicted in Figures 3.2 and 3.3. For example, *supply lead time* may vary per order, making our framework featuring a fixed time length infeasible for some supply chains. Nevertheless, decision-makers can use expected values of varying time lengths to frame their supply chains and understand their exposures to different supply chain risks and demand uncertainty. Companies often possess detailed transactional data of their procurement, production, logistics, and sales activities. Information from these databases can be extracted to form the risk analysis framework in Figure 3.2 or 3.3.

We now conclude the first part of this book that has looked at supply chain management from three different angles to understand its dynamics, complexities, and challenges. First, we have discussed the *economics* of supply chain management and refined our economic thoughts to better understand supply chain dynamics. We have next explained the *fundamental trade-offs*, which lets us depict supply chain complexities in two-by-two matrix form (i.e., Figure 2.2). In this chapter, we have examined supply chain risks and uncertainties to illustrate the challenges of supply chain management. In Part II, which follows (Chapters 4–7), we will delve into four strategies that emerge from our two-by-two matrix typology.

Four Strategies of Supply Chain Management

4 | *Leading the Operational Edge: Supply Chain Integration*

If companies have business models driven by markets more than processes, they tend to quickly respond to rapidly evolving customer demand. These types of companies often introduce several products to the market during short seasons, and they are exposed to high supply–demand mismatches. Those firms may not be good at generating nonoperational profits. For that reason, the costs of supply–demand mismatches can hurt the bottom line. Therefore, they must integrate supply chains to curb the mismatches, which in turn helps increase profits and grow the business.

When Abdullah Kamani immigrated to the UK in the 1960s, he would not have imagined that he could disintermediate the textile supply chain to sell fast-fashion clothes to millennials in the 2000s (Monroe, 2021). Mr. Kamani began business by selling bags at a street stand. He later opened a textile facility operating as a contract manufacturer for retail brands such as Primark and H&M. His son Mahmud extended his father's legacy by founding Boohoo.com in 2006. Boohoo is a UK-based online fast-fashion retailer that generated GBP 447 million in the first quarter of 2022 with a gross margin of 52.8 percent (Smith, 2022).

The success of Boohoo can be attributed to the company's operational model, where the supply chain is very well integrated into the market. First, Boohoo fabricates clothes in the UK rather than outsourcing the production to offshore countries. The company owns a manufacturing facility in Leicester, UK, sited just 160 km (about 100 mi) from London. It also runs three distribution centers in the UK to keep inventory of finished garments. In addition to the manufacturing and distribution centers, Boohoo operates fulfillment centers in seven large cities, such as London, Paris, Los Angeles, and Istanbul, to stay close to customers in dense population zones (Boohoo Group PLC, n.d.).

The simplicity of its supply chain network, where the products flow from the Leicester facility to three distribution centers and the local fulfillment sites, makes it possible to have better control over inventory and logistics systems. Because of this flow map, Boohoo has cut its production batch sizes. Unlike other fashion apparel brands where a minimum production run exceeds 5,000 units, the batch sizes for Boohoo can shrink to 300 units. Thus, demand planners can replenish inventory more frequently in low volume according to market demand. If demand for a new style suddenly surges, Boohoo can replenish stock to fulfill customer orders. If demand is low, no replenishments occur. This helps Boohoo avert excess inventory risk. While many fashion apparel brands, such as H&M, often struggle with excess inventory (Paton, 2018), Boohoo operates without much exposure to supply–demand mismatches, which in turn fuels high growth and profitability.

Cisco also exemplifies the importance of supply chain integration for sustainable growth and profitability (Lee & Shao, 2009). The company has long developed and sold computer network gear such as switches and routers. Since its launch, Cisco has also expanded its menu of products aggressively to more than 300 product families. In 2022, the company reported $51.6 billion annual revenue and $11.8 billion net profit (Cisco Systems, 2022). Cisco enjoys a diverse customer base where varieties of routers, switches, phones, and conferencing systems are offered to businesses, telecommunication companies, and consumers alike.

Cisco owes its success to strategic acquisitions and its integrated supply chain network. It acquired around 100 firms in the new millennium to expand product offerings and hone extant solutions (Cisco Systems, 2024). In September 2023, for instance, Cisco acquired cybersecurity company Splunk for $28 billion (Goswami, 2023). Its diverse portfolio of high-tech products is not produced in-house but outsourced to contract manufacturers such as Foxconn (Lee & Shao, 2009). Outsourcing production may appear quite risky for a technology company like Cisco. First, production activities can be extraordinarily complex when fabricating and assembling thousands of different components. Quality problems seem inescapable when outsourcing production to a manufacturer with average capability. Second, protection of intellectual property becomes more difficult with outsourced versus in-house production. Nevertheless, Cisco has integrated its supply chain very effectively. The company maintains high product quality while controlling all supply chain activities to avoid any loss of intellectual property.

Cisco has long focused on two issues to achieve supply chain integration: (1) supply chain restructuring and (2) IT investments. First, management restructured the supply chain network in the 2000s to reduce its roster of contract manufacturers from 13 to 5 and its list of key suppliers from around 200 to 90. Supply chain partners were selected based on production capacity, manufacturing capability of complex products, product design knowledge, and supply chain agility. While consolidating partnerships to trim the supply chain footprint, the production capacity and supply chain responsiveness were not impaired due to its diligent selection process. Restructuring the supply chain allowed Cisco to focus on a limited number of supply chain allies, monitor their activities closely, pool the inventory risk with fewer sites, and refine operations. As a result, operating lead times are reduced up to 73 percent (Cisco Systems, 2014).

Another benefit of restructuring is that Cisco saw opportunities to innovate its supply chain. Before restructuring, Cisco had been operating in the push model where devices are fabricated according to demand forecasts *before* customers place orders. Due to the uncertainty in demand forecasts for such a fast-paced industry, the push system incurs exposure to the mismatches between supply and demand. Especially in the electronics industry, there is a colossal penalty for excess inventory. Electronics manufacturers incur capital costs tied up to excess inventory and operating costs of physically holding inventory in stock. Beyond these two cost elements, there are price devaluation and product obsolescence costs (Callioni et al., 2005). The cost of price devaluation refers to a falling product price over time. Product obsolescence cost is the disposal cost of an old product where demand vanishes as a new model is introduced. After Cisco's restructuring, it changed its business model from push to a *pull* (i.e., configure-to-order) system. Pull products are built *after* receiving customer orders in the configure-to-order model such that the market demand is served precisely without buffer inventory or bearing any excess inventory risk. Therefore, Cisco eliminated all risks associated with unsold inventory and gained a competitive edge in the electronics industry.

The management team at Cisco has also invested in the IT system to improve visibility and to minimize redundancies in the supply chain. To this end, the team opted to develop a centralized IT system to manage relationships with suppliers, customers, contract manufacturers, and other stakeholders (McAfee et al., 2004). With several business units at Cisco managing different product families, each had wielded much control over developing specific IT solutions. Unfortunately, this created redundant IT solutions such that some units may have developed different tools to address the same issues as the other units. For example, Cisco had *nine* different IT systems checking the status of customer orders in the early 2000s. When order status was labeled "shipped," it meant "shipped to the contract manufacturer" in one system but "shipped to the customer" in another. Here, information was distorted, unleashing uncertainties in the lead-time calculations. To address these issues, management standardized the ERP system, reduced the number of custom applications from 250 to 10, and simplified the operations and business flows. Thus, the IT system became a supporting instrument for new product launches rather than an obstacle. In the end, the company truncated its time-to-market by 30–50 percent (Cisco Systems, 2014).

These examples show the importance of supply chain integration for sustainable growth and profitability. Supply chain integration can be achieved in alternative forms depending on the first three fundamental trade-offs. For instance, Cisco and Boohoo manage the trade-off between in-house production versus outsourcing costs in separate ways such that the former follows an effective outsourcing strategy, while the latter keeps production in-house. Nevertheless, both achieved supply chain integration and minimized the mismatches. Therefore, supply chain integration addresses the fourth fundamental trade-off while being influenced by the first three trade-offs as outlined in Figure 4.1.

There are two main challenges of integrating supply chains: (1) product variety and (2) complex sales and logistics networks. Decision-makers can address these challenges in their integration efforts by following four alternative strategies. Those are effective capacity management, lead-time reduction, delayed differentiation, and operational excellence through systematic cost and lead-time reduction practices. In what follows, we will walk through these challenges and strategies.

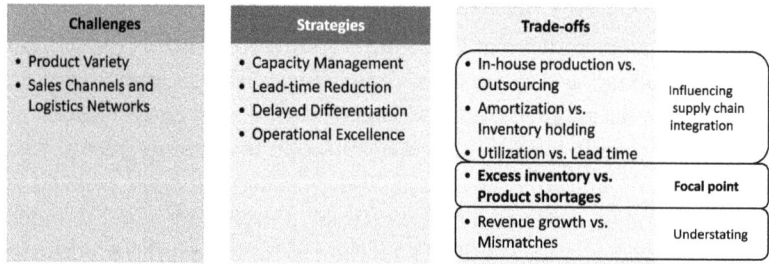

Figure 4.1 Scheme of supply chain integration

4: Leading the Operational Edge

4.1 Operational Complexities

Imagine a farmer in a village who owns a dairy cow. He feeds the cow with grass or soybean, and he milks the cow for sale to other villagers. Here, the supply chain structure is quite simple. The farmer buys soybean meal from a wholesaler such that the only supplier is the wholesaler. There is only one type of customer who is a villager buying milk from the farmer.

Now suppose that the farmer grows the business over years. He has too many dairy and meat cattle. He owns a dairy processing facility where workers make varieties of cheese, butter, and yogurt from raw milk. He also owns a butchering plant where the meat is cut and packaged. The farm has expansive acreage for growing corn and soybean crops – some used as animal feed, the rest sold to traders. Cattle manure is used to fertilize the soil. For this business, the supply chain becomes overly complex. The farmer sells dozens of products to retailers, grocers, diners, grain traders, and others. He purchases various ingredients and processors from a plethora of suppliers to process the milk and meat. He reinjects some outputs as intermediary products back into the supply chain – that is, soymeal to feed animals and cattle manure to fertilize the soil.

This farmer's scenario shows that there are *two* dimensions of supply chain complexity. They are *product variety* and the *expansion of the supply chain network*. Compared to the initial setting, our farmer now sells several dairy and meat products. He has also expanded the supply chain network with countless suppliers, customers, and additional processes along the chain. Such examples are not limited to the agriculture industry. It is common in practice that product variety and expansion of the network emerge as the two main causes of operational complexities firms must address while integrating supply chains.

4.1.1 Product Variety

Customers demand products and services tailored to their specific needs and tastes. However, very few people have the luxury or the chance of getting products and services that are *completely* tailored to their requests. The Air Jordan collection, designed and sold by Nike, has been entirely developed per the preferences of NBA legend

Michael Jordan. Adidas designs the Messi collection based on the ideas of soccer legend Lionel Messi. When common people buy a product, we must shop from a limited menu. Nevertheless, companies have increased their variety tremendously during the last two decades to fulfill the diverse needs of their customers.[1] Amazon, for example, sells more than 12 million products online. This number increases to nearly 340 million for Amazon Marketplace, including external merchants who sell their products through Amazon.com (RTP Editorial Staff, 2016).

While product proliferation helps companies increase their revenues by fulfilling diverse needs of customers, this is often obstructed for two reasons. The first is that customers' *search cost* to obtain product information escalates with product variety. It is not possible for a customer to know the features of every product sold by a big retailer such as Walmart and Amazon. Nevertheless, the Internet alleviates this problem: the websites of online retailers and companies help customers search for products, check for product availability, and submit their purchase orders. In the B2B markets, companies can do the same through platforms such as Alibaba to find a supplier or place a procurement order. Therefore, the Internet has cut the search costs in the market, which in turn induces consumers and corporations to purchase more niche products (tailored toward more specific needs) than the standard ones.[2]

The second obstacle to product proliferation is operating costs that soar with product variety. Fortunately, some manufacturers have recently managed to keep operating costs low while making diverse products through technological advances. For example, additive manufacturing (i.e., 3D printing) uses plastics, powders, metals, or carbon fiber plus adhesives to fabricate objects based on some specifications. This technology enables the production of low-demand items without making large investments. Hence, it has been

---

[1] According to an industry survey of large global manufacturers with revenue summing over $250 billion per year, product variety increased 263 percent from 2010 to 2017 (Mitchell, 2019).
[2] This phenomenon is referred to as "long tail" theory (Anderson, 2004; Brynjolfsson et al., 2011). Markets had typically been dominated by a small list of hot products with 80 percent of total revenue coming from the top 20 percent of products. This 80/20 principle, also known as the Pareto rule, was replaced by the long-tail theory in the early 2000s owing to widespread Internet usage.

adapted in different industries, such as aerospace and construction, to innovate production processes. One Airbus subsidy, Satair, uses 3D-printing technology to manufacture spare parts of old aircraft that are still in use (Bellamy, 2020). General Electric utilizes this technology to make products that are too complex to make by traditional methods.

Beyond businesses, public works and households can use additive manufacturing for construction purposes. The City of Amsterdam commissioned a construction project to build a 3D-printed bridge, which was later completed and sited in Amsterdam (Parkes, 2021b). One Dutch couple owns a 3D-printed house in the Netherlands that was developed in partnership with the Eindhoven University of Technology (Boffey, 2021).

Additive manufacturing makes it possible to produce a range of niche items tailored to customer preference, or even ultra-complex products where traditional manufacturing proves too expensive. Yet this technology is ill-suited for mass production of standard products because its output rate is low compared to traditional methods using assembly lines and CNC machines. Adidas opened its 3D-printing factories (known as the Adidas Speed Factory) in the United States and Germany in 2017. Only three years after launch, the company shut them down due to burgeoning operational costs (Hernandez, 2020). The Adidas Speed Factory failure teaches us that senior executives are often lured by the idea of wider product variety to grow revenues. But such attempts may incur gigantic losses in money and time investments if the benefits and limits of product proliferation are not keenly understood.

Adidas is not the only company that failed in its attempts to diversify product categories. Philips and Lego have also tried to increase product variety, but both ended up with huge losses. Philips was one of Europe's top patent filers in the 2000s. The company had been managing a menu exceeding sixty product types (Mocker & Ross, 2017). Uncontrolled proliferation of products within each category cluttered the operational complexity at Philips such that there were around 10,000 IT applications used by their employees! Due to the operational complexity and increased costs, the revenue plummeted by around 40 percent for the period between 2000 and 2010. In 2011, Frans van Houten was appointed as CEO to manage the operational turnaround. He successfully sold off business units such as lighting and semiconductors to trim product variety. The firm also consolidated the IT systems, as Cisco did, to streamline business operations and enable the integration of products and operations. After winning an operational rebound, Philips recovered revenues and profits. The company also repositioned itself as a healthcare company beyond just electronics to reap hefty margins in the medical business plus leaner overall operating practices.

Lego Group also saw operational problems due to uncontrolled product proliferation in the early 2000s. Lego is a Danish toymaker that sells iconic construction toys that feature the stacking of small Lego blocks (Mocker & Ross, 2017). Owing to its distinctive design, Lego blocks easily connect, allowing kids to construct different shapes and improve their creativity. The interlocking design of Lego blocks was patented in 1958. The patent had been valid for twenty years until 1978. After patent expiration, Lego's competitors copied the design and began eating Lego's market share (Lego Group, n.d.). The reaction of the management team at the Lego Group? Grow product variety. However, Lego could not keep operational complexity under control while expanding the number of different toys. Consequently, Lego had 12,000 unique bricks in 2004. It was reported that some of its designs were not available in the market due to the shortage of a *single* Lego block (Mocker & Ross, 2017). Starting from 2004, the management team focused on the standardization and consolidation of the Lego blocks. They cut the number of building blocks *while increasing the variety of designs*. In other words, the attempts to increase product variety were well integrated into the operational constraints. Such efforts paid off: The Lego Group increased sales and profits steadily after 2004.

Growth in product variety brings *capacity problems* when supply chain resources do not expand at the same rate as the product menu. In fact, decision-makers tend to maintain the same level of resources to produce and market increasingly diverse products. This causes more overtime work, quality problems, production delays, and so on, eventually leading to elevated operational costs. Another challenge of product proliferation is that *new designs go unnoticed* in the market with customers unaware of their features. Reaching customers and informing them of new goods are far from straightforward because customer attention is always limited. For this reason, revenue may not rise sufficiently after companies increase their product variety. Finally, new products may offer much the same features as current products, resulting in mere *product cannibalization*. Here, sales of new products simply replace sales of older ones, leaving total revenue flat. Decision-makers must be aware of these issues in product proliferation. Once they address them, they can boost the bottomline of their companies by widening the product line.

4.1.2 Sales Channels and Logistics Networks

Companies with limited product offerings may suffer operational problems due to complex sales channels and logistics networks. Since Apple launched the first iPhone in 2007, it has released new models *every* year. Although there have been many different iPhone models in the market since 2007, they were rolled out at *distinct* times. Indeed, Apple has wielded tight control over the number of new generations each year. In 2023, for example, the management team introduced only three different versions to the market such as iPhone 15, 15 Plus, and 15 Pro.[3]

Despite Apple's strict control limiting the number of new versions each year, it has often been affected by supply chain problems due to the complex structure. At the center of these problems lies the product complexity where the firm sources different components from forty-three countries on six continents (Petrova, 2018). The iPhones are next assembled by contract manufacturers, such as Foxconn, and then sold in the market via different channels (e.g., Apple Stores, Verizon, BestBuy, Bell, etc.). Given the complexity of *both* sourcing and sales channels, it has been highly challenging for Apple to manage its supply chain activities. In the fourth quarter of 2021, the company lost $6 billion due to chip shortages and manufacturing disruptions (Kline, 2022).

To tackle complex sourcing channels, firms can streamline sourcing activities and trim the number of suppliers and contract manufacturers. As explained before, Cisco pruned its list of contract manufacturers from 13 to 5 and the number of key suppliers from around 200 to 90. Consolidation of sourcing channels is often supported by management teams because such activities do not exert a strong negative

---

[3] Visit the following link for more information about the timeline of iPhone models: https://en.wikipedia.org/wiki/Template:Timeline_of_iPhone_models.

impact on revenues while helping lower costs. However, consolidation of sales channels may not be feasible because management thinks this would risk losing customers to competitors. Therefore, companies tend to diversify sales channels for a revenue boost. Toward this end, firms invest heavily in distribution centers, local fulfillment sites, and IT systems.

To improve sales channels, for instance, Walmart Canada invested in building a mega distribution center in the north Greater Toronto Area (Al-Shibeeb, 2024). It was announced that the distribution center would be replete with many robots, automated systems, and sophisticated ERP solutions to handle complex replenishment and fulfillment activities, as well as product returns. This investment was part of Walmart Canada's strategic plan announced in July 2020 such that the company would invest $3.5 billion over five years to improve online, in-store, and omnichannel sales channels (Walmart Canada, 2020).

Unlike Walmart, many retailers do not have excess capital to make such big investments. Investments in omnichannel capacity may fail to pay off depending on the industry segment and market dynamics. Some retailers keep sales channels more concentrated, refusing to expand them. For example, Primark makes no investment in omnichannel capacity as the company has been refusing to sell any items online (Jack & Frei, 2021). Primark is an Irish, fast-fashion retailer founded in 1969. In 2022, the firm reported GBP 7.69 billion in sales (around $9.5 billion). The management team has clung to its rigid strategy for a long time: All clothes are sold in store, never online. It is quite rare for a retailer like Primark not to sell at all online. Even during the COVID pandemic, the management team made no online sales available while running 305 stores globally (Jack & Frei, 2021). Primark sees the investment cost in local fulfillment centers plus the added cost of product returns (from online sales) outweighing the benefits of online sales. In other words, management estimates operational costs eclipsing any profits to be made online, so this channel has been forfeited.

In supply chain management, operating costs can be curbed by consolidation of sourcing and sales activities. Companies often exert all necessary efforts to consolidate *sourcing* activities. Such endeavors are well justified and supported by officials *if* they do not result in quality issues for products. However, this would not be the case for sales activities. The Walmart and Primark cases reveal two opposing strategies, and firms must weigh the costs and benefits of sales channel expansion before reaching a final decision.

4.2 Strategies to Integrate Supply Chains

When firms are exposed to operational complexities, integration of supply chains requires a comprehensive approach along four dimensions. First, limited operational *capacity* must be managed effectively. Second, companies must reduce *lead times* to improve the supply chain responsiveness according to evolving market conditions. Third, the point of differentiating products must be delayed along the supply chain. Finally, cost *efficiency* must be established at specific points in supply chains so that integration efforts do not end up with escalated costs.

4.2.1 Capacity Management

Businesses build operational capacity to serve customers and stakeholders. For example, logistics service providers must maintain trucks and warehouses to store and transport goods. Manufacturers operate machines and employ staff to produce goods. Hospitals equip intensive care units (ICUs) with a limited number of ventilators, specialized beds, ultrasound devices, and so on. Building operational capacity may require heavy investments, and organizations with large capacities are often deemed leaders in their fields. In the automotive industry, the German automaker Volkswagen has a production capacity of more than 14 million cars per year (Volkswagen Group, 2021). Foxconn, the Taiwanese contract manufacturer of Apple, employs 1.3 million employees at its China plants (Merchant, 2017).

However, large production capacity does not ensure operational excellence or high profits. Tesla has production capacity of two million vehicles per year, just one-seventh of Volkswagen's, whereas its market capitalization is twelve times that of VW in 2024.[4] Tesla attributes its success to popular cars, its innovative business model that eliminates intermediaries from the sales channel, and operational excellence.

---

[4] Tesla = $689.6 billion, VW = $56.6 billion. Visit the following link for more information about market values of the automakers: https://bicersupplychain.short.gy/RsVeB1.

During the COVID pandemic, for instance, Tesla was the firm least affected by the global chip shortage, attaining a service rate of 87 percent for on-time deliveries (Jin, 2022).

It is not necessary for an organization to wield mammoth capacity to achieve operational excellence and superior customer service level. Capacity can be used very effectively. Companies even with a limited capacity would still perform operations very well and minimize the mismatches between supply and demand. This is possible when capacity is allocated strategically in a hierarchical manner. For example, Timbuk2 follows an effective capacity rationing strategy to make both standard and customized bags in its San Francisco facility. This producer of messenger bags, backpacks, and luggage, founded in San Francisco in 1989, offers customers tailored bags where they can select size, color, inside design, and a plethora of functionalities. Or shoppers can simply purchase standard bags without the option to make any changes to them.[5]

Timbuk2 achieves prompt service owing to its successful capacity rationing strategy, where the production of custom bags is prioritized over standard items. Capacity is first used to make customized orders. Customized orders may fluctuate over time creating inefficiencies in production schedules. Idle capacity, after finishing customized orders, is used to make standard products *for stock*. This capacity rationing strategy is also referred to as the "hybrid model," where custom orders are produced in a make-to-order fashion, and standard bags are make-to-stock. This allows Timbuk2 to tap its streamlined capacity at a high rate while fulfilling market demand promptly (Cattani et al., 2010).

The Timbuk2 case exemplifies a manufacturer that rations the capacity by differentiating standard products from the customized ones. Capacity rationing can also be deployed in another way to improve operating efficiency when *all* products are standard and made-to-stock. Here, capacity must be managed according to demand uncertainty of products. In the apparel industry, for instance, it takes 40 weeks for brands to put new collections on sale. For upcoming summer seasons, merchandise planning starts in *September* of the prior year! During the

---

[5] Standard bags are shipped in two business days, but custom bags may need two-week delivery. Visit the following link for more information about processing and transit times of customized and standard bags: https://timbuk2.com/pages/shipping. Timbuk2 delivery times for customized bags are short in comparison to industry standards of a month or more.

production lead time, the brands collect data from various sources, such as social media, product reviews, rival websites, etc. They work closely with merchandise planners and contract manufacturers to adjust the quantities in anticipation of consumer trends (Hunter et al., 2018).

The portfolio of new collections features both classic styles and new ones. The demand uncertainty would be much lower for classic styles given that there is historical data for them. However, new styles would face demand uncertainty, potentially creating a substantial risk of supply–demand mismatches. Apparel brands allocate capacity to minimize supply–demand mismatches by assigning off-season capacity to classic models and peak capacity to new designs. For instance, September through February is considered off-season. During this period, production is carried out for classic models. While demand for new designs remains highly uncertain, planners and the marketing team can amass market information to anticipate demand for each new model. The updated demand data are then used to schedule production of new models after March, where the period from then through June is deemed the peak season. Therefore, products that are made to stock are differentiated according to their exposure to demand uncertainty. Those with low demand uncertainty (classic models) utilize the off-season period, whereas the ones with high demand uncertainty (new models) utilize the precious peak period. This allows retail brands to exploit capacity and minimize the mismatches very effectively.

Some firms use limited operating capacity to offer just customized products and services. Here, they can ration capacity according to customer segments and profits made on each specific offering. For example, NetJets is a US-based aviator that offers *shared aircraft ownership* to their clients. NetJets members book private flights without owning the whole jet (NetJets Inc., 2018). Capacity is limited by the fleet size. NetJets operates more than 750 private jets as of 2023 rationed by a market mechanism where travelers demanding more flexible usage enroll in the ownership program with more options. For instance, the NetJets Share Program is advertised as ideal for individuals and businesses needing over fifty hours of flight time per year. Booking a private flight is possible on just ten-hour notice! However, inconveniences may arise on peak travel days where a new flight requires forty-eight-hour notice (the maximum number of peak days being only ten for the NetJets Share Program). The Private Jet Card ownership program is more suitable for those using twenty-five to fifty hours of flight time. Booking a new flight here is possible with twenty-four-hour notice on a peak day, and the maximum number of peak days is forty-five (NetJets Inc., 2024). Thus, NetJets Share Program owners enjoy more flexibility than Private Jet Card owners. The terms of ownership programs as to notification period and peak days specify how the limited capacity of flight time is rationed at NetJets. In other words, the company sets the conditions of fleet usage and prices, and its capacity is rationed based on these factors.

In these examples, companies develop a rigorous capacity management policy aligned with their business targets. The way limited capacity is used directly impacts the bottomline of firms. Thus, decision-makers must have a well-articulated plan about how to use capacity effectively depending on their business objectives, customer segments, and constraints. Otherwise, supply chains cannot be integrated with markets.

4.2.2 Lead-Time Reduction

In the risk analysis framework given in Chapter 3, operating lead time is considered a source of operational and financial inefficiencies.[6] Firms with long lead times start sourcing and production activities early, thereby holding more inventory along the supply chain. In addition to holding more inventory, such firms must make critical inventory decisions well ahead of market demand realization. Demand uncertainty rises with lead time, and it becomes highly challenging to match supply with demand when lead times get longer. For this reason, companies with long lead times also incur excessive costs of supply–demand mismatches.

Suppose an apparel retailer plans to offer a new model in the upcoming summer season. Demand is highly uncertain such that the sales team expects the demand to be between 10,000 and 100,000 units. Production volume is determined to be 70,000 units when this decision is made forty weeks before the selling season. The sales team next updates the demand forecast between 20,000 and 40,000 after observing customer reaction during fashion shows and on social media ten weeks before the selling season. Thus, the production quantity could have been set at 35,000 if the

---

[6] We refer to operating lead time as lead time shortly.

decision had been postponed to a ten-week lead time before the peak season. The retailer sells 30,000 units of the new model on the market during the selling season. Here, cutting the lead time from forty to ten weeks helps the retailer reduce eventual excess inventory from 40,000 to 5,000 units.[7]

Firms in the retail and manufacturing industries often face excess inventory for one basic reason: *long lead time*. On the one hand, many firms constantly seek offshore supply to reduce procurement costs although procurement from offshore suppliers leads to long lead times. On the other hand, they suffer from the inventory-holding and product-shortage costs associated with long lead times. Beyond monetary loss, inventory pile-up also harms the environment. One investigative report by a British media channel had revealed an Amazon fulfilment center in the UK *disposing of* 120,000 unsold items, such as smartphones and other electronic gear, *in just one week*. Amazon runs 185 fulfillment centers worldwide, and its market share is 7.7 percent of global online retail (Pallot, 2021; Seifert et al., 2022). With 12,000 liters (about 3170.06 gal) of water used to make one smartphone, total water diverted producing items that fail to reach consumers may be estimated 180 trillion liters annually (Seifert et al., 2022). This equals one-fifth of global water consumption of the entire world population. Cutting the lead time addresses not only inventory or mismatch costs but also the water waste and carbon emissions.

Companies can reduce lead times by having their locations near customers and suppliers and avoiding bottlenecks in supply chains. Martin-Brower Company is the largest logistics service provider of McDonald's worldwide (Hancock, 2012). The company provides warehousing, purchasing, and transportation services to McDonald's restaurants. The management team developed an effective logistics network such that warehouses were placed in locations to serve 250 to 700 restaurants in close proximity. They engage McDonald's suppliers and restaurants to manage the sourcing and replenishment activities by

---

[7] The actual demand remains uncertain until the end of the selling season. The retailer observes the actual demand being equal to 30,000 at the end of the season. Nevertheless, the magnitude of the uncertainty decreases over time before the season. The production decision with a forty-week lead time is inaccurate, causing excess inventory of 70,000−30,000 = 40,000 units of excess inventory. The decision with a ten-week lead time is much more accurate, helping the retailer reduce the excess inventory to 35,000−30,000 = 5,000 units.

keeping only four days of inventory. To achieve such an impressive inventory turnover, the firm invested in avoiding bottlenecks in the system. For example, one of the bottlenecks had been the unloading of deliveries at restaurants. To fix this bottleneck, Martin-Brower installed convertible stands to trucks, which can be wheeled smoothly from vehicles to restaurants. This makes it possible to increase the delivery frequency such that most McDonald's restaurants now replenish two or three times weekly. Owing to such efforts, McDonald's serves meals at a high service level while keeping minimum amount of inventory (Hancock, 2012).

Despite its well-known benefits, cutting lead time significantly can be challenging due to high investment costs and supply chain constraints. Manufacturers must often invest in building production facilities near markets or in expanding production to reduce lead times. These types of investments would be costly for many firms, hindering their lead-time-reduction efforts. In these cases, it may be possible to *partially* reduce lead times and minimize investment costs. Manufacturers may consider reorganizing processes or making moderate investments to slightly trim lead times. Such efforts would benefit supply chains significantly while limiting investment costs. The GlaxoSmithKline (GSK) case, which will be discussed later in this chapter, shows that companies can reduce the mismatches through partial lead-time reduction.

In some cases, it is not possible to reduce lead times due to structural constraints that cannot be eliminated in supply chains. In the apparel industry, for example, lead times are unexpectedly long because manufacturing often takes place in Asia. In 2022, lead times even delayed to over a year from around eight months due to supply chain problems such as site closures, shipping delays, and so on. While apparel manufacturers then considered moving production to the United States, they could not do it because of supply chain constraints (Kapner, 2022).

In Asia, several production networks serve the apparel industry. One production network is good at making cotton clothes, while another favors synthetic clothes. Access to deep manufacturing experience and diverse suppliers makes it much easier to plan and manage production in Asia than in any Western footprint. For this reason, reshoring production near US markets would not seem feasible in the apparel industry. Cutting lead times can be possible only after decision-makers address quite serious supply chain issues.

4.2.3 Delayed Differentiation

Firms often sell a menu of products and services by using limited raw materials. For example, apparel manufacturers use *only* yarn to knit different models and sizes of clothes. Dairies sell different flavors of milk, cheese, and yogurt such that all of them are made from raw milk. Service firm offerings are tailored to each customer although they utilize the same equipment and employees each time.[8] When companies use a limited number of resources and differentiate their products over time along the supply chain, they wisely *delay* the point of differentiation. When differentiation occurs *after* demand is known, the mismatches can be minimized.

The Italian fashion apparel manufacturer Benetton has successfully implemented a delayed-differentiation strategy to reduce the mismatches (Benetton Group S.r.l., n.d.; Feitzinger & Lee, 1997). Benetton operates a network of 4,000 stores worldwide and owns well-known brands such as United Colors of Benetton and Sisley. The company offers its clothes in many colors, which is consistent with its marketing policy emphasizing the richness of colors. Therefore, the dyeing operation can be considered the main differentiation point (Camuffo et al., 2001). In the 1970s, Benetton made clothes in sequence of producing yarn, dyeing yarns, and knitting. This sequence of operations forced planners to set the production quantities for each SKU just after yarns were produced. In the 1980s, the company improved its operations and developed a fresh method that makes it possible to color the models *after* knitting. In other words, Benetton revised the sequence: produce yarn, knit, *then* dye. This updated sequence of operations allowed planners to postpone production decisions for SKUs until *after* having reliable information about the market demand. Owing to such efforts, Benetton cut supply–demand mismatches and grew sustainably and profitably (Camuffo et al., 2001).

The Benetton case exemplifies how manufacturers can re-sequence their operations strategically and delay the point of differentiation in

---

[8] Ginkgo Sustainability Inc. (a green energy company based in Canada) exemplifies how service companies can use the same resources but differentiate their services. Ginkgo develops and installs "living roof" to shed carbon emissions in urban areas: https://ginkgosustainability.com. Its roof systems offer such features as LED growth lighting, Wi-Fi user controls, recirculating water tanks, and air filtering. Ginkgo installs fully living roofs *differentiated* per customer site, while most layouts feature *similar* functionalities and components.

the supply chain. Another approach would be to design the products in *modules* so that the modules can attach to each other according to customer preferences. For instance, ASML relies on modular product design to make lithography machines used in chip manufacturing.[9] Making such machines is a daunting task given the complexity of chip manufacturing. Additionally, ASML's customers request their orders to be fulfilled quickly due to time sensitivity of chip manufacturing. ASML tackles these challenges by modular product design and effective supply chain management (Tarasov, 2022).

ASML engineers and designers develop machines consisting of independent modules, each produced at one of ASML's sixty locations and then shipped to the Netherlands for final testing and *assembly*. In other words, the differentiation point is the Netherlands site *where modular assembly* of the machines is done by attaching proper modules in a way that meets customer expectations. After testing the machines, they are *disassembled* for final shipment. ASML engineers later reassemble, install, and test the machine at the customer's production site (Tarasov, 2022). The supply chain network, product modularity, and delayed differentiation strategy all help ASML fulfill diverse customer orders without incurring excessive costs due to supply–demand mismatches, which is important in the electronics industry due to price devaluation and high obsolescence costs of excess inventory. Hence, ASML can sell lithography machines to elite chip fabricators, such as TSMC, Samsung, and Intel, at hefty profit margins. Due to its operational excellence, ASML's 2018 market value topped that of its best client, Intel (Tarasov, 2022).

Product modularity is a highly effective strategy to customize products according to the preferences of customers in a cost-efficient way, allowing manufacturers to delay the differentiation. Consider a three-module product, each module having four different configurations. Here, a company can develop products in 4 × 4 × 4 = 64 diverse ways to address specific customer preferences. Such a variety of configurations helps increase sales by attracting more customers. The modular design also limits inventory costs because only 4 + 4 + 4 = 12 distinct modules

---

[9] ASML is a Dutch company with the market value of more than $240 billion as of October 2023. It employs around 39,000 people (twice the seating in Madison Square Garden) at sixty locations worldwide. The lithography machines made by ASML are extremely expensive, costing more than $200 million. In 2024, Intel paid ASML $383 million just for one machine (Sterlink, 2024).

must be kept in stock. In sum, product modularity helps firms both widen product variety and limit the mismatch costs. Therefore, many companies, especially electronics producers like Hewlett Packard, invest in this approach while developing their product menus and supply chain structures (Feitzinger & Lee, 1997).

4.2.4 Operational Excellence

Supply chain integration helps reduce overhead costs by curtailing the mismatch costs. However, product costs may soar as a result. If the reduction in overhead costs offsets the product cost increase, supply chain integration is deemed feasible. Suppose a company sourcing its products from an offshore supplier pays $10 per unit. After selling products in season, the company ends up with unsold inventory at one third of the initial inventory. The excess inventory is written off from accounts. Thus, per-unit cost of goods sold rises to $15 – that is, $10 / (1–1/3) = $15. The extra $5 is attributed to overhead costs of excess inventory. A domestic supplier asks $13 per unit for the product. If the company sources from the domestic supplier and matches supply with demand perfectly, the overhead cost drops to zero. This makes sourcing from domestic suppliers more profitable than using the offshore supplier *despite* the higher product cost associated with domestic production.

The problem regarding such cost calculations is that overhead and product costs are not static, but they dynamically change over time depending on macroeconomic factors. Therefore, an analysis favoring supply chain integration would be invalid in future. If organizations integrate supply chains while improving cost efficiency, they will achieve operational excellence such that a robust supply chain structure benefits them in the long term. This can be done by systematic cost and lead-time reduction.[10]

Systematic cost reduction is a top-down process such that it starts from the *upstream* operations and moves downstream. Therefore, cost reduction efforts must initially concentrate on the upstream *procurement* and *production* activities. Systematic cost reduction offers two

---

[10] The Kordsa case presented in Chapter 8 illustrates how to digitize supply chains and achieve operational excellence. The manufacturer uses digital technologies to reduce both lead time and costs systematically (Biçer et al., 2022b).

benefits to companies. First, it helps lower total production costs. This benefit is obvious because any type of cost reduction along the supply chain leads to decreased costs. The second benefit is that cost savings at the initial stages of supply chains allow decision-makers to keep more inventory of raw materials and components without incurring any additional cost. When demand turns out to be high unexpectedly, the extra inventory can be utilized to fulfill customer demand.

Imagine that the manufacturing of a product takes place in two sequential steps. Raw materials are transformed to a component in the first step, and components are processed into the finished product in the second step. The cost of operating each step is $10 per unit, including the material costs. Thus, the cost of production is $20 per unit. If the manufacturer achieves 80 percent cost reduction for the first operation, the savings apply to both the component and finished-goods inventory. Then, the cost of production becomes $2 and $12 per unit of components and finished goods, respectively. If the cost reduction is done for the second operation, the savings apply only to finished goods. Here, the production cost becomes $10 and $12 per unit of components and finished goods, respectively.

Systematic lead-time reduction is a bottom-up process such that it starts from *downstream* activities and moves backward. It initially attempts to cut lead times for outbound logistics and final production. Only then does it emphasize shortening the lead time of upstream operations. Like any effort to cut lead times in any stage of supply chains, systematic lead-time reduction contributes to a shorter operating lead time and lower mismatches. Additionally, it helps shorten the delivery lead time in the first place, which translates into elevated demand.

Consider two manufacturers with the same operating lead time of sixty days. The delivery lead time is ten days for the first one, while it is thirty days for the second. It means that the second manufacturer has a shorter production lead time to offset the long delivery lead time. The second manufacturer cannot fulfill any customer order for which the demand lead time is less than thirty days. If a customer demands products in twenty days, only the first manufacturer can meet that demand. Therefore, the first manufacturer is expected to fill more customer orders although they have the same operating lead time. Systematic lead time reduction prioritizes fulfillment activities over upstream operations to eliminate such unnecessary risks of unfilled demand.

4.3 The GlaxoSmithKline (GSK) Vaccines Example

GSK is one of the pharmaceutical giants in the world, which is headquartered in the UK. The company was founded in 2000 through the merger of Glaxo and SmithKline Beecham (Sorkin & Petersen, 2000). Its vaccines business unit (i.e., GSK Vaccines) produces and delivers around 1.5 million doses daily from thirty-seven manufacturing sites.[11]

From operational perspective, there are two challenges of vaccine production. The first one is high demand uncertainty due to unpredictability of epidemics and seasonality. Second, vaccine production is subject to strict rules and regulations. Production must be carried out in batches to guarantee high quality standards. If a problem occurs in the production and cold chain, for example, all doses of the affected batch can be recalled in this way. Vaccine ingredients are purchased from approved suppliers located across different continents. These ingredients form the bulk of a vaccine, which is later filled in vials in different doses. The vials are delivered to customers in the cold chain because vaccines must often be kept between +2°C and +8°C.

Vaccine production typically takes several months due to long supply and production times. The operating lead time for GSK Vaccines was around ten months in average (De Treville et al., 2014). Vaccines are sold to governments and health organizations through a tender process. After GSK bids on a tender, the management team learn the result as late as two months before the delivery date. Thus, the demand lead time is two months in most cases.[12]

Because the demand lead time is shorter than the operating lead time, GSK must start procurement and production before learning the result of tenders. If a tender is lost, the demand drops to zero and the excess stock of

---

[11] GSK Vaccines is one of the key players in the global health sector. Although its market share lagged behind each of Pfizer and Moderna's vaccine business during the COVID pandemic, it recovered after the pandemic and improved the market dominance by gaining two-thirds of the market for the new respiratory syncytial virus (RSV) vaccines (Erman, 2024).Visit the following link for more information about GSK's vaccine products: https://gsk.com/en-gb/products/our-product-areas/#Vaccines.

[12] This duration does not exceed five months even for big tenders. In 2021, for instance, GSK was awarded a large vaccine contract worth more than $600 million by the U.S. Department of Defense: www.defense.gov/News/Contracts/Contract/Article/2845698/. The demand lead time is set at 4.5 months for this contract (i.e., from November 16, 2021, to March 31, 2022), covering the Christmas season, when most businesses stop operations due to holidays.

vaccines results in colossal inventory holding and disposal (if not used before the expiry date) costs. The long-term average probability of winning a tender is around 50 percent. If GSK can reduce the operating lead time to less than two months, supply–demand mismatches can be eliminated. However, this would not be possible due to long supply lead times. The other option is to increase the production capacity to reduce the production lead time so that the ingredients can be purchased before the tender result is known. But production starts after the tender is won. GSK has followed this strategy and expanded the production capacity to reduce the mismatches. In other words, GSK benefited from partial lead-time reduction, capacity management, and delayed differentiation to make the supply chain more responsive to the demand dynamics (De Treville et al., 2014).

The impact of GSK's efforts on the bottomline can be seen in the company's balance sheet. GSK managed to reduce the finished goods inventory by 36 percent from 2019 to 2023. However, the raw materials inventory increased by 34 percent. Because finished goods are always more expensive than raw materials due to value added during production, the 36 percent reduction of finished goods offsets the 34 percent increase in raw materials.[13]

4.4 Conclusion

Supply chains are negatively affected by distinct risks and uncertainties. Beyond these, product variety and expansion of supply chain networks make supply chain management challenging. Companies exposed to all these challenges, risks and uncertainties are inherently vulnerable to mounting losses due to supply–demand mismatches. Integrating supply chains helps companies minimize loss by quickly reacting to supply chain glitches and by fulfilling customer demand without bearing excess inventory risk. Supply chain integration entails these four key aspects:

1. *There is a need for a capacity management policy.* Supply chain professionals must share a mutual understanding about how to use limited capacity to fulfill varying demands of customers.

---

[13] In 2019, finished goods and raw materials inventory were 2.247 and 1.195 billion GBP, respectively. In 2023, finished goods and raw materials inventory were 1.455 and 1.594 billion GBP. Visit the following link for GSK's balance sheet: www.wsj.com/market-data/quotes/GSK/financials/annual/balance-sheet.

4: Leading the Operational Edge 99

2. *Lead time must be reduced to mitigate the mismatch risk.* High investment costs and supply chain constraints may hinder corporate efforts to cut lead times. Yet such constraints can be addressed by decision-makers. Where investment costs soar, companies may consider a partial reduction of lead time.
3. *Delaying the differentiation is essential to manage product variety.* Delaying the differentiation allows companies to defer critical inventory decisions about each SKU until obtaining accurate demand forecasts. Thus, it leads to curbing supply–demand mismatches at the SKU level.
4. *Efforts to integrate supply chains need not put cost efficiency in jeopardy.* Decision-makers can develop hybrid strategies to achieve both supply chain integration and cost efficiency. Toward this end, managers must *systematically* reduce both lead times and costs.

5 | Innovative Business Development: Supply Chain Finance

Supply chain integration would not be appealing for some companies even when the costs of supply–demand mismatches exceed the investment costs to integrate supply chains. Rather than integrating supply chains, some companies find a way to innovate their business models so that their sensitivity to supply–demand mismatches would abate. Although the mismatches would still cause a loss of profit, business model innovations help increase the market value tremendously. For instance, Tesla's market value soared fourteenfold between 2019 and 2021. Sales obviously did not keep pace, rising only 119 percent.[1] How was it possible to increase the market value fourteenfold with revenues growing only 119 percent?

The automaker achieved it owing to efforts to reduce the cash conversion cycle. Tesla's cash conversion cycle *inverted* from twelve days in 2019 to minus fifteen days in 2021.[2] Such a negative cash conversion signals a company using the funds of *external* stakeholders to finance its operations. When a company gets paid by its customers early and delays its own payments to suppliers, the cash conversion cycle can invert. Here, working capital to finance operations comes from these external stakeholders, not creditors or investors. Tesla uses funds of its customers and suppliers to finance operations *plus* generate profits from financial

---

[1] Tesla's market value was $75 billion in December 2019, which increased to $1.06 trillion in December 2021. Total revenue was $24.58 billion in 2019, while it was $53.82 in 2021. Visit the following link for more information about Tesla's financials: https://tradingeconomics.com/tsla:us.

[2] Cash conversion cycle is calculated by using financial data as "Days of Receivables + Days of Inventory – Days of Payables." Here, "Days of Receivables + Days of Inventory" is equivalent to Operating Cycle in Figure 3.2. Tesla's Days of Receivables were 16.88 in 2019 and 12.88 in 2021. Days of Inventory were 59.31 in 2019 and 44.73 in 2021. Days of Payables were 63.85 in 2019 and 72.95 in 2021. Then, the cash conversion cycle is calculated as 16.88 + 59.31 – 63.85 = 12.34 days for 2019, while becomes 12.88 + 44.73 – 72.95 = -15.34 days for 2021. Data courtesy of Morning Star: www.morningstar.com/stocks/xnas/tsla/performance.

markets. Who does not want to invest in such a company that generates hefty profits without demanding any capital from creditors or investors!

McDonald's operates a solid franchise system where 85 percent of its restaurants are run by franchisees (Purdy, 2017). The company generates an estimated revenue of $2.7 million per company-owned restaurant and makes an average profit of $150 K annually. Thus, the profit margin is 5.5 percent for company-owned restaurants. To boost profits, the firm invests in real estate and buys properties. Management leases sites to franchisees. Given that the estimated annual rent for each restaurant accounts for 22 percent of the total annual revenue, the lease income easily exceeds the operating income. Further, the restaurants attract much foot traffic to their locations, sparking gains in property valuations. McDonald's owns real estate worth over $30 billion and earns $4.5 billion of lease income (Purdy, 2017).

In both the Tesla and McDonald's examples, executives successfully generate income from noncore activities. Within the scope of business models, their management teams identify some business opportunities and capitalize on them. Operational activities in such firms should facilitate organizational efforts to generate income from alternative sources without being a bottleneck for any of them. Suppose that a company generates income only from operational activities. Thus, the management team must attempt to reduce both product shortages and excess inventory risk simultaneously to maximize profits. If the company also generates nonoperational income from financial activities, they must aim to reduce the cash conversion cycle and free up excess cash to be used in financial investments. The possibility of generating nonoperational income induces decision-makers to change their objective from minimization of the mismatches to the reduction of cash conversion cycle. To this end, decision-makers tend to liquidate inventory as fast as possible. For example, companies sometimes halt sales of select items during peak seasons and replace them with other goods when their average sales per day decrease. They offer early promotions to liquidate inventory immediately even though customers are willing to buy such products by paying the full price in the long term. These maneuvers seem irrational from the operating point of view when the objective is to maximize *only* operational profits. However, they help managers increase *total* profit when the accounting includes nonoperational activities.

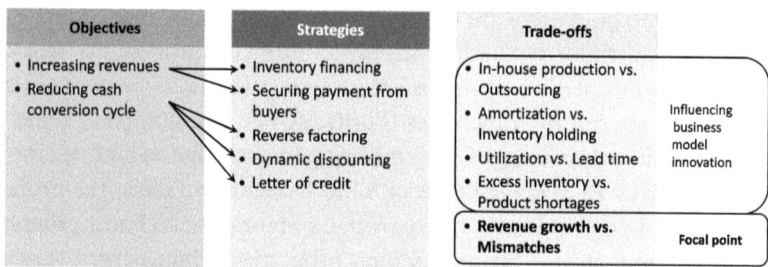

Figure 5.1 Objectives and strategies of innovative business development

Organizations can innovate their business models consistently to alleviate their sensitivity to supply–demand mismatches. To this end, decision-makers must find alternate ways to generate nonoperational income. The easiest path to this objective is to increase revenues (not necessarily operating profits) and shrink the cash conversion cycle. This helps companies extract cash from working capital, and the extra cash can be deployed in financial markets to yield nonoperational profits. Yet such efforts may imperil supply chain performance. Therefore, decision-makers must also cautiously protect supply chains from the negative aspects of reducing the cash conversion cycle. In other words, they must effectively manage the fifth fundamental trade-off – that is, revenue growth versus the mismatches. There exist proven methods to protect both supply chains and welfare of different stakeholders from the efforts of one party to increase revenues and cut the cash conversion cycle. Figure 5.1 summarizes those methods, which we will walk through in detail in the remaining part of this chapter.

5.1 Cash Sources

Curbing mismatches between supply and demand raises operating profits, but not necessarily nonoperating profits. A producer may prefer to order from a domestic supplier to reduce the lead time, which in turn abates the mismatches. If an offshore supplier offers delayed payment terms, however, the domestic supplier would be less appealing than the offshore supplier for a capital-constrained buyer. Here, the benefit of lagged payments would exceed the cost of supply–demand mismatches, making the offshore deal superior.

We often observe these dynamics in global trade. In China, for example, the government strongly supports the export of goods to Western lands. In 2001, the Chinese government launched the export credit and insurance corporation: Sinosure (China Export & Credit Insurance Corporation, n.d.). Chinese producers selling goods to West can earn export credits from Sinosure at low rates. Sinosure has also insured manufacturers against customer nonpayment risks. It offers insurance covering 95 percent of invoiced amounts at a reasonable premium, which is rare in Western countries (IISD, n.d.). Compare this to some insurance companies that are reluctant to underwrite an insurance policy linked to market uncertainty, thus putting US manufacturers at a disadvantage (Steinberg & Wallace, 2020). In the end, the support by Sinosure enables Chinese producers to offer longer payment terms than their rivals, placing China as a better option over domestic sourcing.

Hoping to improve the cash position, supply chain professionals can make suboptimal decisions that aggravate supply–demand mismatches. They may source goods from offshore locations to delay procurement payments as discussed above. They may also sell goods at a discount when customers agree to prepay, growing the sales volume while hurting operating margins. At the core here lies the tendency to improve the cash position by (1) increasing revenues and (2) shortening the cash conversion cycle. An increase in revenue has a direct positive effect on the cash level. Companies must also shorten the cash conversion cycle to keep revenues in their accounts longer. This can be done by postponing payments to suppliers and other creditors. When nonoperating income is a vital part of the business model, supply chain activities must focus on how to collect early from customers and defer payments to suppliers and vendors. Therefore, the focus of supply chain management shifts from curbing the mismatches to enhancing the cash position.

From the perspective of a business cycle, the focus on operational excellence may fade away at the maturity stage of firms – that is, when the chance to earn nonoperational income arises. Business models of start-ups and SMEs are often centered on core operations. Cofounders are expected to specialize in certain processes as they attempt to grow the business by increasing profits from operations. As firms grow, employees and investors suggest new strategies to improve profitability by carefully using the excess cash generated by operations. Here, larger firms may place less emphasis on operational excellence as they seize more options to reap earnings from finance activities that exceed any mismatch costs. The ability to generate extra capital and deploy it wisely would be more important than achieving operational excellence for executives at big firms.[3]

McDonald's also experienced such a shift in their business model that helped the company grow exponentially and become the largest global restaurant chain. In 1948, Dick and Mac McDonald streamlined restaurant operations and started to sell hamburgers in California. Roy Kroc, a businessperson from Chicago, signed a contract with the McDonald brothers to become their franchise agent in 1954. One year later, he opened his first franchise restaurant in Illinois. While expanding the franchise network, Mr. Kroc sought to own land and lease the sites to future franchisees. This allowed him to generate revenues in three ways. First, McDonald's collected franchising fees. Second, the company started to charge rent for its locations. Finally, property value gains helped McDonald's grow total assets. Since then, the fast-food brand has rapidly expanded its business owing to its strong cash level (Haden, 2020).

Business model innovation helps McDonald's maintain low prices charged to customers for their hamburgers, which is exceedingly difficult for restaurants because their gross margins must cover the perishable nature of food. Meal service requires an ample stock of food and ingredients. When demand falls, expired inventory is discarded. Yet McDonald's sells its flagship Big Mac at $3.91 in Mississippi (Vega, 2023), leaving an exceptionally low margin for the fast-food brand. When profit margin is low and perishability risk is high, firms are advised to reduce the stock level. This, in turn, causes stock-outs and customer complaints. However, the service level at McDonald's restaurants is remarkably high. The fact is that McDonald's does not earn money from selling hamburgers, but real estate investments make it possible to attain high service levels and competitive prices in the face of excessive stock charges in the food industry.

To better grasp how McDonald's wins, imagine a fast-food restaurant owner-landlord selling a hamburger at $5 with daily demand of 600 on average. It costs $3 to make a hamburger, so the owner

---

[3] According to a study by McKinsey & Company, firms grow returns to shareholders by 11 percent when they improve cash flows (Govindarajan et al., 2022).

5: Innovative Business Development

generates a profit of $(5-3)*600 = \$1,200$ per day. If the owner sells a hamburger at \$3.10, then the number of visitors is expected to rise to 10,000. Here, daily profit drops to \$1,000. The restaurant loses \$73,000 per year when the burger price is slashed by \$1.90. Thus, the price reduction is not justified from an operational point of view. Now add in property value of \$500 K. The owner also notices that if the restaurant can attract 10,000 customers a day, its property value increases to \$2 million. After weighing the impact of restaurant traffic on real estate value, the burger price cut is justified.

The McDonald's example illustrates that decision-makers can pursue opportunities to increase nonoperational profits. This would help companies elevate total profits and counter the exposure to supply–demand mismatches. However, such attainments may impose serious hardships on supply chains. On the one hand, firms expand their businesses to reap nonoperational profits. On the other hand, high growth impairs operational excellence, putting corporations in a risky situation if ever the ability to generate nonoperational income weakens. According to a study about the growth of retailers, researchers found that retailers are addicted to high growth due to pressure from investors and venture capitalists (Fisher et al., 2017). When high revenues resulting from surging growth do not translate into nonoperational profits, Fisher et al. (2017) suggest that retailers must stop growing their business and focus on improving operational performance. Therefore, corporations that innovate business models to increase nonoperational income must always be ready to undergo an operational turnaround to regain operational excellence. Otherwise, they may suffer competitive disadvantage.

The firms that constantly innovate business models must also consider the impacts of their actions on other supply chain allies. When the cash conversion cycle is reduced by deferring payments to suppliers, for instance, suppliers suffer. Remedial gestures here would include certain supply chain finance methods.

5.2 Supply Chain Finance

When trade occurs between a supplier and a buyer, the parties exchange goods and capital. The supplier delivers goods to the buyer, and the buyer makes payment to the supplier. Before they start to negotiate, the supplier must ideally own the goods and the buyer must have capital. Then, trade would occur without any disruption.

In some cases, however, suppliers sell goods that have not been produced yet, or buyers purchase goods without having enough capital to make payment. Imagine a buyer seeking to buy an electronic device from a supplier. One supplier has gadgets in stock, so the buyer can purchase one for $5,000. Another supplier *can* produce the gadget but lacks resources, asking only $2,000 for the gadget with the same features. The buyer may choose the latter not only to reduce his own expenses but also to promote competition in the supply market in the long term. Such a procurement strategy helps increase the number of suppliers, leading to fierce competition benefiting buyers in the market.

Now let us return to the supplier who has gadgets in stock. Suppose 200 customers are interested in buying gadgets. However, only 10 percent of buyers have enough capital to pay instantly. If the supplier offers a payment term of ninety days, then half of them would be able to buy gadgets. Therefore, market demand grows when the supplier extends payment terms.

In these scenarios, either the buyer or seller can finance the trade. Imagine that *both* parties initially lack the cash to finance a deal. Here, a cash-rich investor or a bank could make the payment to the supplier so it can produce the gadget. Then the buyer uses the acquired gadget to earn profits, now able to make the payment (including the interest costs) to the bank.

Supply chain finance deals with the cash management of corporations engaged in a trade, aiming to find the best financier to facilitate trade. It is important for sustaining corporate operations because many firms need a finance solution for supply chain procurement and sales. Its importance grows especially during economic recessions and global crises. Fintech company Taulia surveyed various suppliers in 2021 and reported that 38 percent of them need supply chain finance to secure timely payment during the COVID pandemic, which was only 27 percent before the pandemic (Basquill, 2022). There exist alternative financing solutions that prove effective depending on characteristics of trade and needs of supply chain parties. They are outlined in Figure 5.1, and they now merit further discussion.

5.2.1 Inventory Financing

In supply chains, cash-constrained buyers must figure out how to finance their purchases before placing an order. The most basic form of supply chain finance is known as *inventory financing*: The supplier lets a buyer pay the invoice sometime after delivering the goods purchased. The time elapsing from actual delivery until receiving the payment is known as the *payment term*, which is also the days of receivables in Figure 3.2. Inventory financing covers this time duration only – that is, the *supplier* finances the trade during the payment term. Suppliers may extend the payment term beyond industry standards (i.e., thirty days) and finance the trade for a long time to increase sales.

The question of whether the supplier or the buyer finances the deal has practical implications. After a sales transaction, the invoice issued specifies conditions as to who would finance the trade. For example, payment terms often include a statement such as *1/10, net 30,* meaning that the standard payment term is 30 days when the supplier finances the trade. If the buyer wants to finance the trade, a discount of 1 percent applies to the invoice amount when paid within 10 days. Buyers with cash on hand may want to benefit from the discount and pay the invoice early. Otherwise, the buyer can wait 30 days to make the payment.

The structure of inventory financing often attracts financial institutions to benefit from early-payment discounts. For example, some big banks act as a buyer to acquire commodities from suppliers (Berthelsen & Baer, 2015). They make immediate payments to earn the discount, later selling goods to buyers with longer payment terms. In other words, banks take ownership of commodities and finance the trade during the payment term to earn a spread. Inventory financing can even widen to a large group of investors by *inventory securitization*. Here, a hedge fund buys inventory (usually commodities or precious materials such as diamonds) from a supplier. Then, it returns the inventory to the supplier on consignment. The hedge fund later issues inventory-backed securities for investors so they can buy a share of the inventory.[4] Investors are repaid at the end when the inventory is completely sold. In this case, a large group of investors owns the inventory and finances the trade during the payment term.

In inventory financing, the discount rates must be well-aligned with current interest rates to avoid any arbitrage opportunity such as occurs when the value created along the supply chain is grasped by financial intermediaries. Toward this end, supply chain specialists must conduct

---

[4] The process of issuing notes that can be traded in financial markets is called "securitization" in finance terminology.

a well-articulated feasibility analysis with *independent* financial advisors to offset any negative impact of inventory financing on suppliers and buyers.

5.2.2 Reverse Factoring

Buyers often attempt to increase payment terms beyond industry standards to improve cash levels and generate additional income from financial activities. However, such attempts may end up with a hefty cost of eroded operational performance where supply lead times or quality problems soar after extending payment terms with a supplier. To avert operational problems, buyers may collaborate with banks toward longer payment terms without hurting suppliers. For example, Procter & Gamble (P&G) decided to delay payments to its suppliers thirty more days (in addition to its existing practice of sixty-day payment terms) in 2013 to free up $2 billion in cash (Goel & Wohl, 2013). To avoid the negative impact of the payment extension on suppliers, the company also introduced a *reverse factoring program* featuring low-cost finance for suppliers (Procter & Gamble Co., n.d.). Suppliers joining this program were not harmed by the payment extension. Some even improved their cash levels as the benefits of reverse factoring exceeded the costs of the payment extension.

Fibria Cellulose, one of P&G's largest suppliers, delivers pulp used to make high-demand products such as Pampers diapers. Before the payment extension, P&G paid invoices to Fibria in sixty days. After P&G's announcement of a thirty-day extension, executives from P&G and Fibria developed the reverse factoring alliance via Citibank (Esty et al., 2016). Fibria even agreed to extend the payment term by forty-five days! Therefore, the new payment term between P&G and Fibria was set at 105 days. Meanwhile, Fibria was paid in five days by Citibank after reducing interest on the remaining 100 days. For the interest calculations, Citi used the corporate rate charged to P&G because it guaranteed payment of the invoices and its corporate interest rate was cheaper than that for Fibria. After enactment of the reverse factoring, Fibria also managed to boost its own cash level compared to the case before P&G's announcement (Dunbar, 2018; Esty et al., 2016).

Supply chains benefit from such a reverse factoring program when buyers have much more credibility than suppliers. Suppose a big buyer (e.g., P&G) procures goods from a supplier (e.g., Fibria). The buyer has a high credit rating that wins access to a low-cost loan at an interest rate of 1.5 percent. Say the payment term is 120 days, and the value of the invoice is $1 million. When the supplier seeks *instant* payment from the bank according to reverse-factoring conditions, the total interest is $1 million*0.015/360*120 = $5 K, and the supplier gets paid $995 K for the invoice upon delivery of the goods. The bank will be repaid by the buyer in full (i.e., $1 million) 120 days later. In the reverse factoring program, the bank applies the *buyer's* interest rate (1.5 percent), not that of the supplier. Assume that the supplier lacks this rating, and its interest rate runs at 6 percent. If the supplier's interest rate had been in force (i.e., in the absence of reverse factoring), then the supplier would have gotten paid $980 K. Therefore, reverse factoring here helps increase the supplier's cash level by $15 K.

Given the benefits of reverse factoring to suppliers, big companies offer this program to their suppliers under specified conditions. They often ask their suppliers to extend the payment term from the standard thirty to sixty days to around six months (Eaglesham, 2020). In 2020, the US-based beverage company Keurig Dr Pepper announced that it freed up $2.1 billion in cash reserves owing to supply chain finance programs with various suppliers. Payment terms with some suppliers were even extended to 360 days as the company harvested returns when allowing suppliers to benefit from its credit status.

Reverse factoring is an effective supply chain finance solution that exploits the credit discrepancy between a supplier and a buyer. Distinct from inventory financing, reverse factoring allows banks to serve as a creditor. However, there are risks related to its use. First, big buyers never offer reverse factoring as a "favor" to their suppliers. To be granted for a reverse factoring program, the suppliers are asked to extend the payment term. It is quite normal because the accessibility to low-rate loans benefits suppliers in reverse factoring. Therefore, buyers may ask suppliers to extend payment terms in return for letting suppliers use their low-rate access. However, the extension of payment terms must be limited such that it has a positive impact on both buyers and suppliers.

Suppose that the payment term on a trade is sixty days. The supplier has access to a bank loan at an interest rate of 5 percent, whereas it is 2.5 percent for the buyer. Reverse factoring makes it possible for the supplier to borrow at an interest rate of 2.5 percent. Assume that the supplier uses the bank loan to finance its operations during the payment term. Without reverse factoring, the supplier needs to have a loan for sixty days with an interest rate of 5 percent. The interest cost in this case is the same as that of a loan for 120 days with reverse factoring. Therefore, extending the payment term to 120 days with the reverse factoring program does not have any negative or positive impact on the supplier while the buyer captures all the benefits of reverse factoring. In contrast, the supplier captures all the benefits of reverse factoring if the payment term remains to be sixty days. Therefore, the supplier and buyer may negotiate a new midway payment term of ninety days to share the benefits.

The other risk of reverse factoring is related to its securitization, which is much riskier than the securitization of commodities and precious materials (cited in the inventory-financing section). Reverse factoring is used for diverse products from consumer goods to soft drinks and electronics. Here, it is difficult to understand and assess market risks associated with such diverse products. Reverse-factoring loans are often granted to suppliers without any rigorous analysis of their business, leading to heavy losses for investors. For example, the collapse of Greensill Capital and its cascading impact on global financial markets exemplify the risks associated with the securitization of reverse-factoring loans (Nelson et al., 2021). To avoid such, companies must enlist established banks with a long history and experience in trade finance.

5.2.3 Securing Payment from Buyers

Suppliers face a perennial predicament when they sell their products to financially distressed buyers. On one hand, they widen the customer base to boost sales and sustain growth. On the other hand, buyers may default on their invoices and hurt the financials of suppliers. To avoid the invoice-default risk, suppliers must monitor the financial stability of their buyers and sense deteriorating financial performance (Schneider & Biçer, 2024). Invoice-default risk is persistent in supply chains such that even some big companies may fail to remit their payments on time. In 2009, well-known automakers failed to pay invoices to suppliers due to the 2008 financial crisis. Many suppliers later declared bankruptcy (Bailey, 2009). In 2020, some retailers failed to make payments to sportswear and fashion apparel manufacturers like Nike Inc. and Columbia Sportswear Co. in the initial phase of the COVID pandemic.

Columbia later reported almost $20 million in bad-debt accounts. Likewise, Nike reported $170 million in bad-debt expenses due to the retailers failing to repay their invoices (Broughton, 2020).

Protecting suppliers from the invoice-default risk is also part of supply chain finance because any default of an invoice by a buyer would have detrimental effects on supply chain activities. Three different strategies can protect suppliers from invoice-default risk. First, suppliers can buy trade insurance or a financial instrument that insures against default. Suppliers often favor trade insurance as their first choice in protecting against the nonpayment risk of their customers. However, insurers may reduce coverage or refuse to write an insurance policy during economic downturns. To replace trade insurance in tough times, financial institutions offer select instruments at lucrative rates. For instance, J.P. Morgan offers *vendor put options* to investors such that the investors insure suppliers against the invoice-default risk and earn a premium in return (Wallace & Steinberg, 2020). Suppose a supplier issues a buyer invoice payable within 60 days totaling $1 million. The supplier may buy a vendor put option with protection percentage of 60 percent for a premium of $50 K. If the supplier gets paid in full, then total revenue generated becomes $950 K after deducting the premium. When the buyer defaults entirely, total revenue is 60 percent of $1 million minus the $50 K premium, equating to $550 K. Premiums and protection rates would depend on the financial leverage of buyers and other factors. Despite its excessive cost, vendor put options effectively protect the financial stability of suppliers, especially when delivering a bulky order after making a substantial capital investment.

The second strategy is to deliver products *after* receiving payment. When suppliers anticipate a high default risk, they best avoid offering any inventory financing and demand upfront payment. Buyers may decline such requests. They may cancel their orders or reduce the order quantity. Here, suppliers lose revenues when they unnecessarily force buyers to make upfront payments. Therefore, suppliers must serve these types of risky buyers carefully. Based on our research, we have identified three red flags that signal invoice-default risk: (1) operating margin, (2) financial leverage (debt-to-equity ratio), and (3) capital structure (Schneider & Biçer, 2024).

When a buyer has a low financial leverage, the invoice-default risk becomes negligible. Such a buyer can get an asset-based loan using equity as collateral and repay the invoices in full even in the presence of temporary cash-flow problems. When a buyer has a high financial leverage, the invoice-default risk can still be low depending on the operating margin and capital structure. In our research, we have shown that suppliers are paid on time by high-leverage buyers when the buyers have high operating margins and robust capital structure. Companies have robust capital structure if they are backed by long-term investors and prestigious creditors. Here, they benefit from the rational behavior of such stakeholders and pay invoices without delay when earning high profits. Yet highly profitable buyers may delay payment owing to agency conflicts among stakeholders. For instance, artists that supplied greeting cards to British retailer Paperchase could not get paid even after a successful financial recovery (Das, 2022).

The last strategy is to help buyers generate revenues so they can pay the invoices on time. As discussed earlier, most McDonald's restaurants (around 85 percent) are operated by franchisees. Unlike other franchisers, McDonald's owns the restaurant sites and leases them to franchisees. Therefore, the company operates like a real-estate company, rather than a restaurant chain, and selling hamburgers helps franchisees pay the rent. Supply chain activities are all designed to ensure that owners reap a steady cash flow, make profits, and pay rent plus the franchise fees.

The profitability of franchisees also attracts new investors who want to be business owners. Such an interest from new investors allows McDonald's to grow its business with minimal capital expenditure. Owing to this business model, McDonald's enjoys the largest franchising network with nearly 41,000 locations in more than 100 countries as of the end of 2023 (Reiff et al., 2024).

5.2.4 Other Strategies to Finance Supply Chains

There may be some inefficiencies regarding the implementation of the supply chain finance solutions mentioned when a supplier and a buyer interact for the first time. Inventory financing could be very risky with no trust between the supplier and the buyer. Vendor put options may protect a supplier from the invoice-default risk. However, this can be expensive, and suppliers hesitate to bear the prohibitive costs. Advance payments, on the other hand, deter potential buyers. Suppliers asking for an upfront payment may incur the opportunity cost of customers lost to competitors. To address these issues, a *letter of credit* may serve as an ideal solution.

Suppose a supplier receives a large order from a first-time foreign buyer with almost no trust between supply chain parties. The payment term is set for thirty days. The supplier wants to ensure timely payment of its invoice made in full. Otherwise, it would refuse to meet customer demand. The letter of credit facilitates trade in this situation. The letter of credit is issued by the *buyer's* bank and guarantees payment by the due date. If the buyer fails to pay the invoice, the buyer's bank is held liable. Because language in the letter may be complex and unclear to a supplier, the supplier's bank acts as its advisor. After the supplier delivers the ordered goods, it gets paid *by its own bank* via remittance from the buyer's bank. Lastly, the buyer's bank deducts the invoice amount from the buyer's account. Two banks, a supplier, and a buyer embody this letter-of-credit arrangement. The buyer's bank is called the *issuing* bank because it writes the letter of credit. The supplier's bank is called the *advising* bank because it guides the supplier as to its responsibilities. Though the banks charge both parties for their services, the fees paid to the banks would be expected to be less expensive than vendor put options.

The lack of trust that occurs when a supplier deals with a first-time buyer is not the only reason to ask for a letter of credit. If a buyer fails to pay an invoice on time due to financial troubles, a supplier may request the letter of credit to mitigate both invoice-default and late-payment risks. Bed Bath & Beyond Inc., a US-based furniture and housewares retailer under financial duress, failed to pay invoices to its suppliers in 2022 (Neuman, 2022). After securing $500 million in extra financing later that same year, the company paid overdue bills to suppliers. Although suppliers were paid, they refused to deliver new orders without letters of credit. After Bed Bath & Beyond announced that it was not providing letters of credit, its suppliers ceased shipments. Lacking supplies and foot traffic, the retailer filed for bankruptcy in 2023 (Fonrouge, 2023).

In inventory financing, the terms determine who will finance the supply chain depending on specified conditions. However, there is a lack of efficiency in inventory financing because there are only two epochs for a buyer to make payment. For instance, the term "1/10, net 30" indicates that the buyer can pay the invoice in ten days at a 1 percent

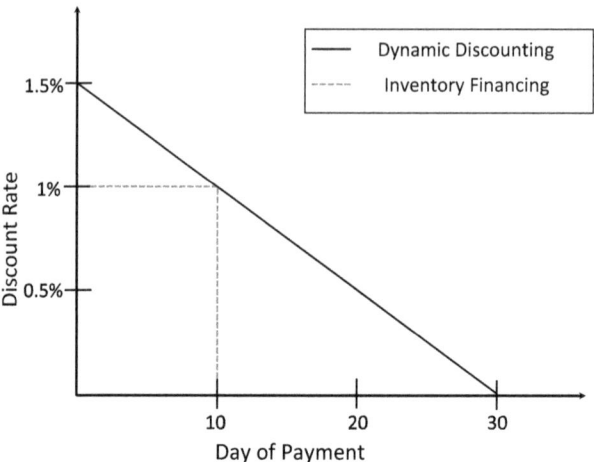

Figure 5.2 Dynamic discounting scheme

discount, or in thirty days after delivery at full price. What if the buyer receives spare cash on Day 11 post-delivery and wishes to remit the invoice? Here, the buyer receives no discount, the same as paying on the last day in this case.

Dynamic discounting is a supply chain finance solution that averts the inefficiency of inventory financing. Figure 5.2 depicts discount rates of dynamic discounting and its relationship with inventory financing. The dynamic discounting scheme matching the inventory financing term 1/10, net 30 is "1.5%, net 30," where a buyer paying the invoice immediately after delivery earns the 1.5 percent discount. The discount rate decreases *linearly*, as shown in the figure, and drops to zero when payment is made on the thirtieth day. If a buyer wants to pay on the eleventh day, the discount rate falls to 0.95 percent, versus none per inventory financing. Dynamic discounting is thus more flexible than inventory financing because a buyer can pay early at its convenience and win some discount depending on the time of payment. This flexibility leads to its adoption in the payment systems widely used in practice.[5]

---

[5] Well-known fintech companies, such as C2FO, Taulia, and PrimeRevenue, offer software services to their customers based on this dynamic discounting solution (https://c2fo.com, https://taulia.com, https://primerevenue.com).

In dynamic discounting, a supplier uploads its invoice to the system developed by a fintech company for payment. The *buyer* can make the invoice eligible for dynamic discounting and propose a discount rate. Next, the supplier chooses the date for payment, and its invoice amount *minus the discount* is transferred to the supplier's account on the selected payment date. Here, the buyer initiates the process by proposing a discount rate. Then, the supplier accepts and confirms the discount rate and payment date.

Another option to dynamic discounting is the *market mechanism* of dynamic discounting.[6] In the market mechanism, the buyer first informs suppliers of a desired discount rate for early payments. Then, suppliers bid discount rates for early payment. Depending on the buyer's working capital and suppliers' offers, some invoices are selected for early payment. There are two advantages of the market mechanism of dynamic discounting over the standard one (i.e., the sliding-scale scheme shown in Figure 5.2). First, the limited cash of the buyer is used to make early payment to suppliers more in need of funds. Suppliers who offer higher discount rates are prioritized for early payment. Second, the total discount is maximized for the buyer who can increase the savings.

5.3 The Starbucks Example

In 2010, Starbucks rolled out a mobile payment app that allows customers to make payments easily and quickly in their locations. The company also developed an effective marketing strategy to promote the mobile app such that the customers who use the app can collect reward points and receive complimentary products.[7] The coffeehouse chain has further improved the app over the years and enticed more people to use it by increasing product variety. It also built new partnerships with food delivery firms, such as Lyft, to boost the loyalty program used in the app (Jargon, 2015). These efforts paid off well in the end. In 2022, Starbucks reported net income of $878 million. Around 20 percent of this income ($181 million) came from prepaid cash yields (Geraldo, 2022; Patton, 2022).

---

[6] C2FO has been using the market mechanism commonly in practice. Visit the following link for more information: https://bicersupplychain.short.gy/YcsIkv.

[7] Visit the following link for more information about history of the Starbucks app: https://bicersupplychain.short.gy/rsR9O7.

Customers load money into the mobile app and receive promotions. This balance can be considered free float at no interest cost. Then, it is used in financial markets to generate nonoperational profits. Some customers also abandon funds in their accounts, which also contributes to nonoperational profits. Such benefits of the mobile come with a risk of deteriorating operational performance. When nonoperational profits constitute a significant amount of total profit, pricing and inventory decisions would be ineffective from an operational point of view, thereby hurting operational profits.

Suppose that a cup of coffee is sold for $3 in a coffeehouse, which is deemed the optimal price. Average monthly demand is 6,000 cups so that the coffeehouse reaps monthly revenue of $18,000. Per-cup cost is $2 after accounting for ingredients, labor, utility, rent, and overhead. This coffee shop makes a $1 margin on 6,000 cups, amounting to monthly profit of $6,000. They can attract more customers in the region and increase total demand to 20,000 cups when the price is reduced to $2.25 per cup. Here, the price cut is unwise because it causes a loss of $1,000 in profit per month.

When the optimal price of a cup of coffee is $3, for example, why do some coffee chains offer rewards or discounts for *mobile* orders? Starbucks offers various rewards for mobile orders, which are not available for regular orders paid at the cash checkout.[8] The mobile app is already helpful for customers: they can order before arriving and pay without waiting in line. Because of its convenience, many customers are willing to use the mobile app instead of waiting in line. Even though it is possible to sell a cup of coffee at $3 through the mobile app, why does a coffee chain offer a discount (e.g., $2.25) for mobile users? What is the motive for this strategy when discounts for mobile orders could cannibalize regular orders and result in profit losses?

Now suppose that there is value in keeping prepaid cash where the coffeehouse can earn 6 percent per month from financial activities. For coffee sold at $3, monthly revenue of $18,000 (ahead of any vendor payables, of course) yields at 6 percent an extra income of $1080. If the price is slashed to $2.25, then our new monthly revenue of $45,000 translates into 45,000*0.06 = $2,700 extra income. Here, the total profit for the $2.25 price tag per cup of coffee now equals

---

[8] Visit the following link for more information about mobile promotions: www.starbucks.ca/rewards.

5,000 + 2,700 = $7,700, while the total profit is running only 6,000 + 1,08 = $7,080 for the $3 price tag. Therefore, repricing to $2.25 helps the coffeehouse boost its profit by 7,700–7,080 = $620, or by 8.75 percent. This case shows that the optimal price for a product or a service depends not only on demand and cost factors but also on nonoperational financial activities. While a myopic analysis of operating profits may yield optimal pricing of $3 per cup, it becomes clear after scrutiny of income from financial activities that the best price may really be $2.25.

Total assets of Starbucks shrank from $29.37 billion in 2020 to $27.98 billion in 2022.[9] When the value of total assets decreases for a company, the inventory level is expected to decrease given that inventory is also included in total assets. Was this a slimming of inventory level? Surprisingly, Starbucks' inventory *increased* from $1.55 billion in 2020 to 2.18 billion in 2022. How did Starbucks worsen inventory productivity as it downsized assets? To answer this, we examine the cash sources of the company.[10] First, Starbucks managed to extend days of payables from nineteen days in 2020 to twenty-two days in 2022.[11] The firm restructured its sourcing to delay payments to suppliers three more days. To negotiate extended payment terms, procurement specialists may have ordered larger quantities, leading to some inventory swell. Second, the company increased current deferred revenues from $1.46 billion in 2020 to $1.64 billion in 2022. Deferred revenues on the balance sheet represent cash deposit to mobile apps in advance of customer visits. Therefore, funds uploaded to the Starbucks app increased $180 million from 2020 to 2022.

The loss of inventory productivity would stem from the company's efforts to persuade customer to use the app. Selling a cup of coffee on site is different from selling it using the app. We often go to a Starbucks close to home or work to buy a cup of coffee in the morning hours. Such a demand already exists for the company. To sell something online, Starbucks must offer a wider menu and promote it in an elegant way to

---

[9] Balance sheet information is given by: https://finance.yahoo.com/quote/SBUX/balance-sheet/.
[10] Cash flow information is given by: https://finance.yahoo.com/quote/SBUX/financials.
[11] Accounts payable were $997.9 million in 2020 and $1,441.4 million in 2022. Cost of goods sold was $18,458.9 billion in 2020 and $23,879.2 in 2022. Days of payable thus equaled 365 * [accounts payable] / [COGS].

win customers. To this end, the company must expand its inventory of coffees, cold drinks, and food to boost app sales while losing efficiency.

While focusing on increasing revenues and nonoperational profits, Starbucks also partnered with C2FO that has a platform to facilitate dynamic discounting practices, so their suppliers can have access to capital to finance their operations (C2FO, 2023). In the end, the coffeehouse chain has followed the principles of innovative business development to grow business and revenues. However, there is also a dark side of innovative business development such that the company has been facing some serious issues regarding deteriorating customer service and perception for the last two years.

Despite Starbucks' gains from nonoperational activities, the management could not align the innovative business development practice with the business objectives perfectly (Haddon et al., 2024). Starbucks has had a long-term vision of being the "third place" after home and work where customers can spend their time (e.g., working on their laptop, reading newspaper). Because of heavy app usage, the company reduced the seating area to have more space for pickup counters of app orders. The increasing store traffic coupled with the reduced seating area put the company's vision in jeopardy. This situation was even criticized by the former CEO and long-time leader Howard Schultz.[12] The variety of offerings has also been increased excessively such that there are now more than 170,000 ways to customize a drink. This causes a substantial loss of operational inefficiency, which leads to high operational costs. Starbucks has increased the prices to offset the elevated costs. As a result, the company reported a 6 percent reduction in the US orders in the second quarter of 2024. The new CEO Brian Niccol was hired to fix these problems and improve customer experience.

5.4 Conclusion

Executives are often lured by the idea of diversifying the income sources of their companies. They tend to innovate business models to reap extra cash in the form of nonoperational profits. To this end, they attempt to

---

[12] In a podcast, Mr. Schultz said, "Everyone shows up, and all of a sudden we've got a mosh pit, and that's not Starbucks" as he was criticizing the impact of the mobile app on store operations (Haddon et al., 2024).

5: Innovative Business Development 119

both increase revenues and truncate the cash conversion cycle to unleash extra capital. They later invest this capital in financial markets to generate profits. When successful, they will grow their business with added traction to improve their cash levels and generate more profits. However, aggressive growth could erode operational excellence. When the income generated in financial markets plummets, loss of operational excellence looms large. Here, decision-makers must have a plan to ensure operational excellence when needed. Otherwise, aggressive growth combined with loss of profits may end up with the bankruptcy of companies.

When executives attempt to harvest nonoperational profits, they face challenges due to: (1) deteriorating financial stability of supply chain parties, (2) nonpayment risk of buyers, and (3) inefficiencies of implementing a supply chain finance method. In this chapter, we have discussed how to address these challenges, which can be summarized as follows:

1. *Supply chain parties can develop an effective inventory financing scheme to protect the financial stability of trading parties.* With a large discrepancy in the creditworthiness of trading parties, executives can exploit this spread by developing a reverse-factoring program.
2. *Suppliers financing the trade may be exposed to nonpayment risk from buyers.* Suppliers must be cautious about the nonpayment risk and assess it by weighing their buyers' financial leverage, operating margins, and capital structure. If the nonpayment risk is high, they can ask for advance payments, buy trade insurance or vendor put options, and even help buyers grow their revenues.
3. *Finally, executives must address inefficiencies when enacting a supply chain finance solution.* For first-time trades, they may prefer the letter of credit over inventory financing or advance payments. For repeated dealings, dynamic discounting may be favored over inventory financing for flexible buyer payment.

Decision-makers would be better off addressing these challenges before innovating their business models. Otherwise, companies may suffer from the loss of operational focus despite some gains of nonoperational profits as demonstrated by the Starbucks case.

6 | *The Premium Business: Market-Driven Supply Chain Management*

Innovating business models to generate nonoperational profits is not the only path to reduce companies' sensitivity to supply–demand mismatches. Decision-makers can also achieve this goal by boosting operating profits. Imagine a retailer who sells an electronic product for a 50 percent gross margin. Suppose the retailer generates revenue of $10 million, and the cost of goods sold is $5 million. The initial inventory is worth $10 million, and the retailer ends up with excess inventory equal to half of the initial inventory level at the end of the product lifecycle. Here, the cost of excess inventory (i.e., inventory write-offs) equals $5 million. Therefore, the cost of excess inventory eats up all operating profits, leaving the retailer with zero net margin. Now consider an alternative case where the retailer reduces the cost of the product by 80 percent. Then, the gross margin increases to 90 percent. If the retailer can still generate revenue of $10 million, the cost of goods sold becomes $1 million. Ending with excess inventory at half of the initial level now costs only $1 million in inventory write-offs. Therefore, the retailer grosses $8 million despite having sold only half the initial inventory.

This example demonstrates that companies selling products at *higher margins* are less worried about supply–demand mismatches because hefty margins offset the cost of excess inventory, making such companies exposed to a lower risk of supply–demand mismatches. Luxury brands exemplify such businesses as they offer premium goods at ultra-high prices. Given the lower risk of supply–demand mismatches, they have different supply chain priorities such that they often concentrate on a robust supply chain that preserves brand value and drives demand from wealthy customers. To better understand these supply chain dynamics, let us first turn our attention to how value is created along the supply chain in the premium business.

The alignment of supply chain activities with business models is crucial to create value for customers in an economical way. For most businesses, value is indexed to the *utility* of the products or services offered. If a product has many features and essential functions, the value of the product elevates. In the luxury industry, though, the value of a product or service is unrelated to the utility offered to customers. Companies have a distinct perspective of the value in the luxury industry: it correlates with the *delight* customers have when they buy and use luxury goods. A former luxury executive, Pauline Brown (former chairperson of North America Operations of LVMH), coined the term "aesthetic intelligence" to describe how firms can shape the customer experience to delight customers (Brown, 2019). Aesthetic intelligence puts customer emotions and delight at the center of product development in the luxury industry, seeking to control and influence customers' feelings toward the luxury product. In this dimension, luxury products differ from utility products as the latter employ design features and utilities in their product development, while luxury goods are developed based on aesthetic intelligence.

The luxury winter-clothing brand Canada Goose uses aesthetic intelligence to increase profits and develop a sustainable growth strategy.[1] Canada Goose aims to induce "customer feel" for the Canadian experience when wearing the brand's well-known parkas. The customers can feel the same as intended by the company if the parkas carry the stamp "Made in Canada." Thus, all Canada Goose products are made in Canada to offer the delight of wearing a Canadian coat or parka (Reiss, 2019). This has implications for its supply chain where *all* production and logistics activities must be carried out in Canada at its eight facilities (three in Winnipeg, three in Toronto, and two in Quebec (Reiss, 2019)).

Canada Goose could have offshored the production of all winter coats and parkas to lower the cost while offering the same features and functions. However, many customers would have stopped buying the brand's parkas at premium prices. Having the same features and functions *alone* does not justify a premium price. Here, an offshoring

---

[1] Canada Goose was founded in 1957 under the name of Metro Sportswear Ltd. In the 1970s, the company launched the brand "Snow Goose," which was later changed to Canada Goose. Since then, the brand has been following a successful marketing strategy such that it collaborates with Hollywood celebrities to promote its products. Owing to these efforts, Canada Goose boosted sales in the last two decades: https://luxstyled.com/which-celebrities-wear-canada-goose-2024-guide/. Visit the company website for more information about its history: https://canadagoose.com/ca/en/our-history.html.

practice could jeopardize the firm and its brand value. When decision-makers emphasize features and functions of products or services without paying attention to aesthetics, luxury companies may find themselves in a fateful race toward commodity status.

Unlike a design ethos aimed at boosting utility value of a product, aesthetic intelligence does not start with customers. As described by Pauline Brown (Brown, 2019), aesthetic products are designed by renowned artists or designers reflecting their own tastes. After such products are developed, they enter the market at high prices. Demand is quite unpredictable given the ontological uncertainty of genuine items first introduced to the market. Despite high uncertainty, luxury demand must be delightfully fulfilled as part of aesthetic intelligence.

Delightful fulfilment of customer demand means a pleasant experience when shoppers first buy the product. To achieve this, fulfilment operations must be quick and convenient while offering knowledgeable, friendly assistance.[2] Therefore, luxury brands must be responsive to the needs of their customers even when demand is uncertain. Such an objective can easily end up with excess inventory when demand turns out to be low. Here, the challenge is that luxury brands must also *avoid* product markdowns while facing excess inventory risk.

The genuine feeling of delight when using luxury goods would fade away if products were marked down at a discount. For that reason, luxury brands often have a contingency plan to wipe off excess inventory without selling them at a discount. For example, Richemont (i.e., the company that is well-known for its brands: Cartier, Piaget, and Montblanc) bought back $567 million worth of watches in 2018 from retail partners after its watches failed to sell at full price. As with other luxury brands, reputation and brand value are much more important than operating profits. While having negative financial consequences, this buyback helped the firm protect its long-term brand value (Bain, 2019; Koltrowitz, 2017).

Supply chain challenges of luxury brands differ from those in other industries. Figure 6.1 summarizes them as well as effective supply chain

---

[2] According to a survey conducted by PwC, shoppers are willing to pay a 16 percent premium on goods or services for a positive experience, and 80 percent of US customers say that speed, convenience, knowledgeable advice, and friendly service comprise such an experience. The survey report is available via: https://bicersupplychain.short.gy/huNtxA.

6: *The Premium Business*   123

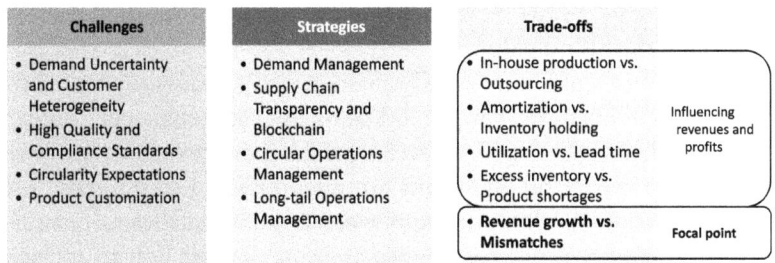

Figure 6.1 Challenges and strategies of luxury supply chain management

strategies and their relationship with the fundamental trade-offs. There are four aspects of the supply chain challenges in the luxury industry. First, it is difficult for luxury brands to manage demand due to high demand uncertainty and customer heterogeneity. Decision-makers must use a mix of judgmental and quantitative methods to predict the distribution of demand. They must next wield insights to develop an inventory policy based on customer heterogeneity. Luxury products are sold to wealthy consumers, collectors, and retail partners. Depending on the shares of these customer segments, a proper production and inventory policy can be developed, reflecting the distinct shares of these customer segments.

Second, luxury brands must closely monitor supply chain activities and ensure that all operations are maintained in environmentally, socially responsible ways. To this end, decision-makers must assess the feasibility of digitalization and blockchain technologies to improve supply chain visibility. These technologies would also help luxury brands authenticate second-hand products and fight counterfeits. Third, luxury producers must innovate supply chains to design circular business models so they can reduce the carbon footprint of their products. Because many consumers tend to justify luxury spending on products deemed environmentally sustainable, there is mounting pressure on luxury brands to develop circular operations.

Fourth, luxury manufacturers are required to increase product variety to sustain growth. Managing the variety in the luxury business is different from doing the same for utility products. There are certain limitations of expanding product offerings that must be addressed by luxury brands. Nevertheless, there exist success stories such that some brands increase product variety substantially while preserving the brand value.³

The challenges of luxury supply chains are not necessarily linked to the mismatches between supply and demand. These challenges hinder companies from growing their revenues if not managed effectively. For that reason, luxury supply chains are often exposed to the trade-off between revenue growth and supply–demand mismatches as demonstrated in Figure 6.1. In what follows, we walk through how to address these four supply chain issues. Then, we discuss how Hugo Boss achieved a substantial increase in revenue and profits by aligning its business strategy with supply chain priorities of the luxury industry. Finally, we provide the concluding remarks.

6.1 Demand Management

The production process of luxury goods is subject to strict quality checks. Raw materials sourced from a limited number of suppliers must meet certain criteria. Procurement and product specialists test the quality of raw materials upon receipt to ensure that raw materials used are of the highest quality. During the manufacturing process, numerous quality checks ensure that customer expectations are fulfilled at a supreme level to merit a willingness to pay a premium to own the luxury brands. Thus, supply chain activities must be initiated well in advance of the targeted product release dates while dealing with high demand uncertainty.

Demand prediction is a challenging task for luxury brands because it requires both good judgmental and quantitative skills. It begins with forecast meetings where experts from different departments, such as product, R&D, supply chain management, marketing, and sales, discuss the product and market characteristics. It is often the case that top executives (CEO, COO, CFO) attend such meetings. After experts make presentations as to the product, target customer segments, and historical sales of comparable items, the demand forecasts are determined collectively. Here, two approaches can be employed. The first is the prediction of consensus demand where specialists agree on a single

---

[3] Hermes has been unusually successful in expanding product variety and boosting sales consistently. Hermes often sells two or three "Birkins" per model (flagship handbag category attributed to the English-French actor Jane Birkin). The Birkin brand thus owes its success to its diverse styles offered to shoppers (Ryan, 2023).

demand forecast for each product. This approach is very efficient, with a single forecast set quickly. The second is judgmental forecasting, such that each expert secretly writes one's own forecast for each product. The average of these values is then used as the demand forecast.

Judgmental forecasting is much better than the consensus approach because it values each opinion of the participants. In the consensus approach, however, one person (e.g., CEO or Head of Product) could dominate others, resulting in lost information. Another benefit of judgmental forecasting is that the average and standard deviation of the forecasts well reflect a statistical distribution of demand. This distribution can then be used in optimization models to determine production quantities and schedules.

German luxury bike manufacturer Canyon Bikes has used judgmental forecasting for its high-end bikes, increasing profits around 8 percent versus the consensus approach (Diermann & Huchzermeier, 2017). Canyon Bikes was founded in 1985 in Koblenz, Germany, and they have been in the market ever since (Canyon Bicycles GmbH, n.d.). They make high-end road and mountain bikes, which are sold in the price range of $1,000 to $9,500. Judgmental forecasting is carried out every year in March. All new bikes are later introduced to the market in September. Thus, procurement (e.g., frames, wheels, brakes, and gears) and production activities take place from March to September. The forecasting practice is sponsored by the top executives of Canyon Bikes where even the CEO and CFO participate. Based on the output of individuals, the mean and standard deviation of forecasts are determined. The forecasts may be biased such that actual demand proves consistently higher or lower. Using data of historical attempts, it is possible to debias forecasts. Suppose the average forecast is 500 units for one model. Weighing historical data, analysts have found that actual demand values were consistently 20 percent higher than average forecasts. Here, average demand is debiased by multiplying the initial forecast with 1.2, making the new forecast equal to: 500 * 1.2 = 600 units. Finally, production levels are analytically set depending on the debiased forecasts and cost factors (Diermann & Huchzermeier, 2017).

Canyon Bikes is one of the best practices of judgmental forecasting for three reasons. First, forecasting activities are sponsored by the CEO with participants sharing opinions equally. No single person dominates or affects another's thoughts. An egalitarian process makes possible a wider collection of information about demand and its statistical distribution. Second, demand distribution is incorporated in an analytical framework to determine the production quantities. This analytical framework uses the cost parameters to determine the production quantities that maximize the expected profit. Finally, the management monitors the actual-to-forecast ratio to understand the forecast bias. Some participants may be overly optimistic or pessimistic about potential sales of new bikes. The company tracks data of historical actual-to-forecast ratios to let the executives realize their biases. The executives could later correct them for better leadership. Owing to these efforts, Canyon Bikes has grown revenues over the years and reached annual revenue of EUR 400 million in fiscal 2023 (Rome, 2023; Storbeck, 2023). Even basketball icon LeBron James invested in the firm to support its growth in the US market (Perez, 2022).

Demand forecasting is the first step in demand management. After forming a statistical distribution of demand via judgmental forecasting, decision-makers must set target fulfillment rates (widely called *fill rate* in the supply chain literature) for each customer segment. Three main customer segments served by the luxury industry are: (1) wealthy consumers, (2) collectors, and (3) retail partners. The first segment intends to use luxury products in daily life. For instance, Hermes sells silk scarves in company-owned stores to wealthy consumers who buy the scarves for their daily usage. When in-store consumers comprise most of the revenue, luxury brands best aim at meeting demand as much as possible by setting a high fulfillment rate. Otherwise, shoppers facing stockouts would switch to other luxury brands, incurring lost profits.

There is a risk for luxury brands such that setting a high fulfillment rate requires companies to produce in large volumes, exposing them to excess inventory risk when demand turns out to be low. Luxury brands cannot easily sell excess items at deep discounts because luxury consumers tend to avoid brands that sell at discount outlets. Here, luxury brands must have a sustainable inventory liquidation plan. One effective approach would be to work with select designer houses, such as Rue La La, that offer limited-time discounts for luxury sales. Rue La La is a US-based company selling luxury items online. The company offers luxury goods at a discount *within a time window* and deletes them later from the website. This allows luxury brands to liquidate excess inventory undetected by regular consumers.

The second customer segment is collectors who purchase luxury products as investments. For instance, the Swiss watchmaker Patek

Phillippe makes around 60,000 watches per year for sale mostly to collectors (Besler, 2023). Unlike consumers who buy the products for their daily usage, collector-investors aim for long-term value appreciation in luxury products that may sell at remarkably high prices, like one Patek Phillippe that auctioned for $5.8 million (Descalsota & Duffy, 2023). Auction sales for old watches make the brand extremely popular for collectors as investments. Hence, Patek Phillippe can charge ultra-high prices for the 60,000 watches made every year. If sales to collectors constitute most of revenue, luxury brands are advised to set a *low* fulfillment rate. Only a select group of collectors would be entitled to buy the luxury products. They must project an impression that their products would soar in value over the years. It is this impression that justifies the hefty spending of collectors on luxury products. In this scenario, products must appear *scarce* in the market.

The last segment features retail partners or agents who buy goods from luxury producers and sell them in the market through their own sales channels. For example, luxury winemakers often sell to merchants. In the Bordeaux region of France, it is almost impossible for an imbiber to buy a bottle of luxury wine directly from a winemaker. All premier winemakers (e.g., Chateau Margaux) in the region have well-designed websites that disclose detailed product information. But no online ordering option appears because winemakers sell all their vintages to merchants.[4]

Merchants form an indispensable part of winery supply chains. They advertise vintages in different markets, set prices, store bottles at proper conditions, and develop keen customer relationships with premium retailers and restaurants. Owing to such efforts, winemakers may focus on the quality of vintages without worrying about marketing, sales, and financial issues. Even the brand reputation of individual winemakers is guarded by merchants as they make every effort to improve the image of luxury winemakers. For instance, they enlist wine connoisseurs to grade high-quality vintages and get their endorsements. This may result in auctions enhancing the image of wine brands. In Canada, one bottle of Chateau Margaux 1990 vintage sold for $15,960 in 2021 under the guidance of two wine

---

[4] We refer the reader to Chateau Margaux's website: www.chateau-margaux.com/en. There was no online ordering option at the time of this writing.

experts.⁵ These types of auctions help luxury winemakers grow brand value that attracts wine collectors to buy their wines.

Characteristics of supply chains differ per customer segment in the luxury industry. If luxury brands sell products mostly to consumers, then they must aim to fulfill the demand of *all* customers who are willing to pay hefty prices. This helps maximize profits in both the short and long term. Direct sales to consumers also make it possible to reap the full potential of broker-free supply chains. When luxury brands sell mostly to collectors, they must limit the availability of wares by producing in low quantities. Such products must appear rare where ownership offers a promising investment. Collectors buy luxury products when they believe prices tend to increase. Finally, luxury brands selling products to merchants must pay attention to value creation by their merchant partners. In this case, brands must work exclusively with qualified merchants that have strong marketing and sales experience. Merchants here are required to *act as the owner* of brands, making every effort to defend the reputation of luxury brands. While paying attention to the implications of customer segments for supply chains, luxury brands must base their critical supply chain decisions on accurate demand forecasts. To this end, they must use the *judgmental forecasting method* to extract maximum information from product experts.

6.2 Supply Chain Transparency and Blockchain

Decisions made downstream in the supply chain are affected by upstream supply chain activities. For example, procurement of raw materials affects production choices. Production activities shape decisions regarding fulfillment of customer orders. To make the right decisions, supply chain professionals must have full visibility of their supply chains. Suppose a manufacturer sets the production schedule based on information that raw materials ordered from a supplier will be delivered in one week. If delivery were delayed for a couple of days, production capacity would be wasted, leading to lost profits. Surely, the manufacturer must know the delivery time before finalizing the production schedule. This is possible if the location of an order can be

---

⁵ Visit the following link for more information about the auction: https://waddingtons.ca/notable-sales/chateau-margaux-1990/.

monitored accurately in real time. Therefore, the manufacturer must establish supply chain transparency to control the flow of goods effectively.

In addition to controlling product flow, supply chain transparency makes it possible for manufacturers to monitor whether supply chain activities are carried out according to quality standards. Buyers of luxury goods often request information about suppliers, materials, and supply chain practices to ensure products are made of the highest quality materials in socially and environmentally responsible ways. In the apparel industry, for example, buyers became very demanding about supply chain visibility after the 2013 collapse of Rana Plaza in Bangladesh (Manik & Yardley, 2013). Jewelry enthusiasts seek supply chain transparency to ensure that their purchases are not funding wars or crimes (Gomelsky, 2023). To address these challenges, companies must establish supply chain transparency so they can provide customers with detailed information about products' journey from raw material sourcing to markets. This information can be linked to serial numbers of products where users could query serial numbers in digital systems to obtain this information.

Traditionally, supply chain transparency has long been deemed an important aspect of businesses because it facilitates the flow of goods and the documentation of supply chain history. Lately, blockchain technology has revolutionized improvements in supply chain transparency. The technology can be viewed as decentralized database management systems where databases are stored at many sites. Each transaction logs as one block in these databases. When a shopper buys a product and makes payment, the buyer requests a private key and uses it to complete the transaction. Then, a block corresponding to this transaction is added to the system. If the owner later sells the product to another, then a new block is created and linked to the prior block using secure algorithms known as hashes. As follow-up transactions occur, new blocks are connected to the chain, forming a product blockchain. When adding the blocks, transactions are verified by users *collectively* according to protocols. Select protocols are carefully developed where each transaction must be verified by separate users and all databases are updated consistently. This makes the technology a secure platform for sensitive operations such as financial payments. Thus, the blockchain can track supply chain footprints accurately so that customers would be able to reach trustworthy information regarding supply chain practices.

There are two important implications of blockchain for supply chain management. First, this technology makes it possible to connect different parties and monitor their activities very effectively. Supply chains involve myriad companies and service providers, all with different digital systems. In this setting, supply chain transparency can be achieved when systems are seamlessly linked and synchronized. To this end, supply chain partners exert much effort to ensure that records in different systems are accurate and consistent. Blockchain can improve the efficiency of such efforts because the synchronization process is exceptionally reliable and fast owing to its protocols.

The second advantage of blockchain is its ease in the authentication of luxury products. Product authentication is critical in fighting counterfeits in the secondhand market. If a proper authentication mechanism is not established, then counterfeits would swamp the market and hurt profits of luxury brands directly. Another threat of counterfeits is that they make secondhand markets inefficient and risky. Owners of luxury products often demand an effective secondhand market for selling their used products at fair prices. Customers may refuse to buy new luxury goods if they think that it would be impossible to resell them in a trusted secondhand market. Proliferating counterfeits would deter potential shoppers from purchasing anything secondhand. Here, owners of luxury goods may not find buyers for their used products, making secondhand markets inefficient. To address these challenges, luxury brands can use blockchain to provide reliable and fast authentication services for their customers.

There have been some professional services in markets to authenticate products through a physical inspection. The experts check products, their certificates, buyer receipts of purchases, product identification numbers, and tags attached to products. Based on their analyses, such professional services identify whether products are original or fake. However, physical authentication is not highly efficient compared to the potential use of blockchain technology due to time and capital requirements.[6]

---

[6] The luxury watch brand Rolex has service centers and authorized dealers worldwide offering authentication services at a cost near $150: https://bicersupplychain.short.gy/vSSrXl. In addition to this cost, customers must spend time to find an authentication service. The time and capital investments (though minor compared to the price of a Rolex watch) are seen as friction in secondhand markets, marring their efficiency. Fortunately, this friction can be eliminated by blockchain.

In the blockchain system, each blockchain is tagged to a digital or a physical product such as a luxury good. There are chronologically ordered, connected blocks in each blockchain where each block represents a different activity. All relevant information as to an activity can be stored in the corresponding block anonymously. Suppose a craftsman assembles a luxury watch. This activity in full detail is embodied as a block into the blockchain. Then, the watch is delivered to a dealer. This is another activity added to the blockchain. Finally, a customer buys the watch from the dealer. The sales transaction including customer information is added to the blockchain as a new block. When the new owner offers to sell the watch in the secondhand market, potential buyers can extract information about all the supply chain and sales history from the blockchain. They first check for matching of owner information in the blockchain with that of watch seller. Then, they match all other blockchain information with product certificates, serial numbers, and so on. This process can be streamlined via online systems developed by luxury brands. Hence, authentication can be done in a rapid and secure fashion.

The blockchain can be considered one of the most important technological innovations transpiring at the center of digital transformation projects among luxury brands. It has the full potential to revolutionize supply chain transparency and authentication, both vital for operational excellence in the luxury market. To fully realize these benefits, three prominent luxury groups (i.e., LVMH, Richemont, and Prada Group) formed the 2021 Aura Blockchain Consortium (Paton, 2021). In academia, the MIT Digital Currency Initiative Lab has further developed blockchain-based verification protocols for supply chain trades (Chod et al., 2020). Digital platforms like Everledger and Tracr also offer authentication services to firms using blockchain. As companies adopt these solutions, blockchain technology will increase in popularity, providing enhanced benefits to luxury brands.

6.3 Circular Operations Management

Global atmospheric content may exceed a critical threshold if certain actions are delayed. Unfortunately, there is an increasing risk of heatwaves, flooding, drought, and crop shortage in future due to global warming if societies do not reduce their carbon emissions (Plumer, 2023). Playing their societal role, corporations face increasing pressure from the public and customers to reduce their carbon emissions. To this end, companies must establish circular operational models so that supply chain activities do not cause substantial damage to the environment and products do not end up in landfills at rapid rates.

Some firms have already begun prioritizing circular business models. Unfortunately, many others lag because they do not benefit *economically* from circularity efforts.[7] Circular operations management is economically sustainable for luxury brands because it has a direct positive impact on sales. In fact, young shoppers justify their spending on luxury goods according to the brands' resourcefulness (Kim, 2023). There is a strong perception among millennials that luxury brands comply with regulations, being environmentally responsible and limiting carbon emissions continuously. Therefore, luxury brands must preserve their circularity reputation and continuously address environmental concerns of young shoppers to maintain high sales.[8]

Five dimensions of circularity prevail in operations management. *First, production must be carried out effectively to avoid wasting limited resources.* Producers with excess inventory have typically used resources to produce goods not demanded by customers. Thus, they increase carbon emissions for no reason. Our 2021 investigation of production-related waste with a group of Swiss researchers (Seifert et al., 2022) has shown this type of waste to be more harmful to the environment than even household waste! Therefore, firms should begin circularity efforts by eliminating excess production. One approach to curb excess production is to cut lead times. As discussed in Chapter 4, short lead times can reduce excess inventory by effectively matching supply with demand. However, reducing lead time is difficult when production involves long quality control processes, such as those occurring in luxury production. Even when brands manufacture luxury items at domestic sites, lead-time reduction may not be possible due to the prolonged production steps. Another approach is to produce goods in scant quantities and introduce them to the market as limited editions.

---

[7] I do not promote the idea that companies must delay the implementation of circular business models for economic reasons. Indeed, I believe that economic factors should not be an obstacle to circularity. Because environmental policies are still lax, however, firms tend to establish circular models if they have public pressure or see economic benefits.

[8] A market survey by Bain & Company has reported the growth in the luxury industry as entirely driven by Gens Y, Z and Alpha. Visit the following link to access the report: https://bicersupplychain.short.gy/t76QTV.

This strategy is more appealing because it allows luxury brands to minimize carbon footprints by streamlining inventory. Another advantage is that luxury brands can sell limited-edition products at a premium because consumers assign high values to scarce items. Accordingly, the limited edition is deemed a prominent strategy in the luxury industry to cut production-related waste and carbon footprints.

The second dimension is to prolong the product's lifetime to where customers may use products for extended periods. Luxury brands pay much attention to product quality to avert quick wear-outs. Owners of such products also maintain their luxury items in good condition. For example, watchmaker Patek Philippe advertises that the lifecycle of their products lasts *generations* owing to its ultra-high-quality standards. Thus, luxury goods wield disproportionate lifetimes versus other products used daily. Given that most luxury brands already achieve extraordinarily long product lifetimes, decision-makers have the privilege of concentrating their efforts toward other dimensions of circular operations management.

The third dimension is the ability and ease of luxury product resale in secondhand markets. Buying a luxury good is an expensive investment even for wealthy people. Customers thus seek flexibility in reselling their luxury items at fair market prices. Such flexibility also aligns with circular operations management because resale diminishes any need for producing new items to fulfill customer demand. To facilitate resale, there must be online services that can easily authenticate luxury products. Also required are brokers who contact and convince the luxury goods owners to resell their holdings. One luxury consignment firm, "The RealReal," allows owners to consign their holdings within its marketplace.[9] According to a *Wall Street Journal* interview with the founder and former CEO of the company, The RealReal has client representatives in sixteen cities who engage wealthy customers and pick up their items for resale on the company's platform. Its business model is based on circularity as they fulfill luxury demand with *used* products (Wainwright, 2014).

The fourth dimension is repairability. Luxury products must function well for a long time so that consumers need not replace them

---

[9] The RealReal is an online marketplace for buying and selling luxury goods. The company was founded in 2011. Its annual revenue was $143 million in 2023, which was generated from the total trade volume of $451 million. Visit the following link for more information about the company: www.therealreal.com/.

frequently. When they wear out, they must be repaired by owners or professional services conveniently. *The final dimension is recycling.* When goods cannot be resold or repaired properly, they must be recycled so that the material can be used to make new units. Luxury brands must locate manufacturing near to market footprints to expedite repair and reuse. Manufacturing facilities have all the necessary expertise about goods produced at those sites. They would diffuse this expertise in their locales. For example, retired plant employees may open a repair shop. Therefore, customers can easily find professional repair services for products when manufacturing facilities are located nearby. Production plants can also use recycled items to produce new ones. Unfortunately, offshore production makes recycling extremely difficult because it is not feasible to collect recycled goods in consumer markets (e.g., the United States) and ship them to an offshore plant. This may elevate the cost of recycling. However, sites near markets make recycling economically viable.

Luxury brands mostly succeed in the first two dimensions of circular operations management. Given the small market size, brands often limit production quantities and introduce new items as limited editions. Luxury products also enjoy long lifetimes owing to their high-quality standards. Yet luxury brands may improve in the final three dimensions. They must address authentication concerns and fight counterfeits to improve reselling efforts in secondhand markets. They also need to improve product design to make repair and refabrication convenient for customers.

6.4 Long-Tail Operations Management

The Internet and growth of e-commerce have reduced the search costs for customers that seek a product in the market. When a businessperson plans for a trip from Toronto to Zurich, for example, she can easily look at Amazon.ca and search for a travel kit and adapter fitting the Swiss tri-plug sockets. One can check pricing and ratings before deciding what to buy. If she often travels to Switzerland, she may buy the specific adapter designed to convert from Canadian to the Swiss socket. Otherwise, she may buy a universal adapter on the Internet. She can also choose a colored adapter as red or blue universal adapters are popular in the market. One can complete all searches and place an order in just ten minutes with twenty-four-hour express delivery for Amazon Prime customers. Imagine how difficult it would be to do all these without the Internet and e-commerce. Finding an adapter to convert from Canadian to Swiss socket would be difficult in only physical stores, so the businessperson could buy a universal adapter. Likewise, finding a colored adapter would be tough outside the Internet.

Customers seek products tailored to their specific preferences. When they do not find the precise specs, they substitute with more generic items having similar features. The convenience of searching goods on the Internet plus its search traffic information allows e-commerce retailers to monitor what products are demanded in the market after analyzing customer queries. Then, they aim to fulfill diverse customer demand by offering a vast menu of wares. Amazon, for example, sells more than 12 million products online. While such product variety raises operating costs, e-tailers can charge a premium for the convenience they offer. Therefore, wider product variety may duly offset any operational costs, helping e-commerce retailers boost bottom-line profits

In 2004, then-editor of *Wired* magazine, Chris Anderson, coined the term "long tail" to describe the evolution of purchasing behavior of customers in online markets (Anderson, 2004). The long-tail phenomenon states that customer purchasing behavior has been shifting from buying standard products at a physical site to ordering more niche items online. Digital manufacturing techniques (e.g., 3D printing) and the Internet promote this long-tail phenomenon by making the production and sales of diverse product lines affordable for firms (Johnson, 2012). For example, many small businesses produce customized, 3D-printed products for sale online through Amazon's or Shopify's marketplaces. Other businesses, where 3D-printing is not viable, still meet long-tail demand by developing production systems that imitate the working principles of 3D-printing technology. If operators can switch production from one product to another without any setup or compromise of quality standards, for example, companies can manufacture long-tail products to fulfill diverse demand through alternate paths.

Luxury brands strive to offer long-tail (niche) products to their customers. However, their assortment is much more limited than regular e-commerce retailers because luxury brands must be hyper-selective in their product offerings. First, products must align with the brand's aesthetic tastes such that brand image and reputation can be maintained. Second, the high quality of products must be guaranteed. Here, luxury brands cannot change their manufacturing practices due to production limits and quality concerns. Nevertheless, they have been constantly exploring some opportunities to widen product variety. Some luxury brands offer their customers the option to configure or customize their orders. For example, the luxury watchmaker Rolex offers a configuration service to customers where they can specify the material, bracelet, and dial of some watches. The luxury brand Louis Vuitton also makes it possible for customers to configure the brand's iconic bags, choosing the shapes of stripes and colors, as well as inscribing initials of their names.

Despite these successful implementations, customization is challenging in the luxury industry due to long lead times. Unlike two to three weeks of delivery time for Timbuk2's customized bags, customers in the luxury industry must wait up to eight weeks to receive their customized orders. Thus, the contribution of customized orders to sales is expected to be lower in the luxury industry (e.g., Louis Vuitton) than the retail industry (e.g., Timbuk2), making customization less appealing for luxury brands.

In Chapter 4, we discussed Timbuk2's effective capacity-rationing methods to produce both standard and customized bags in a flexible production facility. When Timbuk2 receives customized orders, it prioritizes them over standard bag production. This helps deliver tailored bags in shorter times (under two weeks). Does capacity rationing work in the luxury industry? The dynamics of the luxury industry differ from other industries as luxury production processes can be complex, involving strict quality controls. Pauline Brown once remarked: "[Hermes Silk Scarves] quality control is tighter than NASA," emphasizing the role of quality in luxury arenas (Nobel, 2017). Also, luxury goods are made according to certain, well-established (often secret) production methods, limiting operational flexibility needed for capacity rationing. Therefore, luxury brands can make customized products according to customer preferences when buyers are *willing to wait* to receive their orders. Despite the demand for tailored luxury wares, it would be difficult to convert such demand into revenues due to luxury supply chain constraints.

Such lack of operational flexibility often forces luxury brands to find other ways to widen product lines while serving long-tail demand. To this end, they acquire small luxury businesses with heritage and high-quality standards. For example, LVMH has diversified its eyewear menu through an aggressive acquisition strategy. The company launched its eyewear division in 2017 and started to offer products under the names of its in-house brands Louis Vuitton and Berlutti. Next, LVMH bought boutique eyewear brands (e.g., Barton Parreira and Vuarnet) to fulfill long-tail demand (Frank, 2023). Such an acquisition strategy helps luxury brands in two ways. First, it broadens the customer base as existing customers of acquired businesses become new customers. Second, it expands operational expertise as brands learn how acquired companies make their high-quality luxury items. The latter can be extremely relevant toward meeting long-tail demand in the luxury industry. Indeed, gaining new operational knowledge would prove particularly useful in developing niche products without compromising quality standards. For this reason, luxury brands must target small businesses with the best operational practices for acquisition. After finalizing the transactions, they may adopt operational practices needed to make niche items efficiently. This could prove a viable approach toward serving long-tail demand in the luxury industry.

6.5 The Hugo Boss Example

Hugo Boss is a German luxury fashion brand that sells apparel, footwear, and accessory products around the world. It generated revenue of EUR 4.2 billion (equivalent to $4.58 million) in 2023. The company operates in 131 countries and employs around 19,000 people. Geographically, half of the total revenue comes from the European market, around 15 percent from the United States, and the remaining 35 percent from other markets (Grieder, 2023).

Hugo Boss had been struggling to grow sales before the COVID pandemic. Its annual revenue was consistently around EUR 2.7 billion between 2015 and 2019. The annual gross profit was EUR 1.87 billion in 2019. To increase revenues and profits, the company appointed Mr. Daniel Grieder (former CEO of Tommy Hilfiger) as the CEO in 2020. Under his leadership, Hugo Boss created *two product lines* to meet the needs of different customer segments. The *Hugo* product line targets young shoppers seeking contemporary styles, whereas the *Boss* product line is for business and casual wear shoppers. Then, the management diversified the product portfolio significantly under these two product lines. Hence, the company that had been famous for dark suits started to sell bright athleisure clothing worn by Gen Z and famous Instagram influencers (Wheeler, 2022).

These changes were some bold steps for any luxury company that may end up with heavy losses. Nevertheless, Hugo Boss managed them very effectively and increased annual gross profit to EUR 2.58 billion in 2023 from EUR 1.87 billion in 2019. This success is attributed to their organizational turnaround project "CLAIM 5," which was launched in 2021 (Stohr & Westermann, 2021). There are *five pillars* of the "CLAIM 5" strategy, which are well aligned with supply chain priorities of the luxury industry discussed in this chapter. The strategy aimed at reaching annual revenue of EUR 4 million by 2025, which was achieved in 2023.

The first pillar is related to "boosting *brands*," which aims to distinguish customer segments and increase sales for each brand. Boss Menswear category has always had solid sales given the popularity of the brand for suits and business-casual wear among men. While keeping the sales of menswear category at an elevated level, the company started to emphasize the importance of womenswear for the expansion of the Boss brand. Meanwhile, the Hugo brand targets young shoppers whose shopping behavior may be affected by social trends, peers, and celebrities. The company spends heavily on marketing activities, engages famous influencers, and diversifies the product portfolio to increase revenues from the Hugo brand.

While expanding product lines, the management puts so much effort to ensure the highest quality, comfort, and aesthetic levels of their clothes. Thus, Hugo Boss identified the *product* as the second pillar of CLAIM 5 because premium quality of products is important for the brand's image and customer perception as is typical in the luxury industry.

The third pillar is *digital transformation*. The management is dedicated to making ambitious investments in digital technologies to improve circularity, customer experience, and supply chain visibility for the reasons explained above. In 2022, Hugo Boss launched the resale platform allowing customers to resell their clothes, which is part of the company's commitment to circularity (Westermann, 2022). It also implemented the digital twin of the supply chain – that is, digital mirror of operations, which will be discussed in Chapter 8 – to establish supply chain visibility. The company furthermore invested in blockchain technology to enhance customer experience. Unlike some industry practices that promote blockchain for supply chain visibility, Hugo Boss sees the potential of this technology in other areas such that blockchain-based digital showroom would enhance customer engagement for their loyalty members (Westermann, 2024).

The fourth pillar is *omnichannel* retailing. Hugo Boss sells its products online, in company-owned stores, and through select retail partners. The company owns 489 stores as of 2023 (Grieder, 2023, Business Activities and Group Structure). It also partners with select retailers – such as Hudson Bay and Harry Rosen in Canada – to reach more customers. The omnichannel practice helps connect the online channel with company-owned stores so that customer orders can be fulfilled through mixed channels.

Because end users of Hugo Boss's products are consumers, not collectors, the management targets remarkably high service levels. Omnichannel retailing coupled with the management's close control over supply chain operations helps keep service levels high for company-owned stores and online orders. However, achieving high service levels can be challenging in the premises of retail partners. Toward this end, the company replenishes inventory weekly for retail partners. They also pay extra attention to meeting demand of retail partners completely because Hugo Boss faces an 11 percent reduction in order volumes on average when the service level decreases just 1 percent (Craig et al., 2016).

The last pillar is the *growth of revenues*. Hugo Boss identified key geographical areas (e.g., Asia/Pacific) and product categories (e.g., Boss Womenswear) to achieve its growth target. To facilitate its growth plan, it heavily invested in capacity expansion of the supply chain. In 2022, the company increased its production capacity significantly by adding a new facility to their production site in Türkiye. It has also been increasing the capacity and efficiency of warehouses. Through an investment plan worth more than EUR 100 million, Hugo Boss plans to elevate the supply chain capacity from 65 million to 90 million units by 2026 (Grieder, 2023, Sourcing and Production).

The execution of the CLAIM 5 strategy triggered some operational problems such that the company faced 52 percent increase in inventory during the first half of 2023 (Pasquini & Reid, 2023). Focusing on the fifth fundamental trade-off (i.e., revenue growth versus supply–demand mismatches), the management accepted the inventory risk and diligently managed the strategy. Because they achieved the targeted objectives, they are deemed successful from the supply chain perspective regardless of the inventory risk.

The success of CLAIM 5 can be attributed to the management's rigorous identification of supply chain priorities, as discussed above. To excel in demand management, they launched two product lines and improved supply chain operations depending on customer segments. Next, they focused on digital transformation (e.g., digital twin) to increase the visibility of supply chains. Their circularity efforts concentrate on the secondhand marketplace. Finally, they expanded the variety of the Hugo product line and the Boss womenswear category to benefit from long-tail demand and grow sales.

6.6 Conclusion

Luxury companies are less sensitive to supply–demand mismatches due to their hefty margins. Thus, their supply chain practices do not focus merely on perfectly matching supply with demand. *Instead, luxury supply chain priorities are demand management, supply chain transparency, circularity, and long-tail operations management.* In this chapter, we have delved into strengths, weaknesses, opportunities, and risks of luxury operations along these supply chain priorities.

The first supply chain priority of luxury brands is demand management, where decision-makers must characterize the demand for their products. To this end, brands wisely use the judgmental forecasting method to obtain distributional forms of demand. Next, they use demand information to develop an effective inventory policy depending on customer heterogeneity. If most customers are collectors, for example, decision-makers must limit production volume so collectors can later resell their scarce luxury holdings at auctions.

The second priority is *supply chain transparency* that allows firms to better control the flow of goods and document supply chain activities. Luxury brands must excel in supply chain transparency to prove that they produce luxury goods at the highest quality in socially and environmentally sustainable ways. Here, luxury brands would benefit from blockchain technology. This technology is highly promising not only to improve transparency but also to facilitate the authentication of products, which in turn fosters resale efficiency.

The third priority is circular operations management. Younger generations of wealthy customers justify their luxury spending by considering luxury products environmentally sustainable. Therefore, luxury firms must establish circular business models that curb their carbon footprints. They can trim excess inventory to avoid overconsuming limited resources of our planet. They wisely develop mechanisms to avoid product disposal in landfills. Fourth, luxury brands must pay attention to the diverse needs of their customers and develop strategies to meet long-tail demand. If brands improve supply chains along these four dimensions, like Hugo Boss, they can achieve sustainable growth while maintaining high profitability.

7 Economic Theory's Sweet Spot: Lean Systems

If firms do not generate nonoperational profits or sell their products at ultra-high margins, supply–demand mismatches can hurt profits. Supply chain integration helps mitigate the mismatches by improving the chain's responsiveness to fluctuating market demand. However, it would be costly due to investments in capacity expansion and lead-time reduction. The prohibitive cost of supply chain integration is justified for the products with high demand uncertainty, such as occurs when firms sell diverse products through different sales channels. Otherwise, firms must focus on eliminating wasteful activities, excess inventory, and idle capacity along the supply chain by implementing *lean systems* (i.e., also known as lean manufacturing). When the demand for products is stable and predictable, lean manufacturing is highly effective in curtailing the mismatches. Therefore, firms that have a product portfolio consisting only of items with stable demand or companies that can influence customers to stabilize demand may enact lean manufacturing to efficiently curb any mismatch exposure. We consider lean manufacturing *economic theory's sweet spot* because it aligns well with the economic concepts discussed in the first chapter.

Economic theories have emphasized the division of labor and free markets. In early models (i.e., according to Adam Smith), markets are assumed efficient where trade and exchange of goods among buyers and suppliers occur without any friction. When markets are efficient, manufacturers ought to specialize in the development and production of a specific product. Here, flows of goods and supply chain activities occur in free markets automatically. However, markets are inefficient, and firms not only specialize in the manufacturing of a product but also coordinate supply chain activities to offset market friction. Thus, subsequent economic models (i.e., according to Ronald Coase) consider supply chain activities as *factors of production* and isolate them from markets. This view still shapes supply chain practices, where decision-makers are advised to focus on reducing supply chain costs while, wrongly, ignoring the positive impact of supply chain integration on markets.

Aligned with economists' perception of supply chain management being a factor of production, lean manufacturing aims to deploy resources at high utilization rates to cut costs. Its objective is to minimize operating costs by eliminating wasteful activities and idle capacity. Therefore, lean manufacturing principles are consistent with the economist's perception of supply chain management. This consistency can assist in developing a strong grasp of lean manufacturing. Using common economic models, we can better explain the opportunities of lean manufacturing for supply chain management. However, lean manufacturing has some limitations. When demand for products proves highly uncertain, however, a high utilization rate is not viable. Here, manufacturers must keep utilization rates *low* to reserve buffer capacity to deal with uncertainties. Thus, lean manufacturing is not effective when demand uncertainty is high. For that reason, stable demand is a *necessary* condition for lean manufacturing.

Historically, lean manufacturing dates back to the 1960s. After World War II, Japanese manufacturing struggled with productivity issues. Like other Japanese manufacturers, Toyota had inefficient production processes with piles of inventory and defects. Employees had to wait for long setups and component delays. In the 1960s, Taiichi Ohno, an industrial engineer working for Toyota, redesigned the automaker's production system to raise productivity and to tackle its quality issues (Cusumano et al., 2021). Ohno was inspired by the inventory replenishment practices of US groceries where stock is replenished only *after* customers buy products. Following this logic, he set up a small production area operating at lower production volumes. He limited stock levels of parts and components to *periodic* (e.g., daily) demand. If ten cars are sold each day needing four tires plus the spare per car, for example, Ohno set the tire stock level at fifty units.

Ohno later developed an operating system where customer demand triggers fabrication *starting from the final assembly of end products*, moving upstream in production and sourcing. When a buyer orders a car, a new vehicle is produced to replace the one sold. To make a new car, the manufacturer uses five tires from the inventory of fifty tires, thus reducing the stock to forty-five tires. Next, the manufacturer orders five new tires to replenish the system, restoring the stock to fifty. Here, new parts and components replenish what is used. Therefore, inventory is controlled along the production line through a *pull* system. This operational model is famously known as "just-in-time" (JIT) production, which will be detailed in Section 7.2. In the 1960s, JIT production helped Toyota boost inventory turnover by 73 percent, while prominent US automakers failed to improve inventory productivity during that period (Cusumano et al., 2021, Table 2). JIT production also helped Toyota reduce waste in the forms of excess inventory and employee idle time. With these advantages, Toyota reduced both production costs and quality problems.

In the 1980s, the JIT model became extremely popular globally such that US automakers attempted to understand and implement this system in their factories. The International Motor Vehicle Program (IMVP) was launched at MIT by James Womack for that purpose. Researchers at the IMVP surveyed executives and line workers of several automakers, including Toyota, to identify the principles of JIT. Researchers later renamed the Toyota Production System as "lean manufacturing" to make its principles accessible to other firms in different industries (Womack et al., 2007). While coining this term, the IMVP researchers sought the best expression to describe the core principles of the Toyota Production System, which is elimination of waste. According to the Cambridge dictionary, "lean" means thin. The term "lean manufacturing" is therefore consistent with the goal of the Toyota Production System.

Lean manufacturing considers wasteful activities, excess inventory, and idleness as the biggest threats to productivity and quality.[1] Any activity failing to create value for customers is defined as wasteful. Such activities must be either changed or removed. For example, redundant activities not adding to total product value should vanish. Inventory must shrink by eliminating buffer stock because high inventory levels cause needless maintenance and quality problems. Staff must be multi-skilled, collaborating on other jobs while waiting for parts or components. Likewise, setup times and lot sizes must be minimized to cut employee wait times. Low quality is also deemed "waste" in lean manufacturing because customers do not value defects, and the repairs require extra work.

---

[1] According to American Society of Quality (ASQ), lean manufacturing is a set of management tools that improve efficiency and effectiveness by eliminating waste. Visit the link to access the ASQ's website: https://asq.org/quality-resources/lean.

Identifying wasteful activities can be challenging in lean manufacturing. First, wasteful activity must be those that fail to create any value for customers. What is "value" for customers? For lean manufacturing practice and research, unfortunately, the concept of customer value is vaguely defined. Is it aesthetic or utility value? Consider the famous Italian polymath Leonardo da Vinci, who lived in the fifteenth and sixteenth centuries in Italy and France. His painting *Mona Lisa* is judged the most important artwork in history.[2] The aesthetic value of *Mona Lisa* is priceless for many of us. But what about *utility* value? We can still live, breathe, eat, and sleep without viewing artwork. Therefore, utility value is zero. Returning to our main topic: How might lean manufacturing methods increase the *aesthetic* value of any product?

If Leonardo da Vinci had used JIT to replenish the painting, could we have expected a better product than *Mona Lisa*! It seems impossible to define wasteful activities carried out by an artist at work. Therefore, lean manufacturing does not yield any positive impact on reducing waste when a product or a service has a high aesthetic value. The distinction between aesthetic and utility value is crucial for luxury retailers. For example, a Hermes bag would have the same utility value as a standard bag. But its aesthetic value soars over that for others. Luxury buyers esteem aesthetics much more than utility. For this reason, the principles of lean manufacturing *rarely* apply to supply chains of luxury brands.

When a company makes utility products (e.g., middle-class cars), lean manufacturing would be appealing to increase operational efficiency. Nevertheless, it is not easy to develop a lean system and operationalize it smoothly. To this end, companies must identify their wasteful activities and place them in three categories. We summarize these categories and how to establish lean manufacturing in Figure 7.1. For each waste category, lean manufacturing offers a set of tools and methods to design and operationalize a lean system. Those tools and methods help manufacturers manage the second and third trade-offs, which are focal points of lean manufacturing.

The first waste category is *redundancy* that covers unnecessary activities and excess inventory. Suppose that a food company makes biscuits and puts them in small packs where each pack must be 200

---

[2] The artwork has been exhibited in the Louvre Museum, Paris for more than two centuries: www.louvre.fr/decouvrir/les-parcours-de-visite/chefs-d-oeuvre-du-louvre.

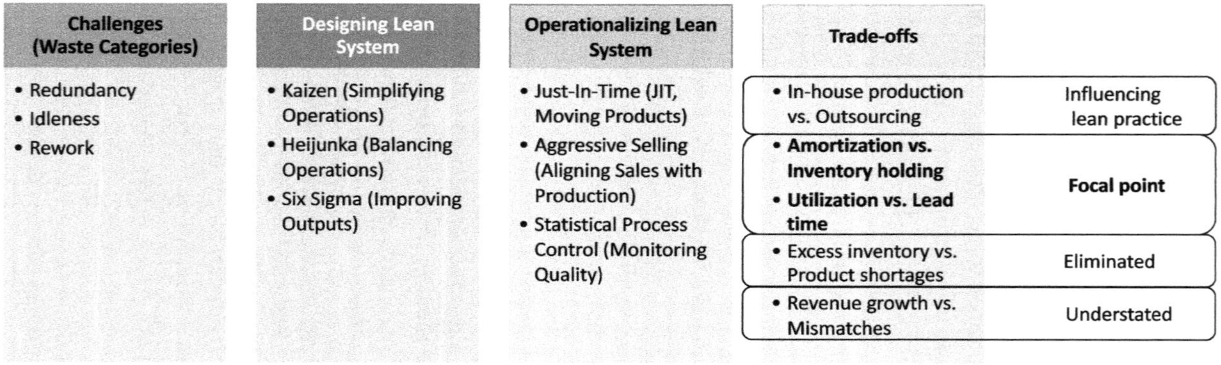

Challenges (Waste Categories)	Designing Lean System	Operationalizing Lean System	Trade-offs	
• Redundancy • Idleness • Rework	• Kaizen (Simplifying Operations) • Heijunka (Balancing Operations) • Six Sigma (Improving Outputs)	• Just-In-Time (JIT, Moving Products) • Aggressive Selling (Aligning Sales with Production) • Statistical Process Control (Monitoring Quality)	• In-house production vs. Outsourcing	Influencing lean practice
			• **Amortization vs. Inventory holding** • **Utilization vs. Lead time**	**Focal point**
			• Excess inventory vs. Product shortages	Eliminated
			• Revenue growth vs. Mismatches	Understated

Figure 7.1 Establishing lean manufacturing

grams in weight. A conveyor belt moves the packs to big boxes after packaging. While packs move on the belt, the system automatically weighs them and identifies those lighter than the targeted weight. Now imagine that a quality controller checks the big boxes to see if weights are lower than standard values. This final quality check is unnecessary given that more detailed control has already been done automatically on the belt.

The second waste category is *idleness*, which occurs when firms' resources are underutilized. Manufacturers make investments to increase production capacity. They build factories, buy machines, and hire people to reach a certain production volume. Some investments have fixed costs regardless of how much capacity is used. A high utilization rate thus reduces the fixed cost portion allocated to each product manufactured. Here, profits are expected to rise when capacity is highly utilized. Otherwise, the manufacturer loses profits due to underutilized capacity. For this reason, lean manufacturing considers capacity underutilization a waste and aims to eliminate this.

The final waste category is *reworking* where manufacturers make extra effort to remedy quality problems. If a manufacturer struggles to fabricate high-quality items, then some would be returned by customers for a refund. In addition to the refund cost (e.g., the full price paid by customers), the manufacturer also incurs logistics costs *and more* to fix quality problems. The total cost of reworking is often remarkably high in any industry. It consists of shipping costs, warehouse processing costs, customer support expenses, repair costs, and so on. In some retail segments, for example, total cost of product returns is estimated to be 27 percent of total revenue (Kapner, 2023). Hence, lean manufacturing aims to establish high-quality standards to eliminate any need for rework.

These three waste categories are nonexclusive as some overlap exists among them. Focusing on how to eliminate them all, lean manufacturing can be established in two steps. The first is the *design* stage where production and supply chain networks are built based on key principles. The second is the *operations* stage where companies use certain tools and methods to operate the lean system.

7.1 Designing Lean Systems

Decision-makers should configure lean systems to make high-quality products efficiently. The efficiency of lean systems makes it possible to reduce production costs and offer products to customers at reasonable prices. Customers buying such high-quality products at cheap prices can thereby maximize their utility, or *value*, which is the objective of lean manufacturing. To achieve this, waste in all three categories must be eliminated.

Redundancy can be avoided by removing any activities that fail to create value. Lean manufacturing offers a set of Kaizen principles to address redundancy. Kaizen is a Japanese term that means "continuous improvement."[3] It has three main aspects. The first one is the *simplification* of operations: Complex tasks must be either refined or divided into simpler subtasks. This helps both decision-makers and line workers have a clear understanding as to the impact of each task on the utility of products. The second aspect is that Kaizen makes it possible to distinguish value-adding activities from non-value-adding ones. After decision-makers simplify operations and assess their impact on the utility of products, they can identify non-value-adding activities and eliminate them. Finally, Kaizen emphasizes that operational efficiency must improve incrementally over time. To this end, firms must develop innovative ideas, test them in practice, document the results, and implement the changes.

Kaizen principles have been widely adopted to improve business systems. Tech firms, for example, have been using Kaizen intensely to improve the customer experience (Varian, 2007). Manufacturers widely use it to streamline operations and cut setup times, thereby helping them optimize the trade-off between amortization and inventory holding costs.

Kaizen is a handy productivity tool that can bolster operating efficiency and profitability for many organizations. However, it may not be useful for those lacking either operational data or a strong understanding of their customers. When manufacturers sell products to *wholesalers*, for example, they may not be able to connect with end users and learn how the end users value the features of their products. Thus, they may not benefit from Kaizen because any attempt to improve operations could spawn severe customer complaints. Other producers may have a strong understanding of customer preferences. However, if they fail to collect operational data about processing times

---

[3] Visit the following link for more information about Kaizen principles: https://lean.org/lexicon-terms/kaizen/.

and machine-labor utilizations for specific tasks, then they cannot identify valueless activities or benefit from Kaizen.

Finally, principles of Kaizen can hardly apply to product innovations for startups. When a startup designs a new item, for instance, the main objective is to market a functioning product. Many non-value-adding activities cannot be avoided during the development stage. Employees at such firms often face extreme pressure to meet strict deadlines and do not have enough time to streamline operations. Any attempt to apply Kaizen principles to new product developments would delay product launches, causing catastrophic results for startups (Varian, 2007).

Lean manufacturing emphasizes *production leveling* (i.e., Heijunka, in Japanese) to both balance operations and streamline product flow, thus reducing the risk of idleness. In supply chains, several activities occur in *sequence* from procurement to fulfillment. If flow rates *differ* in those activities, resources with higher output rates would stay idle, thereby leading to underutilized labor and machinery. Here, the level of underutilization depends on the *bottleneck operation* – that is, the activity seeing the lowest flow rate.

The flow rate of the bottleneck operation determines the throughput of the production system. Any slowdown here wields a negative impact on a product's availability in the market. For that reason, manufacturers must develop some tactics to fully utilize the bottleneck resource. They often keep excess inventory upstream of a bottleneck operation to ensure that bottleneck stages never slow down while waiting for inputs. If bottleneck stages require additional workforce, workers from nonbottleneck operations are reassigned to the bottleneck activity. Therefore, multiskilled employees are a major help in balancing operations.

Production leveling aims to balance workloads across different activities to where all stages operate at the same flow rate. This tunes bottleneck and nonbottleneck operations to the same pace, trimming both excess inventory and capacity idleness costs. This would also allow decision-makers to optimize the trade-off between utilization versus lead times if the process flow rate is set equal to the demand rate.

Efforts on production leveling may not yield positive returns when there is variability in the flow and demand rates. In some cases, such variability can be easily avoided. For example, flow rates are often lowest in the morning hours on Mondays but highest on Friday afternoons for many manufacturers. Employees tend to work hard on Fridays to avoid overtime during weekends, leading to higher flow rates. Decision-makers can enact certain standards and audit employees to avoid such variations in flow rates. In other cases, variability is caused by exogenous factors beyond employee control. Here, *inventory and capacity buffers* help manufacturers manage variability.

Consider a manufacturer that makes reinforcement cords used in the automotive industry. There are four production steps: (1) yarn production, (2) twisting, (3) weaving, and (4) dipping. Suppose that the bottleneck is the twisting operation. The throughput rate of the system is determined according to the demand, which can be affected by the twisting operation. The production rate for twisting is assumed to be 200 pieces of twisted yarns per hour, and the demand rate is 3,200 pieces per day. Then, the manufacturer can have two production shifts to cover the demand where each production shift takes eight hours, making the throughput rate 3,200 pieces per day. If demand fluctuates slightly between 3,100 and 3,300 units, then there may be shortages. When demand reaches 3,300 units, it is not possible to cover full demand with two production shifts. In that case, the manufacturer can process 3,200 units, and there will be a shortage of 100 units. *Inventory buffers* help deal with demand fluctuations: 100-unit buffer inventory could serve downstream of the twisting operation. Then, a total demand of 3,300 units may be covered using the 100-unit buffer inventory to supplement its daily processing of 3,200 units. When the demand drops to 3,100 units, the total capacity of 3,200 units would still be utilized to make 100 units of buffer inventory again.

We next consider the example of a *capacity buffer* to deal with fluctuations in demand. Suppose the output rate is set at 160 pieces per hour, and operating time rises to twenty hours per day. Here, a total daily demand of 3,200 units can be fulfilled after operating the system for twenty hours. Say the bottleneck operation has a utilization rate of 80 percent, calculated by the ratio of output rate to the maximum capacity: 160/200. Thus, a capacity buffer of 20 percent would correspond to forty pieces per hour. When demand increases to 3,300 units, the twisting production rate must accelerate to 165 pieces per hour to cover total daily demand. A capacity buffer makes it possible to fulfill this extra demand without keeping inventory.

Manufacturers can cut production costs by minimizing redundancy and idleness. As a next step, they must avoid quality problems that trigger any product returns or extra rework. Manufacturers ought to set quality standards per the Six Sigma method to minimize quality problems. Six Sigma was first developed by Motorola in 1980 to improve product quality (Lancaster, 1999). At that time, US manufacturers had quality concerns, whereas Japanese products had increased their US market share owing to their superior quality. To address quality issues and compete with the Japanese firms, several US manufacturers adopted the Six Sigma method. It later became popular after Jack Welch at General Electric made mastery of Six Sigma a prerequisite for promotion. Though not originally part of the Toyota Production System (predecessor of lean manufacturing), Six Sigma emerged in lean manufacturing to reduce rework.

The Six Sigma method requires decision-makers to set specification limits for products and their components. If the measure of a product or component is beyond tolerable upper and lower specification limits, it is considered defective. The Six Sigma method permits only 3.4 defects (six standard deviations) per million parts! To achieve such a sterling defect rate, producers work relentlessly at improving product quality. They invest in personnel training as employees learn how to carry out actions that deliver high quality. After finishing formal training, staff are coaxed to propose projects to boost the quality of their tasks. For large-scale quality projects, executives form interdisciplinary teams by bringing Six Sigma experts from different areas together. In interdisciplinary projects, these teams address quality issues that involve different departments.

At the center of Six Sigma lie skilled employees who can apply its principles to practice. To this end, firms spend much time and capital on the education of their workers toward benefiting from Six Sigma. For instance, Sheraton Hotels spent $15 million at the onset of the new millennium for the Six Sigma training of their employees. Though such investments pay off in many cases, failures of Six Sigma projects can also be observed in practice. In 2007, for instance, Home Depot's efforts to use Six Sigma ended up with financial losses and the CEO's departure. To avoid such failures, firms must have a clear roadmap of application areas for Six Sigma and develop a cost-effective strategy to adapt it (Binkley, 2001; Lancaster, 1999; Richardson, 2007).

7.2 Operating Lean Systems

In the design stage of lean manufacturing, supply chain executives must establish operational standards and procedures to design supply chains, aiming to minimize redundancy, idleness, and rework. Kaizen,

Heijunka, and Six Sigma are effective tools of lean manufacturing to configure structural changes in supply chains. To fully operationalize a lean system, manufacturers must complement these methods with the Just-In-Time (JIT) system, aggressive selling, and statistical process control.

First, the JIT system complements Kaizen toward eliminating redundancy along the supply chain. It *operationally* helps manufacturers reduce excess inventory, which is also considered another form of redundancy. JIT is a *pull* inventory control system where upstream production or procurement orders are placed only *after* products are sold to customers. This helps manufacturers shrink inventory levels along the supply chain, which would be impossible in the *push* inventory control system. In a push system, manufacturers try to predict future product demand and use forecasts to schedule production volume. Push system next "freezes" production schedules, forbidding any change in production plans. Simply put, push systems function properly by using demand forecasts and a subsequent lock-in of production schedules. However, JIT operates based on *actual* sales and does not involve any frozen period of production schedules. Owing to this flexibility (not freezing schedules) and reliability (based on actual sales rather than inaccurate forecasting), JIT is a crucial element of lean manufacturing to curtail excess inventory.

To better understand the dynamics of JIT, let us consider a textile manufacturer that makes sweaters in three steps. Workers first produce yarns, dye them in three different colors, and finally knit the colored yarns into three sweater sizes. The manufacturer sells blue, red, and black sweaters in three sizes (i.e., small, medium, and large). Thus, nine SKUs reflect all size-color pairs. The manufacturer keeps ten units of each SKU and uses JIT to replenish inventory. In the JIT system, production orders are managed by *Kanban* cards. One Kanban card can be attached to one group of products. After those products are depleted, the card will be detached, which triggers a production order. For the textile manufacturer, one Kanban card is attached to a box of five units for each SKU. When five units of small-red sweaters are sold, the Kanban card attached is released. This free card triggers an automatic production order. Five units of red yarns will then be used to knit small-red sweaters. After this is completed, the inventory is replenished with the Kanban card attached to the newly produced five small-red sweaters.

7: Economic Theory's Sweet Spot: Lean Systems

Suppose the manufacturer keeps twenty units of each colored yarn where one Kanban card is attached to a group of ten units per color. When the next five units of red sweaters are knitted, ten units of red yarn will deplete. Thus, the Kanban card attached to these will release, triggering a production order to dye ten new red units of yarns. The Kanban card tally sets the upper limit for each item along the supply chain. For example, the textile manufacturer has two Kanban cards per SKU where each card carries five units. Thus, the maximum stock level per SKU is limited to ten units. There are also two Kanban cards for each colored yarn, each card carrying ten units of the given yarn. Therefore, the maximum stock for each colored yarn is capped at twenty units.

The JIT system helps keep inventory within a range. The maximum stock level is set by limiting the number of kanban cards. The minimum stock level is determined according to lead times. In our example, daily demand is assumed to be no more than ten units for each SKU. If the last operation (i.e., knitting) is completed in half a day, the reorder level for each SKU must be set equal to five units to fulfill any demand without being out-of-stock. Here, whenever inventory level drops to five units per SKU, its production order must be placed. The lead time for the first and second operations (yarn production and dyeing) must also be short enough to have an effective flow of products. Ideally, if the lead time to produce yarns or dye them is also half a day, then production flows seamlessly without any substantial accumulation of stock.

Now consider the case where the dyeing process takes ten days. The number of Kanban cards for colored yarns must rise to cover *demand for ten days* – that is, 300 units of each colored yarn given that there are three size options per color and each SKU (size-color pair) has a daily demand of maximum ten units. Thus, there must be thirty Kanban cards for each colored yarn. Such a system would be highly inefficient because inventory piles cannot be avoided at different stages of the chain depending on process variability. If workloads are balanced among operations with near-equal lead times, then JIT can be implemented productively.

Manufacturers must complement Heijunka with aggressive selling to eliminate idleness in supply chains. In the design stage, Heijunka tunes product flow to the same rate along the chain. Once production processes are completed, products reach the market to fulfill demand. Here, steady demand in the market helps manufacturers have a smooth flow of products, thereby eliminating the risk of idleness. Otherwise, fluctuations in demand would cascade upstream in the supply chain and cause swings in product flow, leading to overutilization of some resources while others are idle.

In lean systems, decision-makers emphasize "aggressive selling" methods to keep demand steady. To this end, they set goals for sales representatives so that demand stabilizes as they reach their sales targets. These representatives work relentlessly to reach their goals. They are further tasked to transfer information about customer preferences to production planners. They proactively contact loyal customers, ask if they are happy with their products, and explore whether they have any relative or friend who would be willing to buy the products. When sales lag the throughput, even line workers join sales representatives to increase sales. Therefore, sales practice in lean manufacturing is referred to as aggressive selling (Womack et al., 2007, p.191). Still, this definition does not ensure *efficient* sales activity. In fact, this is never the case!

If we presume the most vital part of an organization to be the costliest one, *sales management* can be considered the *most* essential element of lean manufacturing. Lean manufacturing offers companies an operating cost advantage as elimination of waste along the supply chain works to reduce production costs. Compared to typical mass production, the total cost of producing goods is lower for lean manufacturing. However, the opposite is true regarding the *costs of sales* and customer relationship management. Sales representatives of mass producers are 60 percent more productive than those of lean producers, meaning a higher cost of sales activities for lean firms versus the mass producers (Womack et al., 2007, p.191).

Sales and customer-relationship management are often regarded as the practice of developing sales compensation strategy. Such a strategy has two critical components. First, decision-makers must set a clear goal for individuals in sales teams. For example, sales targets must be ambitious enough to induce salespeople to work hard while avoiding any undue pressure on employees. Therefore, decision-makers must determine the optimal sales targets for sales representatives. Second, executives must have an explicit policy about how bonuses are awarded to those who exceed their targets. After setting sales targets and developing the bonus policy, decision-makers monitor sales representatives to maximize the productivity of sales activities.

In lean manufacturing, however, scant attention is paid to the target-bonus productivity of sales activities. Instead, they prioritize product *promotion and data collection* responsibilities of sales representatives. Regular contact with customers serves as advertising. Rather than investing in marketing campaigns, lean manufacturers rely on their product quality, cost advantage, and *sales representatives' communications with customers* to promote their products. Through their communications with customers, sales agents also learn about customers' changing preferences and transmit this information to demand planners and product designers. Then, planners refine the demand forecasts, and designers develop new products that merit high demand in the market. Therefore, lean sales practices help companies cut advertising budgets and collect accurate information from customers, which in turn justifies their high costs.

The implementation of JIT and aggressive selling will not lower costs if producers have quality problems that necessitate reworking. Therefore, ensuring high quality is instrumental for the success of lean practices. Lean producers often use Six Sigma and Statistical Process Control to ensure high quality. Suppose a manufacturer must produce a part specified 100 cm in length. The upper and lower specification limits of the part are 99.95 cm and 100.05 cm such that customers do not return them when the length is within a tolerance limit of 0.05 cm. Six Sigma aims to always keep the part length within those limits. It emphasizes standardization and a tight control of operations so that the output consistently falls within range.

Manufacturers that establish Six Sigma in the design stage may yet face quality problems eventually for several reasons. Therefore, the quality level needs to be monitored continuously to prevent potential glitches. To this end, businesses must develop feasible technological solutions to *monitor* quality because it is not economically possible to put a quality control (QC) employee for each task. Statistical Process Control (SPC) charts help quality controllers understand whether an alarming situation needs immediate action. To develop the SPC charts, quality controllers periodically (e.g., daily) collect a sample of parts and products fabricated. They measure length or other key specifications in each sample. For each sample, they record the mean value of those observations and the difference between maximum and minimum values. Mean values of sequential samples are logged on the SPC chart, also referred to as the "X-bar chart." The difference values of sequential samples are tracked in the chart known as "the R chart." The SPC charts are highly effective in identifying alarming situations using upper–lower control limits and a long-run average plot. If any point arises outside the control limits, the system is considered out-of-control, and a quality team mobilizes to investigate the root causes. If eight *consecutive* points plot on the same side of the mean line, the system is again considered out-of-control.[4]

SPC became popular in practice and academia in the 1990s via the famous Polaroid case (Wheelwright et al., 1992). Polaroid was a US-based manufacturer well-known for its instant film and cameras.[5] At that time, the firm struggled with quality issues in its production of instant film. Decision-makers tackled these problems by enacting SPC, which in turn helped the company dramatically improve both its productivity and customer satisfaction (Wheelwright et al., 1992). SPC is now deemed an effective tool for monitoring the quality of operations by practitioners. For this reason, it is quite common to see SPC charts in the quality corners of production sites. These charts equip quality controllers to detect any imminent warning situation in production. For example, a machine may malfunction without operators noticing. Such latent problems can be detected by quality controllers studying the SPC charts. Some digital applications of SPC even alert quality controllers automatically about potential problems, even when operators are assuming that operations are under control.

Digital technologies make it possible for organizations to utilize automatic SPC systems where parts are randomly selected for sampling by robots. Their specifications are also measured automatically to update the SPC charts. Rules for classifying a system "out-of-control" can be coded into the software so that quality controllers can be alerted by the software when necessary. For example, General Electric developed such a digital system called CIMPLICITY. In today's digital era, companies can employ a variety of digital solutions to improve their SPC implementation.

---

[4] There are other cases that will also cause quality controllers to classify a system as out-of-control. Such cases are listed on the ASQ's website: https://asq.org/quality-resources/control-chart.

[5] Polaroid was founded in 1937 by Edwin Land. The company was the Apple of the past in the 1970s. After having dominated the global photography business, it went bankrupt in 2001. Visit the following link for more information about Polaroid's history: https://bicersupplychain.short.gy/nvQlBr.

7.3 Challenges of Lean Systems

Decision-makers often face hardships when implementing a lean system. Most challenges stem from inconsistencies between foundational lean *principles* and methods used in practice under the *name* of lean. Lean manufacturing arose from the Toyota Production System (TPS) that focused on eliminating waste. The scope of lean manufacturing has expanded over the years with the inclusion of innovative tools and methods. Practitioners often view *any* attempt to achieve operational excellence as a part of "lean manufacturing," which is not correct (Browning & de Treville, 2021). Without rigid boundaries, decision-makers aiming for leaner systems may often focus their attention on activities *unrelated* to lean manufacturing.

Another inconsistency relates to the definition of *waste*. In lean manufacturing, waste is defined as all activities, excess inventory, idleness, and rework that fail in adding product value for customers. This definition naturally triggers another debate regarding the *value* of a product. Customers assess products differently depending on their preferences. One feature of a product might be considered useless by a customer, while another would value it as the most important. Due to the heterogeneity of customers, the *utility* value of an item can be identified only vaguely. For instance, some people use their smartphones mostly for photography, while others use them to surf the Internet. If a smartphone is worth $700 to the owner, how much of this amount ought to be allocated to its high-resolution camera versus some Internet usability? Understanding the value of each feature is vital in lean manufacturing to note wasteful activities. However, this may not be possible for complex products having many features and uses.

Companies can operate lean systems effectively when the demand is stable. Still, there is no guarantee that future demand, even for standard utility products, will be stable. As the baseball legend Yogi Berra once said, "the future ain't what it used to be." We also observed this during the COVID pandemic when the demand for toilet paper increased sharply, causing stockouts to retailers.

Lean manufacturers use the aggressive selling method to smooth demand fluctuations. But it has limits. If demand changes at an unprecedented rate, the activities of sales representatives will not suffice to stabilize it. This would, in turn, affect the production flow, fluctuating over time according to demand. To manage production fluctuations, lean producers may use inventory buffers placed along the supply chain. Interestingly, the lean manufacturing practice aimed at avoiding excess inventory could pile up stock in certain supply chains. However, this result is not consistent with the *pull* system of JIT where the production order for every single unit is triggered by its demand!

Finally, some opponents of lean manufacturing disparage it as a *push* system with preset inventory targets, not as a pull (Browning & de Treville, 2021). After all, there is no demand at the very beginning when lean practice produces some inventory attached to Kanban cards. If a manufacturer has a diverse product portfolio featuring several niche items, then lean could prove highly inefficient. Niche products are sold infrequently. Some of them are demanded once or twice per year. Applying lean manufacturing here means niche products are produced *before* receiving orders. Such inventories are stored in warehouses for a long time, causing unavoidable inefficiencies.

7.4 The New York Food Bank Example

Lean manufacturing practices are quite common in the automotive industry. For that reason, there may be a misperception that considers lean manufacturing merely an operational system of automaking. However, lean manufacturing has vast application areas outside the automotive industry. One of them is the operations management of nonprofit organizations such as the Food Bank of New York City (NYC) benefiting from lean principles.

The Food Bank of NYC is a nonprofit organization founded in 1983 with the mission of providing food, shelter, senior, and youth rehabilitation services to unprotected people of NYC. The organization has provided more than 1.2 billion free meals to the community since its foundation. In 2023, it spent around $137 million of donations for the distribution and storage of food (McCann, 2023).

One of the challenges faced by the Food Bank is capital restrictions because donations are always limited depending on economic factors. For example, total public support to the Food Bank decreased to $163 million in 2023 from $190 million in 2022. Therefore, cost efficiency of charity operations is critical for serving food to as many people as possible. To improve efficiency, the Food Bank collaborated with Toyota and benefited from lean manufacturing. Using the principles of Kaizen, Heijunka, and Six Sigma, it streamlined the processes in soup kitchens and warehouses.

In 2013, the Food Bank was struggling with long lines and waiting times in their soup kitchens. Toyota engineers carried out a time analysis in the Harlem soup kitchen, where the bottleneck stage was the eating area that can seat fifty people. The engineers changed the operations in three ways according to Kaizen principles. First, the Food Bank volunteers had been accepting ten people at a time. They were waiting for ten people to finish their meals before accepting new guests. Toyota engineers changed it such that the volunteers started to accept people one by one whenever there was an empty seat. Second, they moved the beginning of the line close to food trays so that guests could pick up the food immediately after being accepted to the eating area. Finally, a volunteer was appointed to spot empty chairs. All these changes are well-aligned with the Kaizen principle of utilizing the bottleneck stage at the highest rate. As a result, the Food Bank slashed wait time from ninety to eight minutes, serving more per day (Kadet, 2013).

Second, volunteers in the Food Bank's Brooklyn warehouse had been packing boxes of food items to be distributed to families. Traditionally, each volunteer was tasked to walk around and collect food items. Toyota engineers replaced this process with a conveyor belt such that volunteers put items in boxes as they move. In other words, the organization applied Heijunka to balance operations, thereby cutting the packing time per box from three minutes to just eleven seconds (El-Naggar, 2013).

Finally, the Food Bank changed the boxes to fill each truck fully. Traditionally, it was using cube boxes that are twelve-inch long in all three dimensions. Those boxes were replaced by 16-8-8-inch ones that can easily fill truck containers. Aligned with Six-Sigma, the organization standardized the truck load such that the same number of boxes are shipped each time. Following principles of lean manufacturing, the Food Bank minimized redundancy and idleness, thereby providing more people with food.

7.5 Conclusion

As demonstrated in Figure 2.2, lean manufacturing is a viable strategy for firms when business models are *process-driven* and supply–demand mismatches can hurt profits. Companies that operate lean systems aim to gain a cost advantage over rivals by making products at the lowest possible cost while maintaining high quality. To this end, they must be process-oriented so that operations are designed and deployed to erase all types of waste. At the center of lean manufacturing lies the objective of eliminating waste, which thus helps a producer trim costs and boost quality.

Lean producers are also sensitive to operational trade-offs because supply–demand mismatches can hurt their profits. To minimize the mismatches, however, they cannot instantly adjust product flow according to demand because such an attempt would result in idle resources. Instead, they use "aggressive selling" methods to shape the demand and match it with the level of supply. Given these complexities, operating a lean system is challenging in practice. According to an industry survey in 2007, *only 2 percent* of manufacturers trying to implement the lean practice reached their goals. Such a high failure of lean implementation is attributed to *lack of clarity* in lean systems (Ledbetter, 2020).

Lean manufacturing evolved from the Toyota Production System, in which operations are controlled by JIT. Some methods (e.g., Six Sigma) were later added to lean manufacturing by other companies. Currently, lean involves various methods that can be used to eliminate waste and increase productivity. If decision-makers try to implement all of them simultaneously, it may lead to chaos and inefficiencies. For that reason, they must limit their attention to salient methods crucial to them.

This chapter has grouped major lean manufacturing methods according to waste types. Each group features the most effective method to be used at the design and operations stages, yielding six methods listed in Figure 7.1. JIT, Kaizen, and Heijunka play a pivotal role in TPS. Aggressive selling has been used by Toyota effectively, though not deemed a central tenet of TPS. Six Sigma and SPC were later added to the lean manufacturing palette.

To simplify the list in Figure 7.1, some important methods have been excluded. One of them is *Value Stream Mapping*, which is used by manufacturers to map out activities and to delete those not creating value to customers. Value Stream Mapping seems to contradict the supply chain framework given in Figure 3.2 because some activities in supply chains seek to improve flows of information and capital. Customers do not value such activities although they are necessary for business. There may be some supply chain activities carried out to curtail customer nonpayment risk. Customers do not value them because only sellers are exposed to nonpayment risk. There is always a risk that Value Stream Mapping could end up removing such important activities because it disproportionately focuses on the *value* of products for customers while ignoring information and capital flows. However, both information and capital flows are indispensable for supply chain transparency and financial sustainability. For that reason, we consider the supply chain framework in Figure 3.2 a better alternative to Value Stream Mapping.

Digitizing the Supply Chain

8 Design of Digital Transformation

The five fundamental trade-offs of supply chain management (i.e., given in Part I) lead to the emergence of the four strategies (i.e., given in Part II) depending on business models and firms' sensitivity to supply–demand mismatches. When adopting one of those strategies, decision-makers would benefit from digital technologies for a successful supply chain transformation. Indeed, digitalization helps companies improve the transparency of supply chains, efficiency of operations, and quality of decisions. Despite well-known benefits, digitizing supply chains remains highly challenging. In 2021, firms invested $4.1 *trillion* in digital transformation projects (Loten, 2021). Yet only 26 percent of executives, according to a survey conducted by McKinsey, reported significant improvements after transforming their systems digitally.[1] To minimize the risk of failure, firms must first *design* the transformation of digital aspects of their supply chains. The design of digital transformation involves four steps: (1) operational due diligence, (2) development of data management strategy, (3) comprehension of analytical applications to evaluate their value for supply chain management, and (4) expansion of the potential in digital solutions.

8.1 Operational Due Diligence

Digital transformation projects are costly investments where companies must buy digital systems from service providers and hire technical experts and consultants. Given the prohibitive costs, executives must assess the risks of digital transformation projects and develop some risk mitigation strategies at the beginning. This can be done by conducting

---

[1] McKinsey's survey looks at several dimensions to better understand key factors leading to success in digital transformation. When companies follow a rigorous, actionable strategy, the success rate increases to 79 percent (Bucy et al., 2021).

operational due diligence, which helps decision-makers understand the potential risks and benefits when a digital system assumes control of current operations. Although operational due diligence may delay completion of a digital transformation project, skipping it could lead to negative consequences regarding financials and operations of companies.

Operational due diligence starts with the risk analysis framework given in Figure 3.2. Decision-makers use this framework to understand the exposure of their supply chains to different forms of risks and uncertainties. It also allows them to identify some business opportunities to generate nonoperational profits. Therefore, executives can determine the scope of digital transformation projects after analyzing the framework. Some digital solutions could be used to reduce supply chain risks deemed significant in the framework. Other solutions would be considered toward realizing nonoperational profits.

Next, decision-makers must develop a roadmap to mitigate the potential risks of digital transformation. We call it a *digital roadmap* that sets standards for an effective transformation. There are three aspects of a digital roadmap: (1) simplicity, (2) customer-centricity, and (3) explicitness (Biçer, 2022). First, companies should target *simplicity* when they develop databases and user interfaces of digital systems. This step need not involve any applications of advanced analytics or artificial intelligence. For example, an order management system could streamline the transfer of information to suppliers so that companies can place a procurement order online and monitor the order status on designated web applications. Additionally, the order management system may allow them to receive invoices automatically. These types of systems comprise an integral part of digital transformation because they serve as the backbone of digital ecosystems. Simplicity is key to developing these systems because any pointless complexity embedded into database management practices would invade other digital applications. Additionally, decision-makers must simplify user interfaces to favor the adoption of analytical applications by users.

Digital applications developed in a company are often made available to customers and external parties (e.g., suppliers). To improve acceptance by third parties, platforms must be *customer-centric* so that external stakeholders can meet their expectations by engaging with trouble-free applications. There is an overlap between simplicity and customer-centricity because simple models are naturally well-adopted by customers. Yet customer-centricity differs from simplicity in that it may result in increasing complexity while benefiting customers. For example, e-commerce retailers configure their websites to allow customers to easily select products and place orders. Here, *simplicity* of product selection and order placement helps improve customer experience. Meanwhile, e-tailers try to improve the customer experience with the use of recommender systems, which utilize advanced analytical methods (e.g., association analysis models) and recommend products that merit customer interest. Although integrating a recommender system into e-commerce websites leads to higher *complexity*, it benefits customers toward a better online shopping experience.

Finally, digital applications must be *explicit* enough that all users perceive the same interpretation of user interfaces and dashboards. To this end, performance and risk metrics must be explicitly defined by decision-makers, and visual applications should be transparent enough to avoid any misperception. Terminology in digital applications must also be consistent. In Chapter 4, we cite Cisco's problems regarding inconsistency of terminology in its digital systems – that is, Cisco ran digital applications where the status of a customer order labeled "shipped" meant "shipped to the *customer*" in one platform but "shipped to the contract *manufacturer*" in another. Firms can avoid inconsistencies by making digital systems explicit.

After decision-makers finish operational due diligence, they can outline potential risks and benefits of digital transformation. Then, the design of data management strategies may ensue.

8.2 Data Management Strategy

Data can be considered the atomic unit of digital systems. They are collected from various sources and stored in databases. They are later used to generate information. Visual tools in digital systems make such information available to decision-makers in practical forms. Data also comprise the main input of analytical tools developed for predicting an uncertain variable or calculating a decision variable. Data management is important for digital transformation. Firms often hire technical experts with deep data management knowledge to develop an effective data management strategy and to facilitate digital transformation efforts. However, this task must not be left to external experts alone as they lack the necessary business experience. Instead, decision-makers should take an active role in constructing a robust, efficient data management system and avoid any typical security risks when the access rights of critical information are assigned to unqualified employees. To this end, they must determine business needs and link them to:

1. data *types* needed in the digital systems,
2. database *architecture*, and
3. data *usage*.

8.2.1 Data Types

Digital systems may fail to satisfy expectations of decision-makers when important data are either unavailable or expensive to collect. To avoid these scenarios, decision-makers must have realistic expectations as to digital transformation projects so that analytical applications and reporting tools are built to use available data in their existing formats. In some cases, decision-makers may request new data obtained from various sources. However, expanding the data outreach of digital systems can be costly. Before making such requests, decision-makers must understand data types and how they are maintained.

Data are classified as primary or secondary. Primary data are collected by people *directly* for a *specific* purpose. Analysts and researchers often conduct interviews, experiments, and surveys to collect primary data. The most famous example of primary data would be Charles Darwin's collection of specimens during his trip to South America in 1831, which resulted in Darwin's theory of evolution by natural selection.[2] The primary data collected by Darwin were not reused for another important discovery. Given the amount of time spent by Darwin for data collection, we conclude that primary data are extremely expensive. Company executives may want to support digital systems with primary data to improve the quality of digital applications. However, any effort to collect primary data must be well-justified due to its prohibitive cost.

---

[2] The trip took five years. Darwin studied how specimens differ depending on environment during this time. He observed that finches in distinct habitats develop different traits to ease the gathering of food, thus yielding the theory of evolution by natural selection. Visit the National Geographic's website for more information about Darwin's trip: https://bicersupplychain.short.gy/Ox6n0i.

Secondary data are collected routinely by individuals or firms during daily operations. Retail stores, for example, design checkout stations to collect revenue. Employees scan barcodes of items in shopping baskets, and customers pay for them. Stock levels of the items purchased are then updated accordingly. Checkout data are collected by retailers as part of their daily tasks. Retailers also use data for other purposes such as demand forecasting and assortment planning. Data transformation and handling are important for the *reuse* of secondary data. For instance, the checkout data are transactional, meaning that these would not feed analytical applications directly. Still, modelers can transform transactional data into different forms through encoding schemes. Such encoding schemes are an integral part of all software applications. Once they are applied to transactional data, retailers can benefit from various analytical applications, such as association analysis identifying what items are bought in bundles, analyses of store traffic, demand forecast, customer segmentation, and so on.

The distinction between primary and secondary data has some implications regarding the cost of constructing and maintaining digital systems. If organizations require primary data in their digital systems, they incur excessive costs of data collection. Besides, they would incur maintenance and labor costs because organizations may need to appoint an employee to *manually* enter primary data into systems. Often, secondary data naturally emerge as an outcome of business operations, so these can be added to databases *automatically*. When secondary data are not available in existing systems, organizations incur costs to install interfaces for amassing secondary data and expanding databases to store them. Yet the installation and maintenance for secondary data are expected to cost less than for primary data given the widespread use of secondary data in firms. Decision-makers must scrutinize the characteristics of data types to avoid expensive data management practices. When seeking a digital application fed by new primary or secondary data, for example, they must justify this selection.

8.2.2 Database Architecture

The second key aspect of data management is the database architecture. Firms must build a robust database architecture to collect, store, and retrieve data effectively. Data are stored in *data tables* of databases.

When a customer checks out at a retail store, the transaction is added to the sales transactions data table and stored there. Here, each row in the data table corresponds to one shopping datum tracking the timestamp, products, prices, quantities, payment type, and checkout employee ID. In the database architecture, different data tables must link to each other when they share a common attribute. This is essential for the consistency and accuracy of information kept in databases. Whenever a shopping transaction is processed by an associate in the retail store, for instance, the employee ID must be retrieved from the employee data table. Here, the employee and transaction tables must connect to make such data retrieval possible.

Data tables embody either transactional or meta tables. Transactional tables are dynamic because they are updated frequently. Therefore, they must be managed robustly so that real-time information updates or retrievals will not cause any loss or duplication of data. In contrast, meta tables are highly *static*. For example, employee records are stored on a meta table featuring static data such as employee numbers, job titles, etc. Especially for firms with low turnover, employee records may not even be updated for months. Thus, managing meta tables is less work than for transactional tables.

Transactional tables best occupy *in-memory* databases that use server memory space, so the response time for data retrieval and processing time for data storage are short. This enables real-time database updates without loss of information, which is critical for transactional tables. Conversely, meta tables best serve via *on-disk* databases that utilize the disk space of servers. While response and processing times are longer than for in-memory databases, this is cheaper. This makes *on-disk* appealing for meta tables that need infrequent updates. Depending on the amount of transactional and meta tables, firms must determine the database service provider. Such providers offer in-memory, on-disk, or hybrid services. For example, Redis Labs offers only in-memory, while MongoDB offers on-disk databases (Haggin, 2017). A few providers offer hybrid solutions (e.g., Altibase) where some tables (e.g., transactional) occupy the in-memory segment, other tables (e.g., meta) on-disk space. As part of any database architecture design, organizations must identify the most effective and economical service provider to manage their databases.

8: Design of Digital Transformation

8.2.3 Data Usage

Data usage strategy deals with how to manage data and develop analytical and reporting applications that facilitate supply chain activities. Figure 8.1 presents the data usage process in digital systems. First, data are collected from various sources and stored in databases. These data are then copied to data lakes from databases. Data lakes serve as a bridge between databases and analytical applications to maintain security and robustness of databases. In other words, data lakes actively limit user access to databases as part of data security efforts.

Data transfer from databases to data lakes is carried out based on rules embedded in the workflows. For example, a workflow determines the time and frequency of the data transfer. This would also involve encoding schemes that change data formats during transmission to the data lake. Some tables in databases can merge, and some columns in a data table may be extracted during this step using Structured Query Language (SQL), a programming language for processing information from databases.[3]

Data lakes are finding popularity as a next-generation replacement for data warehouses. Traditionally, data warehouses used in business platforms had allowed users to tap only simple reporting applications fed by structured data in a warehouse. In contrast, data lakes can handle both structured and unstructured data efficiently. They enable the parallel processing and data partitioning of tables so that users can

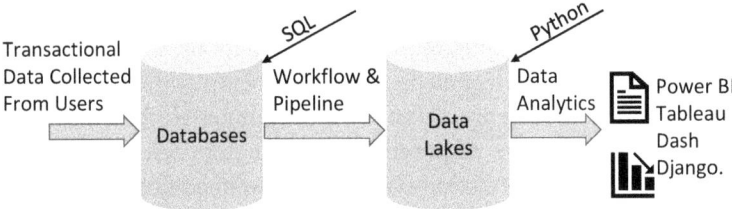

Figure 8.1 Data usage in digital systems

---

[3] SQL was developed by IBM in the 1970s as a query language for relational database management systems (RDBMS). Its commands were later standardized by ANSI (American National Standards Institute) in 1986 and by ISO (International Organization for Standardization) in 1987. Naturally, it then became the standard language for database systems: www.ibm.com/think/topics/structured-query-language.

develop digital tools at a large scale. Additionally, data lakes are often compatible with popular software, such as Python, making it possible to develop analytical applications.[4]

Analytical applications are eventually presented to end users through dashboards as a final interface in data usage. There are some popular dashboard tools in the market such as Power BI and Tableau. Power BI is owned and licensed by Microsoft Corporation, while Tableau is licensed by Salesforce Inc. If organizations have the license(s), using one of these two solutions would be helpful in developing dashboards very quickly. Otherwise, developers can build customized dashboards compatible with Python software. For example, Python features well-known application frameworks, such as Plotly, Flask, and Django, which can be used to configure dashboards. Decision-makers must test alternative dashboard tools and select what will work the best.

8.3 Understanding Analytical Applications

Analytical applications form an integral part of digital systems. Understanding their capabilities is an essential part of designing digital transformation. In business literature, analytical applications also comprise business *intelligence* or artificial intelligence solutions. Regardless of the context where we use them, analytical applications lead to three types of outputs. They are (1) description, (2) prediction, and (3) decision. In fact, any process of intelligence, either artificial or human intelligence, generates these outputs. For example, humans collect information from varied sources through some actions, such as reading books and observing environments. This is the learning process, which is part of human intelligence, but not the output per se. After learning new things, we use the acquired knowledge for description (i.e., describe a situation), prediction (i.e., predict an uncertainty), or decision (i.e., make a choice).

The description capability of human intelligence improves at early ages and throughout the education system. In elementary schools, for instance, kids are often tasked to read a book and explain it to their peers in their own words. Throughout the education system, students

---

[4] For more information about data lakes: https://cloud.google.com/learn/what-is-a-data-lake.

8: Design of Digital Transformation

are often challenged to improve their *description* skills in separate ways. Such efforts continue in professional life as businesspeople may seek structural approaches for that purpose.[5]

People also use their intellect to make predictions. On a windy day, we may look out the window and say: "The apple on that tree will fall in two minutes!" When observing outdoors, we would try to gauge wind speed and see how the apple on the tree shakes. Then, we make a *prediction* with the help of our intelligence. Finally, our intellect helps us make decisions in certain conditions. Here, we need to distinguish making a decision from implementing it. Implementation of a decision comes after the decision is made. It may require physical activity unrelated to our intelligence. Making a *decision*, though, is possible after comparing different alternatives and choosing the one with the best expected result, which is related to intelligence.

Figure 8.2 presents some well-known analytical methods used for only one of description, prediction, and decision. There are also tools that *combine* those methods to carry out complex operations that lie at the three intersections. In what follows, we take a detailed look at these to deepen the reader's understanding of both the potential and limitations of analytical methods.

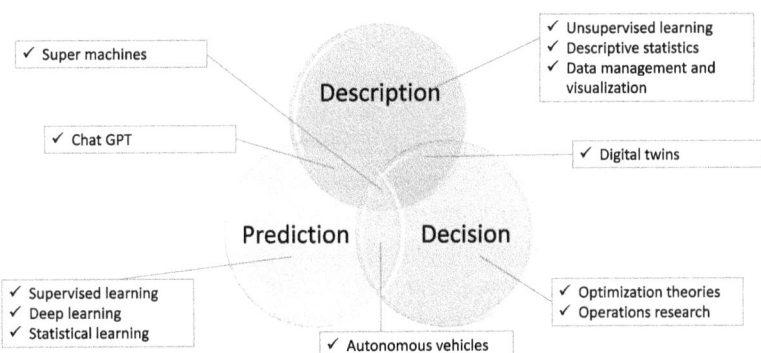

Figure 8.2 Output analysis of analytics and artificial intelligence

---

[5] One approach is the development of compelling stories from data using visual tools in a structural way (e.g., storytelling with data by Knaflic (2015)). This helps executives identify opportunities or find root causes of problems.

8.3.1 Descriptive Analytics

Descriptive models seek to gather information from unstructured datasets. For example, some descriptive methods group data into different clusters, and characteristics of each cluster can next be investigated to identify business opportunities. Other descriptive methods may be used to understand business dynamics by summarizing data in datasets. Before utilizing these, however, modelers must handle unstructured data.[6] Dealing with unstructured data can be challenging in that even experienced modelers may feel swamped. Still, several encoding procedures embedded in programming languages, such as Python, are geared to automatically transform unstructured data into plausible forms. Next, statistical and machine learning models can process the data for description purposes.

In statistical and machine learning, the subfield of unsupervised learning deals with how to cluster data and distill knowledge in the most effective way. Two popular methods of unsupervised learning are worth mentioning because even senior executives need to understand each for evaluating the capabilities of algorithms. They are k-means clustering and principal component analysis.

Suppose that a retail dataset includes sales transactions of customers with loyalty cards. The marketing department would be interested in classifying customers into different segments so they can craft marketing campaigns and promotions targeting each segment. *K-means clustering* can be used to have k groups of customers where k must be selected as an input by the modeler. Though this method forms the clusters automatically using turn-key algorithms, decision-makers must pay attention to two details. First, the k number of clusters must be determined manually. Decision-makers must have strong insight as to potential segments *before* running the algorithm. Based on experience, the number of segments (clusters) is determined and used as an input for the k-means algorithm. The second detail relates to the labeling process assigned by specialists. Ex-post analysis of data is necessary to identify segments for labeling, such as premium versus economy.

---

[6] Data in a table are considered structured if each column in the table has a predefined data format. When there is a text-heavy column including different data formats (e.g., date, string, and integer at the same time), data are classified unstructured.

8: Design of Digital Transformation

When decision-makers pay attention to these two details, k-means clustering distinguishes segments or clusters in datasets very effectively. From a practical point of view, it is important to simplify complex systems. Once data are grouped into different clusters, decision-makers can focus attention on one cluster at a time rather than being lost in a morass of systems. Marketing campaigns can be developed for each segment separately that would maximize the return on invested capital. In supply chain management, this type of segmentation can be applied to products. In the consumer-packaged goods (CPG) industry, for example, companies manage hundreds of different product inventories through certain inventory control and replenishment mechanisms. Products with similar demand patterns may be managed by the same inventory control policy. Product segmentation may thus help supply chain executives match the products with effective inventory control models.

Principal component analysis (PCA) is a data compression technique that renders datasets into more compact and generic forms. PCA is also at the center of many AI innovations such as generative AI, image recognition, and so on. This method can be highly effective as demonstrated in Figure 8.3. Suppose the first table in the figure is the original dataset taking four columns. The first column is just "a" and its derivatives. Similarly, the other columns comprise letters "e," "u," "i," and their derivatives. PCA transforms the first table into a single column that includes only "a," "e," "u," and "i" letters. Thus, PCA reduces the tabular dimension from four columns to a single column, boosting computational efficiency in running analytical algorithms. In addition to the efficiency gain, principal component analysis makes the data highly generic such that it can be used later for matching algorithms and prompt engineering.

OpenAI launched its breakthrough innovation ChatGPT on November 30, 2022. Shortly after launch, ChatGPT became the most

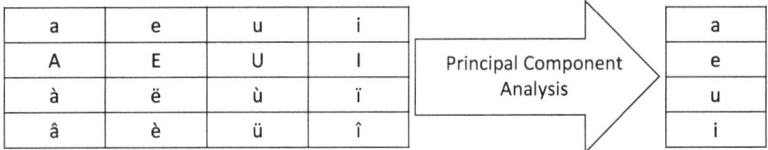

Figure 8.3 Principal component analysis (PCA) and its transformation

interesting and innovative tech buzz! It lured 100 million monthly users in just eight weeks (Hu, 2023). The strong interest in ChatGPT can be attributed to its ability to understand unique sentences correctly and reply with meaningful answers. When a user writes something on ChatGPT, the tool understands correctly what the user seeks. It is a challenging task for an AI tool because our expressions can be unique. Extracting the same meaning correctly from different sentences would be hard for any model. *Prompt engineering* tackles this hardship and is described as the discipline of getting the meaning from unstructured texts. Given its importance for AI tools, prompt engineering is often cited as one of the most important future job skills (Whiting, 2023).

Principal component analysis is deemed the first step of prompt engineering. PCA translates unique user sentences into generic forms, so they can be matched with predefined codes to extract the meaning of each sentence. Our sentences can be unnecessarily long and complex, analogous to the left dataset in Figure 8.3. Principal component analysis can internally transform verbose sentences into compact, simple expressions like the right column in Figure 8.3. Then, ChatGPT interprets what users seek, and it can more likely return the correct output.

Computer language models like ChatGPT are not the only tools using PCA to simplify the representation of data. *Image recognition* also needs a similar technique to deal with the complexity of inputs. Image recognition is a computer algorithm used to identify photos, read handwriting, and detect objects in pictures. It is often embedded in visual tools such as Google's Vision AI. Image recognition algorithms are trained using extensive datasets. However, it is almost impossible to yield exact matches of, say, handwriting. Human handwriting is quite unique and elusive in training for exact forms. Image recognition first divides the scanned handwriting into different grids and obtains pixel information per grid. Pixel information forms a numeric value that reflects the *intensity* of the picture in each grid. Therefore, a scanned piece can be represented by a matrix where each entry is the pixel value of its corresponding grid. Such a matrix can be complex and difficult to understand by computer. However, principal component analysis distills the matrix, as shown in Figure 8.3, and makes it possible to match with writing samples in the training datasets.

K-means clustering and principal component analysis embody *unsupervised* learning. *Machine learning* algorithms are divided into two: supervised and unsupervised learning algorithms. Supervised learning has a target variable with historical information such that fine-tuning the model parameters is carried out based on the historical information. Demand models used by retailers exemplify supervised learning. Retailers are interested in predicting the demand for products to optimize their procurement and replenishment decisions. Demand predictions depend on explanatory variables such as weather, price, store location, and season. When developing a demand model, the influence of each explanatory variable on total demand is tracked by testing how historical demand outputs are affected by explanatory input variables. We therefore call demand models *supervised learning* methods because past values of the target variable (i.e., demand) are available in datasets. In unsupervised learning, there is no target variable whose past values can supervise the model development process. Without paying attention to a specific variable (e.g., demand), unsupervised learning involves detecting clusters in data and simplifying complex datasets. Unsupervised learning is thus deemed a *descriptive* analytics method that describes the working dynamics of a system. After analyzing the results of descriptive analytics, decision-makers may better understand complex systems, thereby allowing them to identify business opportunities.

Not all descriptive analytics are as complex as k-means or principal component analysis. In statistics, summary tables may include key information about a variable: the mean, standard deviation, or maximum and minimum values. They can powerfully convey the range and expectation of variables. Such tables can be presented visually featuring histograms and boxplots. Visual tools also serve as a part of descriptive analytics. Descriptive analytics techniques (regardless of being either complex or simple) are helpful for decision-makers to draw insights from unstructured, complex datasets.

8.3.2 Predictive Analytics

Supply chain executives make decisions that would have both short- and long-term effects on profits. Procurement decisions in the manufacturing industry exert a direct impact on revenues for the next few quarters. Merchandising decisions in the retail industry shape inventories over the next year. At the time these decisions are made, it remains impossible for executives to foresee the future. Hence, those decisions are made under *uncertainty*. Predictive models are crucial in dealing with uncertainty, and they help decision-makers in two distinct ways. First, an effective model can generate accurate forecasts that minimize the degree of uncertainty. Companies often invest in predictive models to improve accuracy. For example, some retailers, including Walmart and Walgreens, have announced investments in model upgrades to better predict demand (Young, 2023). They previously used predictive models that rely on historical data to forecast future demand. Such models can effectively capture the impacts of seasonality and trends on future demand. But they cannot capitalize on weather information and social media posts to improve forecast accuracy. Walmart has begun feeding weather information into its predictive models to forecast demand for winter items such as snow shovels, plows, and road salt. Drugstore chain Walgreens now scans social media posts citing flu to forecast demand for flu-antiviral drugs (Young, 2023). Such efforts pay off when the improvement in demand forecasts allows decision-makers to base key decisions on more accurate information.

Second, predictive models let decision-makers understand the *range* of uncertainty and its impact on profits. These models use salient inputs – for example, historical demand, weather forecasts, and social media posts – to generate demand forecasts. The outputs of such models are the expected demand and its standard deviation. Using this information, planners can set a range of demand within upper and lower limits. Range information is especially useful for framing possible minimum and maximum demand values. Decision-makers determine order quantities for products based on the demand range. If a product sells at a high profit margin, the cost of missing a sale opportunity outweighs the cost of keeping excess stock. Here, order quantity would be near the maximum value because retailers do not want to forfeit the upside potential of demand uncertainty. If the profit margin is low, the cost of excess stock outweighs the cost of a missed sale opportunity. Here, order quantity would be near its minimum to help retailers avert the risk of unsold goods.[7]

---

[7] A well-known method, known as the critical-fractile approach, optimizes the inventory level depending on the profit margin and the cost of excess inventory (Biçer, 2023). The critical fractile of a product is found by the profit and cost values, and it yields the optimal service level that optimizes the trade-off between excess inventory and product shortages.

Most companies fail to benefit from predictive models because they do not integrate the model outputs into decisions effectively. This results from the isolation of predictive models from the optimization of decisions. While firms often utilize predictive models to find *expected* demand forecasts, they mistakenly view these forecasts as *realized*. Here, executives enact ordering decisions assuming that actual future demand is the same as predicted. In other words, they *ignore uncertainty* inherent to these forecasts and base their decisions on limited information. The ideal approach would utilize an integrated model that uses the statistical *distribution* of demand forecasts to optimize decisions. In other words, the ideal approach loses less information by utilizing fully extracted content.

In my research, I have observed that such an integrated approach leads to up to 40 percent extra profit versus the isolated approach (Biçer et al., 2022). The development of an integrated model brings the added challenge of accurately characterizing the statistical distribution of demand. This would require a detailed analysis of all uncertain elements that contribute to total demand uncertainty. Uncertain elements must also be combined in the analytical model consistently in the way they form true demand. Such analytical model development efforts are known as the *uncertainty modeling approach* (Biçer et al., 2022).

The uncertainty modeling approach deals with how the demand is formed in practice. Therefore, it focuses on the customer journey from product search until the purchase to train the model. Unlike many forecasting tools that use periodic (e.g., monthly) demand values, uncertainty modeling explicitly tracks how demand data are formed. Then, it aims to better predict demand by using the developed model.

The importance of uncertainty modeling cannot be explained in a better way than the Wald's *survivor bias* (Biçer et al., 2022). During World War II, Abraham Wald was a scientist in a statistical research group that was analyzing post-mission aircraft to predict areas targeted by enemies. The research group detected the frequently struck parts and suggested that those parts must be strengthened as they were mostly targeted by enemies. Wald resisted this suggestion and argued that *aircraft damaged at other parts were lost*. Only those that survived returned to the airbases, and the dataset did not include the lost aircraft. After analyzing how the data were formed, Wald pointed out the risk of survivor bias such as occurs when the initial assessment of the research group was based on limited data. He advised that *unstruck* parts must be strengthened, which was accepted by the military officials.

We also observe such a need for scrutinizing how data are formed in the business-to-business (B2B) environment, where buyers place bulky orders periodically from suppliers. Here, the number of distinct orders per month can be uncertain. Suppose that a supplier receives between nine and thirteen distinct orders from its buyers in a month. For each order, the order quantity and demand lead time can also be uncertain. The quality demanded per order ranges between 3,000 and 25,000 units, with demand lead time between three weeks and three months. Characterizing total demand is challenging in this case. Nevertheless, uncertainty modeling attempts to develop a predictive model that treats total demand as a blend of these three uncertain elements. It is much easier to explore trends and patterns of uncertain elements *individually* than to analyze overall uncertainty of total demand. Then, these elements are consolidated through analytical and simulation methods to have a statistical distribution for total demand. This, in turn, helps decision-makers improve both their forecasts and decisions.

The power of uncertainty modeling is not limited to B2B practices. In the retail industry, shoppers visit physical stores or e-commerce websites to buy products. Consider the online purchase case. The number of customers seeking a product category is uncertain. Suppose that it ranges from 15,000 to 20,000 per day. Customers choose one of the items in a product category or exit without buying anything. The probability of choosing a specific product is uncertain. The demand for a product is simply the multiple of "the number of visits" times "the choice probability for that product." The uncertainty modeling approach that weighs the characteristics of these two variables would lead to better demand forecasts.

In the agriculture industry, crop yield uncertainty is a critical issue that impacts food prices and commodity markets. Uncertainty modeling here can better predict yield. For example, sugar refineries induce farmers to grow sugar beets by setting the purchase price *ahead* of the growing season. However, they cannot wield full control over farmers who make the decision of what to plant depending on several factors. Therefore, the total land to be used for growing sugar beets is uncertain for refineries. While crops are growing, weather (humidity, sunshine) exerts impact on the crop. During the growing season, humid and sunny weather results in high-quality sugar beets. Whether the season will be humid and sunny is also uncertain. Finally, the sugar content in beets depends on the *harvest* temperature. Mild temperature for a harvest campaign leads to beets with high sugar content. Therefore, yield uncertainty for sugar refineries can be modeled as the combination of these three uncertain elements: farmland, weather, and harvest temperature. Uncertainty modeling thus helps decision-makers in the agriculture industry predict crop yield accurately.

Despite its effectiveness in improving forecast accuracy, one of the biggest challenges of uncertainty modeling is the difficulty of consolidating uncertain elements into a predictive model, especially when simulation studies prove infeasible. Nevertheless, recent advances in AI and cryptography have made uncertainty modeling possible using an innovative method: the fast Fourier transform (FFT).

Uncertain variables differ in statistical distribution. Developing a predictive model that includes uncertain variables in the way they form the final demand can be challenging. Suppose that a manufacturer runs a central facility to fabricate goods and sell them in three different countries. It has a long-term presence in one country where the demand model has a normal distribution with a known mean value and standard deviation. In the second country, it sells items through retailers. The manufacturer receives orders periodically from retailers and demand is modeled according to a process that depends on the rate of received orders. In the third country, the product is on the market for a limited time. The manufacturer has demand values for a few months, insufficient for fitting any statistical distribution or stochastic process. Therefore, only empirical data of demand exists for the third country. Decision-makers are interested in predicting the total demand to make production decisions related to the central facility. Total demand must be modeled as the summation of three uncertain variables with distinct characteristics. Such a modeling approach is possible by utilizing the fast Fourier transform, which is used in cryptography to represent data in very compact ways. This method has been used to refine demand forecasts and improve supply chains (Biçer et al., 2018; Biçer, 2023).

8.3.3 Decision (Prescriptive) Analytics

Supply chain professionals make several decisions to manage the flow of goods along the chain and fulfill customer needs: how much to order from a supplier, how much to produce, what to sell at what price, and so on. These crucial decisions must be made after carefully analyzing demand patterns, supply chain constraints, and logistics costs. Otherwise, organizations may incur losses. For example, the UK government purchased large volumes of personal protective equipment (PPE) during the COVID pandemic in 2021 without analyzing supply chain constraints. After receiving the PPE, they realized their lack of warehouse space to store it all. It cost the public GBP 436 million in additional charges to keep the PPE in containers (Editorial Staff, 2022).

US retailer Target also suffered from wrong product assortment decisions in 2022 such that their profit margin dropped to 2 percent from 5.3 percent in the second quarter. CEO Brian Cornell later announced that the retailer would take prompt action to liquidate inventory and free up space for items customers wished to buy (Repko, 2022). Another case is vaccine-maker Moderna, which is one of top players in the innovative vaccine development. Moderna struggled to adjust its production network according to post-COVID dynamics, resulting in suboptimal production decisions due to supply chain constraints. This cost the company $2.2 billion in inventory write-downs in 2023 (Ridley & Talukdar, 2024).

To avoid such circumstances and to curtail losses, decision-makers invest in analytical models that best help improve their decisions. Operations research is an analytical field that aims to find optimal solutions for complex problems. It takes as input the *state variables*, *constraints*, and *objective function* and generates as an output the optimal decision. The first step in operations research is the mathematical formulation of a real-world problem. This is also deemed the most difficult step because casting a complex, real-world problem into a mathematical framework can be daunting. To this end, decision-makers must have a strong understanding about the framework of mathematical formulation that involves three essential factors: (1) the set of variables, (2) the set of constraints, and (3) the objective function.

The *set of variables* involves both state and decision variables. State variables are those needed to describe the current situation when a decision must be made. Suppose a procurement manager wants to place an order to buy raw materials from a supplier. The available stock of the raw material is one state variable in this setting. If this amount is exceptionally low, then the order quantity must be large enough to cover production needs. If it is high, then the procurement manager

8: Design of Digital Transformation 183

would place a small order. The decision variable is the output of the mathematical model, which is the order quantity in this procurement example.

The *set of constraints* forms limitations executives must pay attention to when making decisions. In the procurement case, there may be a capacity constraint where total inventory of raw materials cannot exceed the capacity limit. The supplier may set constraints, such as the minimum order level where the procurement manager cannot place an order less than this level. Ignoring such limits would be detrimental for firms. As in the case of the UK government's procurement of PPE, a lack of understanding of the constraints could end up with hefty costs for organizations.

Finally, an *objective function* defines the goal of decision-makers. It can be formulated as the total *profit* or average profit that decision-makers attempt to maximize. The optimal decision serves as the best action to maximize profits. The objective function can also be total *cost* or average cost. Here, decision-makers attempt to minimize cost. Objective functions differ depending on the context of the problem. For example, it can be total *distance* or travel *time* for a transportation problem. If a logistics firm is concerned about the fuel cost, then trucks may be routed with the aim of minimizing total distance. If delivery responsiveness is the major concern, then routes must be determined with the objective of minimizing travel time.

After the set of variables, constraints, and objective function are defined in a mathematical model, the best action is generated by utilizing a suitable operations research model. Optimization tools are often embedded in various software so that little theoretical knowledge is required to use them. For example, Google makes them available to developers under the name of Google OR-Tools.

Operations research models are divided into two main categories. The first is *deterministic* models that cannot incorporate any uncertain variable into solution procedure. Uncertain variables are often replaced by their expected values in deterministic models. Suppose, for example, that a delivery worker receives 200 parcels on a specific day that must be delivered to a region. What is the optimal route to complete deliveries most quickly? This is a difficult decision because the driver's route should cover all 200 addresses and be the fastest. Adding to this complexity, traffic time is uncertain and may change unexpectedly for specific roads. Disregarding the uncertainty in traffic, decision-makers can use the estimated duration for each road and determine the optimal route accordingly. It may be difficult to incorporate any uncertainty in this problem, which could make the solution intractable.

Consider a manufacturer that uses 100 different resources to make 1,000 different products. Each product has a different profit margin and consumes different amounts of each resource as an input, and resources are limited. Thus, the producer must determine production levels so that total resources consumed in fabrication do not exceed available levels. Adding to the complexity, demand is uncertain. However, incorporating demand uncertainty in this setting would be tricky, rendering the solution intractable. An alternate approach would be to replace future demand values (though they are not known yet) with their *forecasts* and assume that future demand is known to decision-makers. This makes the problem tractable, and executives may forge a useful, but not optimal, solution.

Replacing an uncertain variable by its expected value is a strong assumption because supply chains are surrounded by several uncertainties as to demand, supply, and yield uncertainties. Therefore, outputs of deterministic models may misguide decision-makers if uncertain variables are merely replaced by their expected values. To address this shortcoming, decision-makers can utilize deterministic models for scenario analysis: using predictive analytics, specialists can obtain a range of forecasts for uncertain variables. They can later conceptualize the forecasts as actual values for uncertain variables. They can run a deterministic model several times for alternative scenarios before making their decisions. Here, assigning forecasts to uncertain variables will allow decision-makers to craft an effective, but not optimal, solution to a complex problem.

Operations research models can also be *stochastic* where uncertainty about some variables (e.g., demand and yield) is characterized by a stochastic model. Ignoring uncertainty may be unwise in cases where decisions made by removing uncertainty (i.e., replacing an uncertain variable by its expected prediction) could prove irrelevant. When people hike difficult and long trails, for example, they do not rely just on weather forecasts. Forecasts for upcoming days may be nice and dry, yet serious hikers plan for unexpected rainy or other adverse conditions. They cannot ignore forecast uncertainty because an unexpected rain storm would seriously threaten human life during a hike.

When a procurement decision is made for an item with a remarkably high profit margin, demand uncertainty cannot be ignored. Replacing a demand variable by its predicted value may impose serious financial consequences in such a case. Suppose that a company sells a luxury product at a 90 percent margin. The demand is uncertain with an expected value of 100 units. Here, it is unwise to order just 100 units although it is the expected value. This would forfeit any upside potential from the demand uncertainty. When demand exceeds the expected value, the firm loses the 90 percent margin for each unit of lost sales. If demand is at least 200 units with a probability of 10 percent, then ordering 200 units is better than ordering 100 units to improve the expected total profit.

Stochastic modeling deals with decision-making under uncertainty. These types of models can be either static or dynamic. In *static* models, a decision is made at a specific time, and no follow-up decisions are made in relation to the original decision. Suppose, for example, that a ski resort sells stylish winter jackets for only three months. They change product assortment completely every year depending on new styles and trends. These jackets must be ordered from a contract manufacturer before October for availability during the ski season. No extra replenishment can be made during the season due to the brief seasonal window and long procurement lead times. Therefore, the procurement decision is a one-off where no further adjustments ensue. We refer to these types of models as static models.

The objective function in static models is formulated based on the *expected* profit value. Suppose the resort can sell all jackets with 90 percent probability and generate $10,000 profit in total. With a probability of 10 percent they end up with unsold jackets, and the resort earns just $2,000 profit in total. Therefore, expected profit becomes 0.9 × $10,000 + 0.1 × $2,000 = $9,200. The objective function can be formulated as the sum product of probabilities and profits when there is uncertainty about some variables. For a given set of constraints, the optimal decision can be found by employing appropriate stochastic models. Static stochastic models, indeed, slightly differ from deterministic models in that the objective function needs to be reformulated by considering the expected values.

Deterministic approaches can be used to solve static stochastic models after making small adjustments.[8]

In dynamic models, problems cover *sequential decisions* over time where a decision today will impact others in the future. Formalizing a dynamic problem is quite different from static stochastic models or deterministic models. First, the scope of state and decision variables must be narrowed. Given the complexity of dynamic models, it would not be possible to assess the optimality of all values of state and decision variables. Instead, modelers must form different clusters to define states and actions. For example, the stock level may serve as a state variable in the static model example. Here, stock levels can be converted into three clusters, such as: (1) low stock, (2) medium stock, and (3) high stock to define the states and thus manage the complexity of dynamic problems. The decision variable in the static model may be order quantity that can be converted into a set of actions: (1) no orders, (2) moderate order, and (3) aggressive order. If the state is (1) – that is, low stock – and executives take the first action (no orders), then the state on the next day will *probably be* the same. If the second action is taken, the state *probably* goes from (1) low to (2) medium stock. If the third action is taken, it *probably* goes from (1) low stock to (3) high stock. For each state-action pair, the company generates a specific profit.

After defining the states and actions and calculating profit values, the modeler must next compute the *probability* of transitioning from one state to another when a certain action is taken. The modeler can later run an appropriate algorithm to find the optimal set of sequential decisions.[9] Most real-world problems can be formulated as dynamic models. Suppose a museum manager wants to attract more visitors to exhibitions in the museum. If the number of visitors is high on one day, it is also expected to be high on the next day.[10] If the number of visitors is low, the manager can advertise the exhibition on social media to

---

[8] The Lagrange duality theorem of optimization makes it possible to develop an alternative representation of deterministic models. Static stochastic problems can be solved by the Lagrange duality coupled with some parametric analysis techniques (e.g., Biçer et al., 2022b).

[9] Dynamic model algorithms solve problems iteratively. There are two well-known iterative algorithms, which are value-iteration and policy-iteration algorithms.

[10] This stems from the fact that visitors often talk about exhibitions and induce their friends to visit the museum, which is referred to as "word-of-mouth" marketing. This marketing strategy relies on visitors sharing their experiences, and it does not cost the museum anything.

attract more visitors. However, the advertising cost could be so high where its benefits may not suffice to offset the cost. Therefore, the manager needs an analytical model to determine the optimal policy.

Suppose that there are few visitors in the museum, and the manager wants to spend money to advertise the exhibition on social media. The advertising cost is estimated to be $1,000, which would increase the number of visitors by fifty the next day. The ticket price is $10 per person. Here, the museum can earn additional revenue of $500 the next day that can be attributed to the social media expenditure. Given that the cost is much higher than the added revenue, the manager might decline the social media spending. This could be a big mistake because the benefits of social media spending cannot be confined to the short term. After social media advertising, the visitor count may increase far beyond the next day. There may be steadily high demand for exhibitions owing to the word-of-mouth for *several* days. Thus, it is not only the increase in the number of visitors the next day but also ongoing high demand that can be attributed to the social media spending. A *static* approach here would wrongly advise decision-makers to not advertise on social media. Only a *dynamic* approach would help the manager grasp the true, long-term benefits of social media and induce one to make the ad investment.

Analytical tools are important to facilitate decision-making processes. Before developing such tools, executives ought to understand their problems and outline factors that describe the current condition of their systems (i.e., state variables). They must also outline constraints and potential actions. Then, they need to analyze the sources of system uncertainty to decide whether the uncertainty can be ignored. If yes, then *deterministic* models as given by Google OR-Tools may be used to find the optimal set of decisions. Otherwise, they must consider *stochastic* models, either static or dynamic.

The supply chain field is overwhelmed by hundreds of solution providers that offer optimization tools for complex supply chain problems. However, *optimization is not unique*. Various optimization approaches may work for any single problem. Decision-makers should not delegate to consultants the decision of how the optimization is to be performed because they would tout their own tools: "to the man with a hammer, every problem's a nail."[11] Instead, decision-makers must explicitly

---

[11] As documented by the law of the instrument, people tend to have a cognitive bias of over-reliance on their own skills (McDonald, 2022).

specify what they need – for example, a *dynamic* optimization approach that does not ignore uncertainty (*stochastic* modeling) toward generating the optimal set of actions.

8.4 Boosting the Potential of Digital Solutions

When decision-makers focus exclusively on one of prediction, description or decision, they can craft an effective analytical tool to facilitate supply chain management. There are many academic theories addressing the salient issues of developing descriptive, predictive, and prescriptive models. These theories have been taught for decades in *engineering* schools as part of Industrial Engineering and Operations Research programs. They have also been taught in *business* schools in Operations Management and Business Analytics programs. Even in *science* departments, mathematics and statistics curricula feature courses about predictive modeling and optimization. If an organization targets an analytical application with a single capability (i.e., description, prediction, or decision), then it can easily hire graduates from these programs to develop the analytical tool that would yield a positive impact on their supply chain activities.

However, breakthrough innovations in digital transformation lie at the *intersections* of these three types shown in Figure 8.2. In other words, analytical tools that can *jointly* perform at least two tasks (e.g., both description and prediction in one model) are more likely to prove superior in the market. For instance, Generative AI (e.g., ChatGPT) lies at the intersection of description and prediction. Prompt engineering would be done by unsupervised learning, which is a descriptive analytics method, so it can understand unique user utterances and transform these into more generic forms. Generative AI also utilizes a *predictive* analytics method to predict the next word in the sentence. To this end, it updates words iteratively until the machine output nearly mimics human output.

To tackle challenging problems in supply chain management, decision-makers need to adopt a solution method from the intersections of Figure 8.2. In one project with a consumer-packaged goods (CPG) company, for example, we developed an analytical model to improve the accuracy of demand forecasts (De Treville et al., 2014). This CPG company has featured over 700 different SKUs sold in the European market. Some of them have been on this market for a long

8: Design of Digital Transformation

time, whereas some others have been recently launched. Because demand data of newer SKUs are limited, their demand forecasts would prove wrong. Nevertheless, their forecasts can be improved if a product with a *similar* demand pattern is identified in the product portfolio. Then, information about the demand pattern of a similar product can be used to improve the forecast accuracy of the newer SKU. Our research applied unsupervised learning to sales data, which helped us classify SKUs into distinct clusters depending on the demand characteristics. We introduced some variables to capture differences between clusters (referred to as "cluster-level fixed effects" in econometrics). After finishing this step, explanatory variables belonging to each cluster were next used to improve the demand forecasts of each SKU. Our analytical framework thus intersects description and prediction. First, unsupervised learning is used for *description* where it helps identify to which cluster a new SKU coheres. Subsequent *predictive* modeling is employed to generate accurate demand forecasts.

AI systems utilized by autonomous vehicles jointly perform prediction and decision. Autonomous vehicles can be used on some roads and highways with caution when both road and lane lines are visible. Otherwise, the sensors do not work properly, risking the life of passengers. To utilize the AI system of such vehicles, the descriptive environment must *already* be complete. Then, the AI system can *predict* the actions of other cars, such as whether another car on the road will change lanes or the one ahead will stop. Based on predictions, the system makes *decisions* to prevent road accidents and transport passengers safely.

Recent advances in *big data* analytics can be partly attributed to regularization methods in machine learning, which also utilize prediction and decision analytics. Big data analytics aims to predict values of uncertain variables using a large dataset. In healthcare, for example, doctors conduct research to understand which parts of human DNA correlate with certain diseases. For rare diseases, the sample size of healthcare datasets is limited, but a plethora of explanatory variables (i.e., various parts of DNA) appears in models. Such models suffer from an *overfitting* problem where a predictive model trained on a slim dataset fits data perfectly. But it fails to yield an accurate prediction for a new case because new observations can be unique and completely different from those in the training dataset. To solve this issue, researchers apply regularization methods to regulate the model-fitting process using an optimization model. Given that optimization is part of *decision* analytics, regularization methods lie at the interface of prediction and decision.

A further version of regularization can be applied to supply chain management. In B2B, buyers place procurement orders to suppliers where demand lead times vary. Demand lead times of some orders can be long enough to form *advance* demand. Advance demand information is a critical variable that helps forecast total future demand. Meanwhile, advance demand is the portion of total demand that buyers have *already* committed to purchase. For that reason, it can be considered the minimum threshold for total demand prediction. If a predictive model returns demand forecast below the advance demand, then the model would need refining given that total demand can *never* be less than advance demand. Thus, advance demand serves as both a predictor and a *constraint* when predicting total demand. An appropriate predictive model must integrate predictive analytics with optimization methods, thus interfacing prediction with decision.

Another important digital innovation for supply chain management is *digital twins*, which lie at the nexus of description and decision. A digital twin of a system is a *virtual* environment that replicates the real-world system. It allows decision-makers to test their hypotheses without disturbing their businesses. According to a Gartner survey conducted in 2023, 60 percent of supply chain leaders were either piloting or planning to implement a digital twin of their supply chain (Lavelle & Ruane, 2023). The digital twin is a descriptive tool that allows users to overview the entire system and its pieces. Activities carried out by different supply chain teams are visible to all users of the digital twin. The digital twin is also a decision tool where executives can change the parameters of decision variables and track the outcomes. For managers opting to change strategy, a new one can be tested in the digital twin without any detrimental impact on the business.

Digital twins do not produce any predictions for uncertain variables. Instead, they are often programmed to *simulate* values of uncertain variables and calculate the outcome. For example, demand is almost always uncertain where it may be modeled by a statistical distribution with a known mean value and standard deviation. The digital twin uses this information to generate a demand value from the statistical distribution. Then, the cost and profit calculations are carried out for this demand value. If the digital twin is run again, it would generate

8.5 The Kordsa Example

Kordsa is a Turkish manufacturer of reinforcement composites such as tire cords and construction reinforcement technologies.[12] It produces tire cords in *four sequential steps*. The first is *yarn production*, where polypropylene is processed into polymer yarns. This step is a continuous process such that it is not possible to stop the operation.[13] The second step is *twisting operation*, where two yarn threads are twisted to strengthen the material. Third, twisted yarns are *woven to make raw cords*. Finally, raw cords are *dipped into a chemical bath* to reach the technical specifications (strength, elasticity, etc.) demanded by customers. The last three steps are carried out according to batch production such that each type of product is manufactured in large volumes. Here, the machines must be set up before starting to produce each type of product. The polymer yarns produced in the first step are of a single type. Using the same type of yarns, Kordsa produces a large variety of tire cords by differentiating the product along the last three operations.

Kordsa has a diverse product portfolio such that it manufactures tire cords to different technical specifications depending on tire brand and type (e.g., winter, all-season, truck, SUV, off-road, etc.). It faces high demand uncertainty due to market volatility and seasonality of tire sales. Given its diverse product portfolio coupled with high demand uncertainty for each SKU, operational excellence is crucial in earning profits and meeting customer demand at a competitive price. To this end, the management team reduced both lead times and costs over the years systematically. Kordsa also invested in data management and

---

[12] Kordsa operates across four continents with thirteen facilities and employs over 5,000 people globally. The manufacturer has been the global leader in the tire-cord market for several years. One-third of the World's automobiles and two-thirds of airplanes have tires reinforced by the cords produced by Kordsa (Biçer et al., 2022b).

[13] Any machine breakdown in yarn production may cause colossal costs (e.g., a few million dollars) due to long setups that require clearing production pipes and long quality inspections.

business analytics to facilitate efforts to achieve operational excellence. It has a long-term collaboration with SAP to collect and utilize data at various stages of the supply chain. Additionally, it formed an internal business analytics team and collaborated with academia to implement innovative technologies.

Analytical projects at Kordsa span across descriptive, predictive, and decision analytics. Regarding descriptive analytics, for example, Kordsa uses image recognition in its process-monitoring tools to identify an unusual pattern in its products. If a problem occurs during the weaving process and threads are not connected at the highest quality, the monitoring tool immediately detects the problem and stops the weaving operation. Kordsa's data scientists also developed some reporting dashboards to monitor KPIs.

To predict demand, its data scientists devised a machine learning regularization model with the help of academic partners (Biçer et al., 2022). Kordsa sells products to other companies, not end consumers. Its buyers place intermittent orders periodically. For example, a buyer would order ten to twelve times in a month. However, it is not clear what products are to be demanded for each distinct order and in what quantities. Demand lead time may also differ for each order, varying from two weeks to three months. Therefore, demand uncertainty can be attributed to the uncertainties regarding the number of distinct orders, the quantity demanded for each order, and the demand lead time for each order.

Customer orders with a demand lead time of more than a month are labeled advance orders. The tally of advance orders makes into advance demand information. As discussed in the previous section, this information is used as a constraint and a predictor simultaneously. Kordsa's predictive model characterizes such dynamics correctly and generates accurate demand forecasts (Biçer, 2023).

Kordsa also utilizes advance optimization tools to optimize their inventory decisions. Its planners must determine the production volume for each SKU and set the schedules of the last three operations depending on the output rate of polymer yarns. They attempt to use yarns effectively to produce different SKUs so that demand for diverse types of cords is fulfilled to the greatest extent possible. Here, the optimization tool facilitates inventory management by determining the order volume for each SKU according to the evolution of demand forecasts.

Owing to these investments in digital technologies, Kordsa achieved substantial cost savings as well as sales growth. Additionally, the manufacturer gained extensive experience in using analytical technologies to manage operational complexities. This encouraged the executive team to expand the product portfolio through strategic acquisitions. Kordsa acquired some advanced manufacturing firms (e.g., Microtex Composites and Axiom Materials in the United States) to increase the market share in different business segments.[14]

8.6 Conclusion

Digital transformation projects can be quite risky for organizations. Many attempts to digitally transform supply chains often fall short of initial expectations. Organizations should not hurry digital transformation to avoid such a result. Rather, they must have a well-thought-out design stage for digital transformation before launching any implementation. The design stage must begin with operational due diligence, which helps decision-makers determine business needs (i.e., expectations from the project), understand the risks, and develop a *roadmap* of the project. Next, they must frame a data management *strategy* to: (1) determine what data must be collected by digital systems, (2) design the database architecture, and (3) configure the data usage plan. The data management strategy is deemed the backbone of digital transformation for achieving its objectives and developing effective analytical applications.

Decision-makers must also understand the capabilities of analytical applications in three dimensions: description, prediction, and decision. Finally, they must try to broaden the potential of digital transformation by exploring the most productive applications. If business applications exploit only one of description, prediction, or decision, projects may be completed with easy success. When decision-makers attempt to achieve digital transformation by developing analytical tools that lie at intersections of the three dimensions, the risk of failure increases. Yet risk and return are positively correlated in business. Breakthrough innovations in digital transformation are all at those intersections. Thus, executives must determine the path of digital transformation based on their risk appetite and ROI targets for digital investments.

---

[14] These acquisitions were made after 2019 – that is, when Kordsa started to benefit from analytics investments: https://bicersupplychain.short.gy/UE5Kzc, https://bicersupplychain.short.gy/1tYdYa.

9 Integrating End-to-End Digital Transformation

Companies reach a certain level of digital maturity after the design stage. Next, they can implement digital transformation so that digital technologies enable end-to-end *synchronization* and *transparency* of supply chain activities. Analytical models (description, prediction, and optimization) and dashboards in digital systems play a key role in the synchronization of activities. Decision-makers employ analytical applications so they can easily coordinate operations with external and internal stakeholders. Supply chain transparency can be established when digital systems allow decision-makers to monitor information flow (as demonstrated in Figures 3.2 and 3.3). To this end, important operational and financial transactions must be recorded in real time and stored in a database. Digital applications must also make it possible to retrieve such transactions from their databases easily.

Digitalization efforts to make supply chains synchronized and transparent are obscured by risks and uncertainties. For example, product shortages due to supply disruptions or unexpectedly high demand may imperil the synchronization of fulfillment activities. Nevertheless, companies often have contingency strategies to mitigate these risks and uncertainties. To realize full potential of digital transformation, its implementation must address not only synchronization and transparency needs but also deployment of contingency strategies.

When unprecedented events unfold, decision-makers must update their short- and long-term plans. Organizations handle these situations by developing and updating their sales and operations planning (S&OP) practice. Thus, the contingency strategies are involved in S&OP, which is regarded as a cross-functional, enterprise-wide practice where business objectives and long-term strategies are translated into sales and operational plans. These plans often cover two or three years of time horizon in practice. The first year is strictly monitored to meet short-term business objectives. The second-year plan is developed

9: *Integrating End-to-End Digital Transformation* 195

Sales & Operations Planning	Sales & Operations Execution	Classes of Digital Applications

• Horizon: 2-3 years
• Key aspects
  • Demand planning at category level
  • Supply planning of critical raw materials
  • Supply-demand consolidation
  • Profit-loss (P&L) analysis
	• Horizon: Operating lead time (e.g., 2 months)
	• Key aspects
	  • Demand forecasting
	  • Supply management
	  • Inventory management
	  • Order management
	  • Sales and Fulfillment management
		• Descriptive tools
		• Real-time activity monitoring
		• Predictive models
		• Optimization
		• Customer Relationship Management (CRM)

Figure 9.1 Key elements of end-to-end digital transformation

based on rough demand forecasts. The third-year plan is considered future projections.

The activities that fall into operating lead time cannot be planned loosely because they must be executed directly to fulfill customer demand. Therefore, the activities during operating lead time constitute sales and operations execution (S&OE) practice. S&OE forms the basis of end-to-end supply chain management. For that reason, digital transformation efforts must be well-aligned with S&OE. A robust and effective S&OE practice will naturally result in superior S&OP, leading to the achievement of more strategic business objectives. Figure 9.1 summarizes characteristics of S&OP, five key aspects of S&OE, and five classes of digital applications.

In the following, we will walk through these concepts and discuss how to establish end-to-end supply chain management through digital transformation.

9.1 Sales and Operations Planning (S&OP)

S&OP starts with an *annual operating plan* (AOP) where executives set revenue, growth, and profit targets. They also determine key performance indicators (KPI) for sales and supply chain divisions.[1] For sales teams, *annual revenue credit* is often considered the most effective KPI. To better understand how it is calculated, suppose that a product's wholesale price is $10 per unit. The percentage of revenue credit is set

---

[1] There are different views regarding the scope of AOP and S&OP. In some cases, companies only determine revenue targets in AOP before a fiscal year. The KPIs are later set in S&OP.

at 20 percent. If the sales team sells 100 units of the product, the company makes $1,000 in revenue. Then, the sales team collects revenue credit of $200 (i.e., 20%*1,000). One of the advantages of annual revenue credit is that it allows sales teams to do promotions effectively within some limits. When sales executives offer a discount of 10 percent, for example, they will lose 10 percent of the revenue credit. Nevertheless, if such a promotion can help increase demand from 100 to 300 units, their revenue credit still increases to $300. Total revenue credit collected in a year amounts to annual revenue credit. Sales teams of each product category are requested to meet their annual-revenue-credit targets every year.

For supply chain teams, service level, product cost, and inventory turnover are common KPIs. Supply chain executives must achieve high service levels for all product categories while keeping product costs at low levels. They are also expected to achieve a high inventory turnover because the higher the inventory turnover, the less the working capital needs. In some industries, such as consumer-packaged goods, supply chain executives are tasked to fix the product cost for one year. The cost fixation becomes critical for products that have a high percentage of revenue credits. If the product cost is $7 per unit in our example, an increase of $2 in the product cost would cause huge losses although the total cost of $9 after the increase is still less than the wholesale price. This results from the fact that 20 percent revenue credit gives salespeople the flexibility to offer products as low as $8 per unit. Such a flexibility would be costly if the product cost cannot be kept under control.[2]

Supply chain executives are required to fulfill their targeted goals. To this end, they develop S&OP, monitor their performance, and update the plan when necessary. They organize S&OP meetings frequently (e.g., monthly) to compare past plans with current realizations (Grimson & Pyke, 2007). As risks and uncertainties arise in the supply chain, decision-makers may detect a major difference between targeted and realized

---

[2] The revenue credit percentages cannot be changed easily depending on cost fluctuations because promotional campaigns are planned according to revenue credits. The planning and execution of promotions may take a *long* time because such activities require involvement of external parties such as marketing agencies, retailers, and so on. Manufacturers cannot cancel promotions after an increase in supply chain costs nor accept losing money. For that reason, supply chain teams face pressure to keep costs low and stable.

values in KPIs. To address such deviations, they discuss alternative contingency plans in S&OP meetings and adjust both short- and long-term plans.

S&OP has two key components regarding the coordination of flow of goods along the supply chain. They are demand and supply planning. Demand planning is often done at the category level because SKU-level forecasting would be inaccurate for a long horizon. After demand planning, decision-makers develop supply plans that detail strategies for procurement and logistics to make products available in the market according to demand plans. It is often the case in practice that supply and demand plans would not match easily. The reconciliation of demand and supply plans requires much attention and effort from planners. On the one hand, demand planning is a top-down approach that shows target sales to achieve revenue targets. On the other hand, supply planning relies on operational dynamics more than revenue targets because firms aim to keep inventory just enough to meet demand.

Decision-makers also monitor the performance of sales and supply chain teams in S&OP meetings according to profit and loss (P&L) statements. If total sales volume for the previous month is significantly lower than the initial demand plan, the executives try to identify the reasons. Likewise, they attempt to address supply chain inefficiencies if supply chain costs increase. The performance of sales and supply chain teams is recorded in separate P&L statements. Here, the goal is to manage sales and supply chain operations such that business objectives are fulfilled in the end. If business objectives are not realistic, S&OP makes senior executives aware of this fact so that more realistic objectives are set. Otherwise, it allows sales and supply chain teams to make progressive improvements toward the successful completion of business objectives.

9.2 Sales and Operations Execution (S&OE)

Sales and operations plans that fall into the operating-lead-time horizon must be executed smoothly to meet customer demand and achieve performance targets. For that reason, operating lead time is deemed the frozen period for S&OP because short-term plans within that period cannot be changed. Execution of such plans can be incredibly challenging. First, S&OP is a high-level planning process that does not detail any short-term execution plan. Next, it would be exceedingly difficult to develop an effective execution plan because it requires the optimization and synchronization of several supply chain activities. The S&OE practice aims to address these challenges by focusing on five distinct aspects of supply chain management: (1) demand forecasting, (2) supply management, (3) inventory management, (4) order management, and (5) sales management.

S&OE structure is quite generic in practice. Even software providers specialize in one of these aspects. For instance, SAS is effective in demand forecasting; Blue Yonder offers innovative solutions for supply management (especially for lowering sourcing logistics costs); Manhattan and Slimstock are both popular for inventory management; o9 Solutions and JD Edwards are effective for order management; and Salesforce is popularly used for sales management.

9.2.1 Demand Forecasting

Demand forecasting is one of the most difficult yet important tasks of supply chain management. It is difficult because even advanced predictive models often fail to produce accurate results for a long horizon. For that reason, demand planners group SKUs and forecast total demand for a product category (summing up several SKUs) when planning for a long horizon, such as occurs for S&OP. Demand forecasting at the category level is often based on historical sales such that a time series model uses past sales data to generate long-term predictions.[3] However, such efforts have little value for S&OE because decision-makers require SKU-level demand forecasts to carry out activities in the short term. Unfortunately, SKU-level demand forecasting is challenging even for a short horizon. Decision-makers ought to utilize more advanced models based on hierarchical methods to produce reliable forecasts for each SKU (Kök & Fisher, 2007).

Demand forecasting is used for S&OE to develop a *short-term mix* strategy and a *medium-term volume* strategy. A short-term mix strategy aims to set a plan for how many units per SKU must be made available in different markets. If a retailer sells 1,000 different SKUs in fifty stores, for example, the mix strategy must show how many units

---

[3] The popularity of time series methods for forecasting at the category level can be attributed to their flexibility of explicitly incorporating seasonality, trends, and autocorrelation in forecasting tools.

per SKU will be made available in each store during the short term. If the retailer has a powerful forecasting tool that generates accurate forecasts for each SKU at each sales spot, an effective mix strategy can be implemented to perfectly match supply with demand.

When it is not possible to predict demand for each SKU at each sales spot, decision-makers must group data by having some data clusters. Suppose the retailer operates in five regions with ten stores in each region, totaling fifty stores as written above. The retailer also has one distribution center in each region. Therefore, each distribution center supplies inventory to ten retail stores in their region. Inventory replenishments take place biweekly. The retailer also sources products from a manufacturer such that the manufacturer supplies inventory to five regional distribution centers once every month. Here, S&OE involves two critical questions:

1. How much to order from the manufacturer to each distribution center each month?
2. How much to replenish from regional distribution centers to stores biweekly?

If the retailer can generate weekly forecasts at SKU level for each store over one month, both questions can be answered easily, leading to a successful S&OE. Otherwise, often the case in practice, demand forecasting must be performed at the *distribution center* level. In this setting, the demand per SKU is *aggregated* to cover sales in the ten stores served by each distribution center. Then, each store must pull inventory from distribution centers on a biweekly basis. Here, decision-makers are often challenged by the actions of stores that may order excessively to guarantee enough stock for critical SKUs. This would put S&OE at risk because excess inventory in one store would cause a product shortage in another store. To avoid such imbalance, decision-makers must control the flow of inventory from distribution centers to retail sites. They often check historical sales patterns of stores, contact store managers to understand the rationale for excessive ordering, and try to convince the managers to trim order levels.

The other usage of demand forecasting for S&OE is the development of medium-term volume strategy, which aims to set a plan for how much capacity to reserve for key resources. Companies need workforce, equipment, and raw materials to execute several operations during the operating lead time. The amount of such resources is ideally determined based on some demand clusters. For example, the workforce planning in each distribution center depends on total demand for all SKUs in each region. When total demand is expected to increase sharply, distribution centers may consider hiring seasonal workers to keep up with increasing demand.

These dynamics of short-term mix and medium-term volume strategies are not limited to retailers. Manufacturers may also produce a variety of products using a common raw material. Here, procurement activities are planned and executed ideally by considering total demand of all the products rather than each SKU separately. In such circumstances, accurate forecasting of demand clusters helps improve the S&OE practice through an effective volume strategy.

S&OE involves both upstream and downstream decisions. Upstream decisions are related to procurement and early production stages, whereas downstream decisions are about replenishment of inventory in retail outlets. For upstream stages, volume planning is more important. As products move downstream, the variety increases due to product differentiation along the supply chain. Then, mix planning becomes important for downstream operations. S&OE must facilitate a smooth transition from upstream volume planning to downstream mixed planning by effectively managing supply, inventory, orders, and sales and fulfillment activities. Demand forecasting plays a key role in establishing such a smooth transition.

9.2.2 Supply Management

Supply management deals with the procurement of raw materials and other key resources so that production and other downstream activities continue without any disruption. It is part of volume planning because raw materials are often used for production of not a single SKU but several items. Therefore, forecasting tools must predict the future requirements of raw materials by utilizing a method developed for demand clusters as it is the case for volume planning.

To develop a forecasting model for demand clusters, manufacturers must link sales information of final products to raw materials. Raw materials can be used for the manufacturing of several products in different quantities. Manufacturers keep the information of raw material requirements in Bills of Materials (BoM). A bill of material has a tree structure that documents all components and raw materials used as inputs for each product. Using BoM and historical sales data, decision-makers can reach information of historical raw material requirements that are used to produce the number of items sold in past months. Manufacturers must use such historical requirements information for forecasting of demand clusters and developing volume plans. Then, they must reconcile volume plans of raw materials with demand plans of finished goods. After reconciliation, they can schedule procurement activities so that finished goods are made available in the market according to initial plans.

While scheduling procurement, decision-makers must consider production and logistics constraints that have an impact on levels of products, components, and raw materials. Demand plans often ignore these types of constraints although *supply* management is affected by them heavily. When a manufacturer undergoes technical maintenance for certain machines, for example, product supplies become limited. Likewise, a quality problem at one of the suppliers causes delays in raw material deliveries, leading to unmet demand plans. Procurement teams are responsible for developing contingency plans and addressing these issues so that market demand is fulfilled as planned. This can be challenging during turbulent times such as the COVID pandemic. That challenge also makes supply management a standalone practice rather than a follow-up procedure stemming from demand planning.

9.2.3 Inventory Management

Inventory management deals with the development and implementation of inventory policies. Such policies are designed according to product characteristics, cost parameters, and supply chain constraints (e.g., capacity limits and contractual agreements with suppliers). For example, perishable goods or seasonal items are best replenished through *single-ordering* policies at retail sites. In other words, retailers order those items in face of demand uncertainty and sell them in the market at full price for a short period. After the selling seasons end or "best-before" dates of perishable items expire, retailers can no longer sell them. Then, they must order new items to meet the demand during the next period or next season. For durable products that are sold in the market year-round, retailers must use *multiple-ordering* policies where unsold inventory at the end of one period can be sold during the next period. Therefore, retailers must consider period-ending inventory before placing a new order, whereas they write off the unsold inventory for the single-ordering case.

The design of inventory policies has implications for demand-supply planning practices. Suppose that demand planners of a retailer develop a plan and reconcile it with the supply plan. Then, they estimate the sales in the next month to be 10,000 units. The retailer follows a multi-period ordering policy to replenish inventory *weekly* from a supplier. During the next month, the inventory will be replenished four times such that the retailer will receive 2,500 units in each replenishment. Therefore, the retailer will make 10,000 units available to meet demand. However, the demand in the first week of the month turns out to be 3,500 units, and total demand for the remaining three weeks is 6,500 units. In this case, the retailer may fail to meet the first week's demand. Here, actual sales may fall below 10,000 units due to the heterogeneity of customer orders during the month.

Now consider the single-ordering case where the retailer makes 10,000 units available at the start of the month. The retailer can now meet the whole demand of 10,000 units during the month regardless of heterogeneity in orders. Even though the amount of inventory received from the supplier is the same in both cases, *sales differ per the inventory policy*. Thus, inventory policies have a significant impact on the execution and achievement of demand and supply plans.

In a single-ordering policy with demand uncertainty, decision-makers aim to optimize order quantities that minimize the expected value of excess inventory plus any product shortage costs. Therefore, the single-ordering policy optimizes the *trade-off* between excess inventory versus product shortages. In this setting, the optimal order quantity is derived by the *newsvendor* model – often regarded as the most famous analytical model in the inventory literature. In the *multi-ordering* policy facing demand uncertainty, decision-makers attempt to determine the optimal *base-stock level* that minimizes the expected value of the inventory holding plus product shortage costs. At the end of each period, decision-makers check existing inventory and place an order to restore the base-stock level. Although ordering policies differ in single versus multi-ordering cases, they face this same trade-off, which is between excess inventory versus product shortages. This trade-off relates directly to the supply–demand mismatches.

There is also another trade-off of inventory management, which is related to the control of excess inventory: the fixed ordering versus inventory holding costs. Suppliers often ask buyers to cover *shipping* costs in their procurement orders. Producers also incur *setup* costs when starting a new production run. These types of costs are *independent* from order volume. Each procurement or production order incurs such a fixed cost regardless of order levels. Large orders reduce the fixed cost per unit, but this leads to a rise in the inventory *holding* cost, which is the cost of capital tied to inventory plus the cost of *handling* inventory in warehouses per period. Small orders escalate fixed costs per unit, but the inventory holding cost drops. In the inventory literature, the Economic Order Quantity (EOQ) model optimizes this trade-off when demand is stable. The EOQ model helps decision-makers calculate the optimal order quantity that minimizes the sum of fixed plus any inventory holding costs. For uncertain demand, this trade-off is affected by the uncertainty. Here, the optimal policy becomes the *reorder* model as suggested in the inventory literature. There are two outputs of the reorder model: order quantity and reorder level. Decision-makers place the order quantity *when* inventory drops to reorder levels.

Firms can use these inventory models in digital systems to optimize inventory decisions depending on product characteristics and costs. When inventory dynamics are too complex to be optimized by one of these models, companies can use *digital twins* (detailed in the prior chapter) in their systems to improve their inventory decisions.[4] Therefore, digital systems can help guide decision-makers toward optimal procurement and production quantities.

Another benefit of digital systems is that they help control the ordering behavior of managers and avoid irrational inventory decisions. There is always a risk in supply chains for professionals to make a potentially irrational decision based on subjective viewpoints. The use of a digital solution avoids such risks. For example, the US-based retail chain

---

[4] Inventory theories cannot deliver any optimal solution for some complex problems. For example, consider a manufacturer selling a perishable item through different channels. Customers in each channel have different acceptance levels of the remaining shelf life. One channel does not accept products less than ninety days of remaining shelf life. Another channel keeps this threshold at 120 days. Adding to this complexity, demand and operating lead time are both uncertain. The manufacturer follows a reorder policy to replenish inventory. There is no analytical solution to optimize the parameters of the reorder model. Nevertheless, manufacturers can deploy a digital twin to improve inventory management.

JOANN changed its inventory allocation policy after implementing an analytical model that optimally allocates limited inventory in distribution centers to retail stores (Ferreira & Jagabathula, 2020). The retailer's planning team used to place over 60 percent of total inventory of seasonal products in retail stores at the beginning of each selling season, even though this approach was not optimal. The analytical tool identified this issue and started to place less inventory in retail stores at the beginning but replenish stocks more frequently. This innovative approach helped JOANN increase operating margins.

Inventory management is carried out successfully when firms develop an optimal inventory policy and implement it smoothly. Then, they can realize the targeted benefits of demand and supply plans and improve bottom-line profitability. Digital solutions prove crucial as they facilitate inventory management and ensure the execution of well-matched demand and supply plans.

9.2.4 Order Management

Decision-makers place *orders* for procurement, production, and other activities so that products move from upstream suppliers to downstream customers. Here, we differentiate order management from supply and inventory management in that order management is an activity management system that is integrated into digital technologies. It helps decision-makers inform employees about activities that must be performed in the near future.

Order management involves three steps. The first one determines the scope and mechanics of orders. For procurement orders, the purchasing team must determine the products, their requested quantities, budget, and delivery due dates. This information sets the *scope* of a corresponding purchase order. The second step is negotiation, where stakeholders work to reach an agreement on the terms and conditions of an order. For example, the supplier may request higher prices for each product ordered or want to delay the delivery. The purchasing team attempts to reach an agreement on price and delivery date during the negotiation process. The last step monitors activities to ensure that all stakeholders fulfill responsibilities as planned. Suppliers often share the tracking numbers of their shipments so that buyers can monitor the logistics of their orders.

Digital systems help improve order management practices. However, two challenges arise in digital solutions for this purpose. First, the stakeholders of order management are heterogeneous in their diverse technical knowledge and constraints. Therefore, digital systems must be simple and convenient enough to be used by any person regardless of analytical savvy. Second, order management must be carried out easily through different channels such as in-person, by phone, or fully online. To this end, digital systems must be integrated with other channels to forge a seamless order management practice. To better understand how such integration can be achieved, we look at the finance industry because banks and financial firms set lofty standards for channel integration.

In April 2024, I received my replacement debit card from Dutch bank ABN AMRO at my Canadian address. My card could not be activated because I was not in the Netherlands at the time, and I had blocked my card from use outside Europe. So, I called the bank and talked to the agent. The agent informed me that activation could be done after talking to the Chatbot on the phone, connecting to the bank's app, and later returning to the call with him. He first forwarded me to the Chatbot so I could enter my account number by phone. Chatbot next connected me to an app where I answered security questions and completed the activation. Finally, I returned to the call with the agent for confirmation. The entire process took under four minutes, including the waiting time. In such a sensitive transaction, my request was done securely with the involvement of the agent, Chatbot, and digital platform. Retailers and manufacturers must adopt a similar seamless workflow to handle procurement, production, and other order activities. Otherwise, heterogeneity in the analytical savvy of stakeholders could create problems.

In digital systems, the order management workflow must follow the sequence of three steps discussed (i.e., determination of scope, negotiation, monitoring). For a procurement order, the buyer must specify the scope of the transaction by filling out online inquiry forms: product information, bid price, requested delivery date, and payment terms. Then, the buyer transmits the form to the supplier for review and updates. Next, the parties start to negotiate. The supplier may change some of the terms in the inquiry form and send it back to the buyer for its response. Negotiation proceeds as the parties alter the terms in the inquiry forms received. Negotiation ends when they reach an agreement or one party cancels the inquiry process. If agreement is reached, the parties then sign the contract digitally. Monitoring starts after signing, and the supplier enters information as to the planned delivery date and keeps the buyer informed about potential delays. After products are shipped for delivery, the supplier can share the tracking number and link to the logistics service provider so the buyer can track the shipment. Finally, the order management system must tie into the payment system to remit the supplier in line with the agreed conditions.

The management of procurement orders is simpler than that of production and activity orders in digital systems. Production and activity orders deplete inventory (e.g., raw materials) and consume resources. Digital systems must ensure that all order management is carried out successfully given the inventory, labor, and machine constraints. For a *production order* issuance, the production manager determines the quantity plus the planned start and finish dates in the first step. Line workers next receive the order on their screens and check the availability of resources and raw materials in the second step. Production problems may delay the production run associated with an order. For example, labor shortages, machine breakdowns, or lack of raw materials may halt production. The production manager and line workers set a start date for the production order after verifying such factors. The last step monitors the production run so that resource usage and inventory levels are controlled and updated from raw materials to final goods.

In *procurement orders*, workflows are developed in ways that maximize the efficiency in transacting with an external party (i.e., the supplier). They emphasize inter-firm transactions (i.e., digital signatures of contracts and payments) without tracking resource usage because the suppliers assign their own resources and deliver goods to buyers. In contrast, workflows of *production orders* focus on resource utilization and intra-firm activities without having any digital signature and payment functionalities. *Activity order* is another type that combines the workflow functionalities of both procurement and production orders: firms may simultaneously assign their own resources while buying a service from another company to complete a task. For example, some companies outsource production to contract manufacturers while employing quality controllers and production engineers to control the activities of the contractors. They may also supply contract manufacturers with raw materials and components. Therefore, an activity order to complete production using a contract manufacturer must involve both inter-firm and intra-firm workflows. To this end, activity orders must be embedded in digital systems in a flexible way so that digital solutions can all handle extensive negotiation cycles, resource utilization, inventory control, and payment transactions.

Order management systems are often considered the *input* layer of transactional databases. When a new order is placed or an activity associated with the order occurs, transactional databases are updated accordingly. Using the data in these databases, companies can develop various analytical tools to improve supply chain management. When digital solutions are designed flexibly, firms can develop an effective, smooth order management system. To this end, software developers set the workflows, define a computer object or module that offers the functionalities of activity orders, and connect both workflows and objects with user interfaces and databases. Such a framework can be used to manage the transactions of all procurement, production, service, and complex activity orders when the computer object or module is designed to cover a wide range of tasks.[5]

9.2.5 Sales and Fulfillment Management

Sales and fulfillment management deals with the activities from receiving customer orders until their fulfillment. It differs from order management in two ways. First, orders are created by decision-makers in order management systems, whereas sales transactions are initiated by customers. Thus, order management starts with internal stakeholders, while sales management is launched by external stakeholders. The second difference is related to how sales and orders are managed in digital ecosystems. Sales transactions are preserved in sales databases, whereas order management transactions are stored in activity databases. There may even be more aspects distinct to sales versus order management systems. Nevertheless, digital solutions for sales and fulfillment management can be developed by following the same steps as order management: (1) determination of the scope of sales, (2) negotiation, and (3) monitoring.

Customers navigate e-commerce websites before placing orders. They survey products, their availability, pricing, customer ratings, and product recommendations to determine their shopping lists. The first step of sales management covers activities from navigating

---

[5] Object-oriented programming in computer science can be useful in developing order management systems because it allows creating an activity order module. Such a module would be used for procurement, production, and activity orders given the high complexity of activity orders.

e-commerce websites to forming shopping lists. Digital systems facilitate this phase by making all necessary information available for customers. They would also use association analysis tools to recommend products to customers so they can effectively fill their shopping carts. Then, a negotiation step starts when customers do not need products immediately. Here, they delay the purchase and save their shopping carts in e-commerce accounts. They can later look at social media and company websites to collect more information about products. They can watch YouTube videos uploaded by influencers explaining the positive and negative aspects of products. Finally, shoppers may buy none, some, or all items in their carts. This negotiation stage involves all such activities until the customer places the order. It is also referred to as *the customer journey analysis* in digital marketing. Digital systems track digital touchpoints to help decision-makers link sales transactions to certain touchpoints. For example, 80 percent of sales may be triggered by an emotional YouTube video, with the remaining 20 percent from X (Twitter) posts. Customer journey analysis helps identify these percentages so that decision-makers learn the contribution of each touchpoint to the probability of purchase. Therefore, they can better allocate the marketing budget to key touchpoints (Danaher & van Heerde, 2018).

Customer journey analysis can help decision-makers better control sales management. When seeking to liquidate excess inventory, for example, managers can examine the history of customer journeys and identify a group of customers mostly apt to purchase the unsold inventory. This practice is referred to as *demand sensing*, where companies attempt to understand which customers would like to buy what products. Businesses can further promote products to customers through the most effective touchpoints. This is referred to as *demand shaping* such that companies use pricing and promotions to induce customers to buy certain products. Demand sensing and shaping are vital for e-commerce companies to sustain profitability and growth.[6]

Firms cannot realize the full potential of demand sensing and shaping if they do not correctly track the contribution of distinct touchpoints toward total sales. Adidas had been using a flawed model that

---

[6] According to a market survey conducted by Deloitte, 71 percent of professionals believe these activities exert a significant, positive impact on their companies. The access to the market survey is available via the link: https://bicersupplychain.short.gy/J3HtIx.

attributed sales to the *final* touchpoint of the customers (Vizard, 2019). Suppose a shopper watches a YouTube video of an Adidas product and opts to buy. Before placing the order on the Adidas website, the customer also checks the Facebook reviews. The attribution model that Adidas had been using until 2019 links this sale to the Facebook page as it is the final digital touchpoint. The company later improved the attribution model by using advanced analytics and econometric models, thereby reducing its media expenditures.

The last step of sales management is the monitoring of the fulfillment activities where customer orders are delivered rapidly at the highest quality. Digital solutions make it possible to track the timing of fulfillment activities and process real-time information as to the location of shipments. They make this information available to customers and decision-makers alike. Customers can thus accurately see when to expect delivery. After receiving their products, customers can give feedback about their fulfillment experience and rate the fulfillment performance of the e-commerce platform. Decision-makers use the tracking information to plan downstream fulfillment activities (e.g., last-mile delivery operations). They also apply analytical tools to understand how fulfillment activities impact customer satisfaction.

In China, for example, Alibaba's logistics arm Cainiao Network (hereafter Cainiao) excels in the monitoring and control of fulfillment services. It achieves fulfillment excellence through innovative digital solutions developed by the Alibaba Group while benefiting from the logistics capabilities of select independent couriers. In addition to serving Alibaba's customers, Cainiao makes its services available to other Chinese e-commerce firms, such as JD and Pingduoduo, although they compete with Alibaba in the Chinese e-commerce market.[7]

Cainiao uses innovative digital solutions based on *edge-computing technology* to monitor and control fulfillment activities.[8] They also utilize the logistics capabilities of its couriers to operate a dense supply

---

[7] Three big e-commerce platforms serve Chinese customers: (1) Alibaba, (2) JD, and (3) Pingduoduo (PDD). The market leader Alibaba cofounded the Cainiao Network as its logistics service provider with chosen couriers in 2013. Though Alibaba Group owns 63 percent of the Cainiao Network, JD and PDD also use Cianiao's services to better fulfill their customer orders. In other words, the Cainiao Network is an open logistics service provider for businesses regardless of whether they compete with Alibaba in the market (Ge, 2024).

[8] For more information about how Cainiao capitalizes on Alibaba's technology: https://alibabacloud.com/en/customers/cainiao-logistics.

chain network with its many fulfillment centers plus the 170,000 post stations for in-person pick up of orders. Owing to these investments in digital technologies and logistics capabilities, Cainiao can deliver express orders in half a day, reaching a volume of 1.5 billion parcels and serving over 100,000 merchants and brands in 2023 (Cordon, 2023; Qu, 2023). Beyond improving its fulfillment transparency and delivery speed, Cainiao uses digital systems to also understand how to enhance customer satisfaction.

Cainiao's customers appreciate getting updates about their orders nearing the end of fulfillment activities more than at the beginning (Bray, 2023). Suppose a customer order is delivered in five hours. During this time, the customer receives five alerts via Cainiao's mobile app. If the median alert (third one) is sent to the customer in the first hour, the density of alerts will decrease toward the end of fulfillment. Cainiao customers do not like that. Instead, they prefer to receive the median alert in the *fourth* hour and have more frequent alerts toward the end of delivery. Executing fulfillment activities in a way that sends the median alert in the fourth hour yields the same impact on increasing customer satisfaction as reducing the delivery time by 27 percent (Bray, 2023). Using a variety of analyses in digital systems, Cainiao better understands the *psychological* aspects of customer satisfaction and improves its execution of fulfillment activities.

9.3 The Slimstock Example

We have already discussed that digital transformation efforts must integrate S&OP into digital applications because synchronization of supply chain activities must be coordinated according to sales and operations plans. We now look at how Slimstock develops software solutions that can effectively achieve end-to-end supply chain integration while focusing on the excellence in S&OP and S&OE.

Slimstock is a software solution provider headquartered in the Netherlands. It was founded in 1993, and it has around 1,400 customers (e.g., manufacturers with annual revenue of 5–50 million USD) operating in more than sixty countries as of 2023. Slimstock serves those customers from its offices in twenty-two different countries with more than 450 employees. Its software Slim4 utilizes advanced analytics for inventory management and demand forecasting tailored to customers' needs. It also allows decision-makers to develop detailed sales and operations plans according to revenue targets.

One of the critical issues regarding S&OP is the reconciliation of supply and demand plans. As discussed earlier, demand and supply plans do not often match in practice. Slimstock addresses this issue by following a bottom–up approach that starts with rigorous modeling of the S&OE practice. To this end, it classifies demand patterns and utilizes an effective forecasting method for end items.[9] Next, Slimstock optimizes inventory decisions along the supply chain by determining optimal safety stock and order quantity depending on operational and financial constraints.

The forecasting tool is also used in S&OP to develop *high-level* demand plans (i.e., by use of forecasts for demand clusters) that break down the annual revenue target along product category, province, and sales channels dimensions. If a company has two product categories sold in two provinces through two channels, for example, there exist eight category–province–channel triplets (i.e., 2 × 2 × 2). Then, the demand plans must show revenue targets for each triplet. Slimstock uses aggregate forecasts coming from the forecasting tool to allocate the annual revenue target to the triplets.

Slimstock's inventory tool helps develop supply plans such that procurement and capacity requirements in supply plans are directly obtained from the inventory tool. It also identifies supply bottlenecks that may jeopardize the fulfillment of demand plans. Utilizing both forecasting and inventory optimization, Slimstock can advise decision-makers as to contingency strategies to improve bottlenecks.

Finally, the executive dashboard in Slimstock's software provides decision-makers with performance metrics while highlighting gaps in sales projections. Decision-makers later focus on the highlighted points in monthly S&OP meetings toward a successful execution of sales and operational plans. Given the software's strengths regarding S&OP and S&OE, Slimstock is seeing an increase in customer satisfaction and retention. The company reported a 97 percent retention rate in 2023. According to Gartner's industry survey, the overall rating of Slim4 is 4.5 out of 5, with 91 percent of Slimstock users recommending it to other companies.[10] According to Oliver Wight's industry survey of

---

[9] If the demand is intermittent, for example, Croston's method is used as suggested in academic literature (Shenstone & Hyndman, 2005).

[10] Gartner is an American research and consulting firm that conducts technology surveys. It collects verified reviews from actual users of supply chain software

companies that implement S&OP, 52 percent of Slimstock's customers reported an increase in revenue by 10–31 percent, with profits rising more than 25 percent (Correll & Palmatier, 2014).

9.4 Conclusion

Digital transformation of supply chains is a long journey that must start with a robust design process. The previous chapter discussed the design aspects of digital transformation. After decision-makers understand the risks (operational due diligence), benefits (value of analytical tools), and challenges (data management), they can begin to design digital solutions. Next, implementation must focus on S&OP and S&OE and align digital applications with the five stages of S&OE. We identify five classes of business applications, shown in Figure 9.1, that can be used in various stages of S&OE:

1. Decision-makers can use *descriptive analytics* to observe historical sales and existing inventory levels of products, components, and raw materials. Descriptive analytics can be useful for demand forecasting, supply management, inventory management, and sales and fulfillment management.
2. *Predictive modeling* is instrumental in managing uncertainties in the supply chain. Such applications are used to predict demand, supply disruptions, and machine breakdowns. Therefore, demand forecasting, supply management, and inventory management would benefit from predictive analytics tools.
3. *Optimization* can help determine the optimal values of decision variables subject to different supply chain constraints. As a part of S&OE, executives must decide on how much to procure from suppliers, how much inventory to hold, and how to allocate limited inventory to customers. To facilitate these decisions, optimization tools can be effectively integrated into supply management, inventory management, and sales and fulfillment management.
4. Decision-makers and line workers use digital systems to monitor activities and to ensure product flow from upstream suppliers to

solutions. Slimstock secures a remarkably high rank in Gartner's list. For example, 82 percent of the Canadian Kinaxis's users recommend its Maestro platform to other companies. This value stays at 82 percent for Blue Yonder's Luminate platform: https://bicersupplychain.short.gy/MgBPZs.

downstream customers. To this end, *real-time activity monitoring* must be embedded in supply management, order management, and sales and fulfillment management systems. Such monitoring applications rely on data engineering systems such that information transfer between user interfaces and databases occur both rapidly and consistently.

5. *Customer relationship management* (CRM) applications play a crucial role in improving sales and fulfillment management. CRM applications help salespeople determine potential buyers of their company's products. Such applications are referred to as *demand sensing* tools in practice. Demand sensing can be essential for sales management because it allows salespeople to determine strategic channels to place inventory. Another use of CRM applications is that salespeople can develop effective promotions to increase sales, which is referred to as *demand shaping*. Relying on CRM tools, companies can form effective promotions tailored to customers' expectations and increase the efficiency of sales and fulfillment operations.

10 Closing Remarks

Supply chain management has long been regarded as the practice of having the right products at the right time in the right place to fulfill customer demand without keeping excess inventory. Such a perception makes its ultimate objective perfect matching of supply with demand. However, this objective can tackle only one of its five trade-offs – that is, excess inventory versus product shortages. As outlined in Figure 2.1, there are four other trade-offs related to supply chain management. If one of the other trade-offs is more important than the one between excess inventory versus product shortages, decision-makers will be better off refining their objectives. This can be achieved by taking a comprehensive approach to supply chain management and delving into its trade-offs, economics, strategies, and digital aspects. Only with a comprehensive approach can decision-makers be transformative enough to use the right tools and methods and align supply chains with rapidly changing business dynamics. Otherwise, efforts to transform supply chains may end up with huge losses due to their complexities.

Supply chains are often extraordinarily complex for three reasons. First, there are diverse actions, agents, and decisions in supply chains. These structural aspects cause complexity in supply chains. Second, there are different risks and uncertainties contributing to supply chain complexity. Chapter 3 is completely devoted to an in-depth discussion about supply chain risks and uncertainties. Finally, supply chain executives face the challenge of identifying dominant trade-offs in certain settings. We cover supply chain trade-offs in Chapter 2 with follow-up discussions in Chapters 4–7. Any misidentification of supply chain trade-offs leads to ambiguity in the objectives and priorities, which in turn contributes to supply chain complexity. Thus, supply chains may break up in disarray due to their *structural complexity* coupled with *risks and uncertainties* in the *absence of clear objectives*. In this book, we attempt to address these issues by uncovering the fundamental trade-offs of supply chain management, their economic causes, and strategic implications.

Although there is a common (mis)perception that supply chain management's objective is ever-perfect matching of supply with demand, other objectives may arise in different contexts. For example, matching supply with demand is less important for luxury brands than fast-fashion retailers. Thus, its objective can be the coordination and monitoring of operational, information, and capital flows in the luxury industry. The World Economic Forum defines supply chain management as the backbone of economic systems, implying that one of its objectives is to improve economic welfare. Another objective can be to facilitate the achievement of business objectives. These objectives are all semantically different, which is unique to supply chain management. For example, it is much easier to have a common objective for other business areas such as finance, accounting, and marketing. Even standards of accounting are so universal that firms in different countries use generally accepted accounting principles (GAAP). When it comes to supply chain management, divergence starts with objectives at the very beginning. This explains the pall of ambiguity as to the roles of supply chain management for firms. Why is it difficult for supply chain practitioners and academics to agree on a common objective? Why is there such ambiguity as to supply chain practice?

The roots of this ambiguity date back centuries ago. Adam Smith's theory on economic liberalism asserted that nations could create wealth by division of labor and market efficiency. Division of labor lets workers focus on what they do the best and become more proficient, a cornerstone of improved productivity in economic systems. There is also a need for efficient markets so people can trade goods and services without any difficulty. In an efficient market, trade occurs without any contractual or search costs. Prices in an efficient market must reflect the true values and costs of products. In this economic environment envisioned by Adam Smith, goods flow naturally in the market. Here, supply chain management is regarded as a *self-functioning module* in the marketplace.

Markets are inefficient in practice such that there are secondary costs to exchange products and services. Prices rarely reflect the true values and costs of products. Therefore, supply chain activities must be coordinated by a group of decision-makers. This need for coordination seems to isolate supply chain management from markets, promoting the idea of supply chain management serving as a mere *factor of production* where executives focus on cost minimization.

Supply chain management is neither just a segment of markets nor a factor of production. It indeed resides *between* markets and production. In efficient economic systems, supply chains are more integrated to markets such that market pricing coordinates the flow of goods. When markets are inefficient, supply chain management is more oriented toward production. This positioning of supply chain management contributes to the ambiguity of what defines it in practice. Hence, it can be daunting for decision-makers to identify supply chain objectives and priorities.

This book has proposed a framework that identifies effective supply chain management strategies according to business models and firms' sensitivity to supply–demand mismatches (Figure 2.2). The framework is built upon our detailed analysis of supply chain trade-offs such that each proposed strategy in the framework deals with certain trade-offs effectively. For example, fast-fashion retailers and automakers are sensitive to the mismatches. They mitigate the mismatch risk via supply chain integration and lean manufacturing, respectively. However, firms may ignore the mismatches partially or completely when they are not much affected by them. When companies can sell their products at hefty margins (e.g., luxury brands), for instance, they become less sensitive to the mismatches. Likewise, the sensitivity to the mismatches fades when companies have an innovative business model, which makes it possible to generate nonoperational profits (e.g., supply chain finance). In this book, we discuss these strategies in detail (Chapters 4–7) and explain how to align supply chains with business models.

10.1 Strategic Implications

Supply chain trade-offs have important implications for firms' growth and operational turnaround strategies. Only with the identification of dominant trade-offs can decision-makers align supply chains with business models. Otherwise, they seek to grow their markets without having clear objectives nor any alignment between supply chains and business models. We have already discussed a few examples where growth efforts of organizations ended up with huge losses in the absence of supply chain alignment (e.g., Philips). We now look at another interesting example: Hershey Company, a US-based chocolate brand.

10: Closing Remarks

Hershey is exposed to demand uncertainty, which is typical for chocolate makers. Here, demand uncertainty results from price fluctuations because chocolate makers adjust their selling prices according to volatile cacao prices (Hoppe & Petroni, 2024). This makes Hershey sensitive to supply–demand mismatches because the chocolatier does not have an innovative business model to generate nonoperating profits significantly. It also does not sell their products at hefty margins. Combining these characteristics together, supply chain integration is the right strategy for the chocolate maker.

Hershey had sought an ambitious growth strategy before 2015 to increase revenues. It had started to operate in different markets beyond the United States and Canada without paying attention to supply chain integration. This caused serious financial problems that came to surface in 2016. Mondelez International even attempted to acquire the financially strapped Hershey, which did not come to fruition. Then, the chocolatier crafted and implemented an operational turnaround plan that aligned supply chains with business goals. To this end, it downsized in some markets and focused more on the United States and Canada.[1] It acquired popcorn and salty snack brands, which are popular in the US-CA footprint. Hershey also invested in a new US factory (thirty years after their last factory launch) and configured operational flexibility in its existing plants.[2] Owing to its operational turnaround, Hershey elevated both its revenues and its stock price in just five years (Cohen, 2022).

The Hershey case exemplifies the role of supply chain management in shaping growth strategies. The chocolatier first tried to expand geographically and increase revenues, which did not go well due to inconsistencies between its growth strategy and the dynamics of integrated supply chains. Then, the company decided to focus on the North American market (keeping the logistics and sales networks compact as suggested to integrate supply chains) while increasing product variety to

---

[1] According to a *Wall Street Journal* article (Cohen, 2022), Hershey's strategy of "scaling back internationally and sharpening the competitive edge at home" is contrary to the company's traditional strategy. In 2023, the company underwent organizational restructuring, and its European division became a standalone business (Bhalla, 2023).

[2] Visit the following link for more information: https://bicersupplychain.short.gy/rNMprL.

grow revenues. The new strategy is consistent with the dynamics of integrated supply chains, leading to fulfillment of business goals.

One of the factors that helped Hershey achieve operational turnaround is having retailers as intermediaries in the supply chain. Hershey sells its products through retailers, distancing itself from consumers. In the food industry, it is highly challenging to fulfill consumer demand in an economical way without having an innovative business model (e.g., Starbucks and McDonald's). Nevertheless, food companies can integrate supply chains via sophisticated digital technologies, which makes it possible to *sell their goods to end consumers* and *generate high profits*. There is always a possibility of developing an effective supply chain strategy to grow business regardless of the business complexity. In this sense, one of the supply chain integration (and digital transformation) best practices is the Dutch online grocery Picnic, which was founded in 2015 as an online food delivery company.[3] The company operates in the Netherlands, Germany, and France with 2,000 small electric trucks and fourteen fulfillment centers. Picnic runs no stores or pick-up points. Orders are prepared in one of the fulfillment centers and delivered to customers. Customers placing orders before 10:00 p.m. receive them the next day within a twenty-minute window (Lindert, 2022).

Picnic's integrated system collects data from four sources: (1) its online app, (2) trucks, (3) fulfillment centers, and (4) customer intelligence.[4] The company uses cloud systems such as Amazon Web Services and Snowflakes to connect customer orders with trucks and fulfillment centers. It also utilizes Salesforce systems to collect customer feedback from social media, online apps, and WhatsApp messages. If a customer tags Picnic on a social media platform, for example, the system processes the post with Natural Language Processing (NLP) methods. This information next feeds the demand sensing, shaping, and forecasting tools. The firm also uses weather forecasts in various locations through Snowflake's cloud solution for demand forecasting. Demand for seasonal items (e.g., ice cream) is strongly influenced by weather. Using real-time weather information

---

[3] Picnic's website is https://picnic.app/nl/.
[4] Visit the following link for more information: https://join.picnic.app/team/strategy-and-analytics. Information about Picnic's working dynamics is extracted from the articles under "Interesting reads" section on the website.

and forecasts, Picnic improves forecasts for such items and fulfills demand with ultra-high service levels.[5]

Demand and supply planning activities are maintained under a Master Planning Process. Data analysts at Picnic use SQL to develop ad-hoc queries and prepare strategic reports that help decision-makers plan demand and supply. Picnic also simulates digital twins to improve inventory, procurement, and fulfillment decisions.[6] Its digital system identifies bottleneck operations dynamically depending on varying supply–demand traits. Then, replenishment orders are placed to store buffer inventory in key locations.[7]

Picnic relies on a trading platform to manage procurement and order-to-cash workflows. This platform facilitates the formation, negotiation, observation, and remittance of orders with the suppliers. It also tracks messaging to easily sense procurement and supply lead times for each procurement order.[8]

Overall, Picnic excels in applying digital solutions to achieve end-to-end supply chain integration. Owing to its success, the company has consistently grown its European customer base and raised $388 million in 2024 from The Bill and Melinda Gates Foundation and German retailer group Edeka to sustain its growth targets (Van Campenhout, 2024). Indeed, Picnic had reached unicorn status in 2020, just five years after its founding (Westermeyer, 2020). Given Europe's saturated retail market dominated by big players, Picnic's success is incredibly important to show the merits of digital transformation for business growth.

10.2 Interactions with Tax Policies

Policymakers can benefit from our insights to increase the efficiency of tax policies. For instance, we emphasize the importance of capacity

---

[5] Visit the following links for more information:
  https://diginomica.com/rethinking-retail-picnic-delivers-data-driven-approach,
  https://bicersupplychain.short.gy/4D3Set.
[6] For more information about how Picnic simulated their system using Python: https://jobs.picnic.app/en/blogs/2023-in-a-nutshell-ride-along.
[7] For more information about Picnic's warehouse and inventory management system: https://bicersupplychain.short.gy/lWwprX.
[8] Visit the following link for more information about Picnic's use of the supplier management and trading platform: https://www.b2be.com/blog/picnic-partners-with-b2be-for-supplier-management/.

management and effective asset utilization in supply chains. When the amortization cost of an asset is extremely high compared to inventory holding costs (i.e., the second fundamental trade-off), decision-makers must utilize the asset at a remarkably high rate. Furthermore, they are better off seeking process innovations to increase the output rate of the asset. Decision-makers may achieve productivity gains if the ownership of valuable assets remains stable in an economic system. Here, policymakers wisely promote *asset retention* when an asset's contribution to economy increases with the length of ownership by certain people.

Unlike asset retention, productivity in consumer markets increases as individuals trade products easily. In consumer markets, the utility value of products decreases over time. After the utility of holding a product diminishes for an individual, the product must be sold to another person so that maximum utility is extracted during its lifetime. Here, policymakers wisely promote *product trade* when a product's contribution to economy increases with the frequency of ownership changes. From the supply chain perspective, tax policies must promote trade and market efficiency for downstream consumers but asset retention for upstream suppliers.

Taxes can be categorized into three as corporate, individual (including investors and shareholders), and consumption taxes (Andersson, 1992). At the corporate level, executives pay close attention to corporate tax rates as well as taxation of interest payments and dividends. Interest payments of corporate debt are often tax deductible, whereas dividends are paid out from after-tax income. At the individual level, there are savings, investment, and income taxes. Saving taxes comprise interest income and wealth taxes on individuals' savings. Investment taxes consist of dividend and capital gains taxes. When governments increase the capital gains tax, for instance, investors prefer receiving dividend income rather than selling their investments. This would help them avoid paying hefty capital gains taxes. Finally, consumption tax is the Goods and Services Tax (GST). When people buy groceries, for example, they pay GST. It is also known as the Value Added Tax (VAT) in many countries.

To promote asset retention for upstream suppliers, policymakers may consider raising the *capital-gains* tax. This can be effective to avoid short-termism in investment decisions (Sarin et al., 2022). Higher capital-gains tax rates would steer investors to focus on long-term projects that reward persistent efforts leading to higher long-term returns. ASML is one of the most innovative companies in the world with a market value equaling hundreds of billions of dollars. It was founded in 1984 in the Netherlands when the tax rate was 60–70 percent in that country.[9] It took ASML a long time to gain the expertise needed to become a multi-billion-dollar corporation, and higher capital-gains tax rates prompted the company's evolution by coaxing its founders and investors to embrace long-term objectives.

After corporations utilize their assets efficiently, they make some goods or offer services. The *corporate* tax rate and GST for trading goods and services must be *low* so that corporations can sell goods in the marketplace, pay high wages to their employees, and earn a profit. This would help them preserve capital to finance operating expenses, so they can utilize their assets and increase productivity in nationwide economic systems.

In sum, policymakers may attempt to render upstream suppliers *inefficient for trading assets* by raising the *capital-gains* tax rate, thus promoting supply chain management as a factor of production for *upstream* operations. Here, decision-makers focus on the efficient utilization of valuable assets. However, policymakers must make markets *efficient for trading goods and services* by reducing both the corporate tax rate and GST. This would promote supply chain management as part of the market for *downstream* fulfillment and trading activities. The alignment of supply chain management, taxation, and economic incentives can yield productivity gains and foster the innovation culture and welfare of nations.

10.3 Corporate Social Responsibility

On April 24, 2013, the Rana Plaza factory in Bangladesh collapsed due to unregulated and poor working conditions, which killed more than 1,100 garment workers (Yardley, 2013). This disaster triggered widespread protests in Western countries toward apparel brands linked to the Rana Plaza. The Clean Clothes Campaign identified those companies and contributed to the public awareness of poor labor safety in the apparel supply chain (Rahman & Yadlapalli, 2013). Recent reports

---

[9] Individual tax rates were as high as 72 percent for high-income people, and corporate tax rates were between 45 and 48 percent in the Netherlands at that time (Rosendaal & Wetendorf, 1981).

have also revealed that Rana Plaza owner, Mr. Sobel Rana, violated the Building Construction Act and bribed officials in obtaining the required permits (Talukder, 2024; Yardley, 2013b).

These incidents forced apparel brands to take proactive steps toward establishing work safety in their supply chains. Since then, brands have been working with various stakeholders to improve labor safety at their contract manufacturer sites. For example, they have made great strides in installing fire systems and raising salaries as well as commissioning independent organizations to inspect contract manufacturer sites. Many contractors were blacklisted after these inspections (Paton, 2020). All these efforts are centered on supply chain transparency. In other words, apparel brands invested in supply chain transparency to guarantee the conformity of their partners to work safety standards. Therefore, having a transparent supply chain clearly helps corporations achieve their corporate social responsibility goals.

The Rana Plaza disaster demonstrated that corporations are increasingly being held responsible for supply chain activities outside their boundaries. Because supply chains involve complex activities spanning different countries (and even continents), it may not be realistic to expect a company to take responsibility for all operations executed by their external supply chain partners. Therefore, the complexity and dispersion of supply chains may hinder corporate social responsibility efforts. For that reason, decision-makers must have a clear understanding about the scope of supply chain activities that fall into the boundaries of corporate social responsibility. Only with such an understanding can they improve business objectives to sustain profitability while fulfilling social responsibilities. Then, supply chain management facilitates the (improved) business objectives as emphasized in this book.

Historically, the idea of corporate social responsibility was refused by some economists (e.g., Milton Friedman) because corporations' sole responsibility had been considered to make profits (Friedman, 1970). According to Friedman, corporations are only responsible to their shareholders, and decision-makers do not have any right to use shareholders' money for social purposes. After decision-makers generate profits for shareholders, they can use the money to serve society in separate ways. Here, corporations' sole duty is to generate profits *while conforming to regulations.*

The problem regarding Friedman's view is that regulations are often incomplete in practice (Fowlie, 2009). It is not possible to write a regulation for every conceivable situation in supply chains. Furthermore, supply chains may span several countries subject to different regulations. When regulations in different countries conflict, supply chain activities would be performed in direct conflict with each other. Here, decision-makers must establish *regulatory compliance* such that they conform to written regulations. Additionally, they must establish *voluntary compliance* such that supply chain management becomes consistent with moral values regarding social, environmental, and cultural norms. Decision-makers may refuse voluntary compliance because there is no written rule or law enforcement to punish them for disobedience to these norms. However, such a refusal would be difficult given intense pressure for corporate social responsibility. If decision-makers can avoid a disaster at a negligible cost (compared to total cost of the disaster), for example, they must do it. Otherwise, they may face protests and the loss of loyal customers, causing much higher costs.

To improve the adoption of corporate social responsibility, companies must strictly conform to written regulations governing their supply chains. Next, they must develop such a voluntary compliance scheme that details supply chain standards (consistent with social, environmental, and cultural norms) and contingency strategies to be taken when the standards are not met. Here, companies can collaborate with nongovernmental organizations (NGOs) to set the standards. Finally, they must invest in supply chain transparency to monitor operations.

We observe an effective exercise of corporate social responsibility in the global palm oil supply chain. Palm oil consumption has a devastating impact on the deforestation of rainforests in Indonesia and Malaysia. Palm oil is a commodity ingredient of many food products, cosmetics, even biofuel. It constitutes nearly 40 percent of the world's vegetable oil volume. Indonesia and Malaysia jointly account for 85 percent of the world's palm oil production. In these countries, more than 3.7 million hectares of rainforest (almost the size of Switzerland) were cleared to produce palm oil (Brown et al., 2015). After being aware of this environmental damage, many food companies cut palm oil from their supply chains or declared that they would only use palm oil produced sustainably (Phillips & Morris, 2015). They invested in supply chain transparency that verifies palm oil usage from sustainable sources. They also expanded supplies by replacing palm oil with sunflower and rapeseed oil (Cohen, 2024b). Although restructuring the supply chain causes additional costs, those companies accepted the loss of profits to protect the environment.

10.4 Implications for Investment Analysis

We have discussed economic implications of supply chain management for investment analysis in Chapter 1. The economic view that regards supply chain management as a mere factor of production leads corporations to invest in centralized systems, where a single factory produces items in large volumes to supply different markets. Such a system proves ineffective in the presence of supply chain risks and uncertainties, resulting in colossal mismatch costs. To avoid sunk investments in ineffective systems, decision-makers must identify supply chain trade-offs before restructuring supply chains. This helps increase the return on investments at the firm level.

We now look at the implications of supply chain trade-offs for the investments in capital markets. Investments can successfully generate high returns when investors do not overlook the supply chain implications of their investments. In stock markets, for instance, share prices of publicly traded firms increase with their profitability. In the retail industry, executives would tend to keep excess inventory in their accounts to inflate their operating margins. This strategy helps increase share prices in the short term while hurting profits in the long term. Retail investors often assess the supply chain performance, especially inventory metrics, of their target firms to understand whether juicy margins are sustainable. When the market value of excess inventory becomes lower than its cost, such as occurs at the end of each selling season, keeping excess inventory in accounts makes it possible to report higher operating margins than their true values. In this case, excess inventory reported as *regular* inventory in financial statements rather than as cost of goods sold (when sold at discount) or inventory write-offs may fool naïve investors in the short term. Investors are wisely advised to analyze both margins and *inventory turnover*. If profit margin rises sharply while inventory turnover *decreases*, high margin may prove illusory. If *both* metrics rise at the same time, then high margins may be real and sturdy. When fund managers scrutinize supply chain management to shape their investments, they can achieve high returns on their portfolios. For example, a fund manager, David

Berman, has used inventory productivity as a key metric in his investment strategy to achieve a competitive edge over rival funds (Raman et al., 2005).

While investors like David Berman earn high returns on their investments, many others who ignore supply chain dynamics end up with huge losses. For example, trucking startup Convoy had developed a platform where firms buy freight services from truck owners or logistics companies. Convoy was popularized as the "Uber for freight," and it raised $160 million from investors. With the last funding round transacted in April 2022, the startup soared to a market value of $3.8 billion (Berger, 2023; Griffith, 2023). Convoy investors may have thought the startup would disrupt the freight-shipping arena as Uber did to traditional taxi. Its business model appeared extremely attractive as it resembles that of Uber. Freight shipping is a big market, and the same business model worked great for Uber. Why not for Convoy now?

Uber offers its service to individuals having short demand lead times. In other words, demand is signaled and fulfilled rapidly in that market. To serve customers, Uber uses slack capacity in the supply market given that any person owning a car can be an Uber driver. In the freight business, however, there is no slack capacity. Unlike cars, not every household owns a truck. Besides, demand lead time is much longer for freight transportation compared to ride-hailing. Therefore, client firms have much time to plan and schedule shipments from their suppliers. Unlike Uber riders, Convoy's clients (i.e., corporations) may contact logistics firms and negotiate prices *ahead* of shipment. They use the Convoy service only when trucks fail or for expedited orders. Otherwise, it is challenging for Convoy to penetrate the shipping market.

The business model of Convoy had been misaligned with the procurement dynamics in supply chains. Convoy should have aimed to facilitate the *contingency* plans of procurement activities. For example, companies often negotiate flexible contracts with suppliers where order quantities can be changed by, for example, 20 percent during the selling season. If they need to increase the order level according to the contract, they may use a platform service to manage the shipment of any additional amount. Here, an ideal business model for the platform would have been based on a dynamic pricing mechanism that enables truck reservation in advance. This would allow Convoy to collect reservation fees from regular customers, registration fees from stand-by customers, and commissions from truck owners.

To better understand the merits of dynamic pricing, we can look at its applications in other businesses. Dynamic pricing is an effective revenue management method for monetizing the capacity of costly resources. It helps airlines and hotels sell their seats and rooms effectively and generate high profits. In such a setting, companies offer their resources (seats for airlines, rooms for hotels, trucks for transportation) at reasonable prices when customers book well ahead of the planned usage date. Early booking information helps decision-makers gauge potential future demand, reducing demand uncertainty. If demand is expected to be high, firms raise prices to maximize profits. Otherwise, they trim prices to utilize capacity.

In a dynamic pricing scheme, customers may need to remit a penalty fee for cancellation. Airlines often require partial or full ticket price as a cancellation fee. Hotels are more flexible than airlines in offering free cancellation to their customers. The management of no-shows is crucial for airlines and hotels. They use predictive analytics to forecast the number of cancellations. Based on such forecasts, they accept more reservations or sell more tickets than capacity, known as "overbooking" in revenue management. Or they form a list of stand-by consumers to fill the eventual no-shows (Glusac, 2024).

Convoy could have used such a dynamic pricing model with stand-by customers to align its platform with supply chain dynamics. In this case, clients could have used the platform to reserve trucks for potential extra shipments after they had negotiated contracts and planned the shipment with their logistics service providers for original delivery. If they had canceled their transports, other companies with flexible schedules could have used the idle truck capacity. Here, Convoy could have collected reservation fees from regular customers. It could have also charged stand-by customers a registration fee, so they could use idle capacity cheaply.

Convoy attained peak market value in 2022 due to the unprecedented need of expedited orders during the COVID pandemic. After supply chains returned to normal, the firm closed operations. Convoy would have operated successfully if its business model had been aligned well with supply chain dynamics.

To summarize, all these examples in the book show that decision-makers cannot execute business models successfully, design effective economic systems, or devise profitable investment plans if they fail to adequately address supply chain challenges. Then, it would not be possible to solve more serious problems such as wasting limited resources of our planet. My ambition in writing this book comes from my strong belief that urgent global problems can be solved only by placing supply chain management at the center of solutions. Only after having a supply-chain-centric view can we develop robust solutions to pressing global issues.

Glossary

Aesthetic Intelligence: Coined by Pauline Brown to describe luxury brands' ability to shape customer experience to delight customers.

Aggressive Selling: The sales practice carried out by lean manufacturers to reduce demand fluctuations.

Annual Operating Plan: An executive plan that sets revenue, growth, and profit targets.

Annual Revenue Credit: A performance indicator for sales teams.

Base-Stock Model: The inventory model that optimizes the multiple-ordering problem for durable goods in the absence of setups given demand uncertainty.

Bill of Material: The document showing all components and raw materials used as inputs for a finished good.

Buffering: Keeping either extra inventory or idle capacity to deal with sudden increases in demand.

Cash Conversion Cycle: The time length during which a firm must finance operations.

Consignment Inventory: Inventory that is physically stored in a retailer's locations while being recorded on the manufacturer's balance sheet.

Cross Docking: The practice of keeping inventory in distribution centers just for a limited time before the products are shipped to retail stores.

Data Lake: Data intermediary that stores data used for reporting tools while maintaining security and robustness of databases.

Days of Payables: The time elapsing from when a buyer receives ordered goods until when the payment is completed.

Days of Receivables: The time elapsing from when a seller delivers goods until receipt of the payment.

Decision Lead Time: The difference between operating and demand lead times, which is considered an indicator of the mismatch risk.

Glossary

Demand Lead Time: The time window between a customer order and its requested delivery time.

Demand Sensing: Companies' attempt to understand which customers would like to buy what products.

Demand Shaping: Inducing customers to buy certain products through pricing and promotion strategies.

Digital Twin: A digital tool that mirrors operational systems.

Direct Shipping: The practice of shipping goods from manufacturers to retail stores without stopping at distribution centers.

Disintermediation: A strategy carried out by some suppliers such that they reach end customers and become competitors of their buyers.

Dynamic Discounting: A mechanism that allows buyers to pay their invoices any time until the end of payment term and receive a discount.

Economic Order Quantity: The quantity that optimizes the ordering decision with setups in the absence of demand uncertainty.

Epistemological Uncertainty: The uncertainty created by supply chain stakeholders to receive short-term benefits.

Inventory Financing: Suppliers' act of financing trade during the payment term.

Inventory Securitization: The practice of owning inventory (precious materials) and issuing notes to investors so the investors can share the ownership of the goods.

Inventory Turnover: Inventory productivity metric that gives how many times inventory is fully replenished per annum.

Letter of Credit: A financial instrument used to facilitate trade when there is no trust between a supplier and a buyer.

Long Tail: Coined by Chris Anderson to describe niche items tailored to specific needs of customers.

Newsvendor Model: The inventory model that optimizes the single-ordering problem for perishable or seasonal goods given demand uncertainty.

Ontological Uncertainty: The uncertainty resulting from unknown unknowns, which is also known as deep uncertainty.

Operating Cycle: The time elapsing from the instant when a manufacturer starts operational activities until revenues are collected from customers

Operating Lead Time: The time elapsing from the beginning of procurement activities until the delivery of final goods to customers.

Procurement Lead Time: The time window that covers search activities, negotiation, assessment of suppliers, contracting, and the final physical delivery of ordered raw materials.

Production Lead Time: The time elapsing from when the raw materials are received until the completion of production.

Reorder Model: The inventory model that optimizes the multiple-ordering problem in the presence of setups given demand uncertainty.

Resource Acquisition Time: The time elapsing from when a resource is available until it starts to serve a customer.

Resource Idle Time: The time window during which a resource remains idle.

Resource Utilization Time: The time window covering service time for a customer.

Vendor Managed Inventory: An inventory management system in which suppliers control replenishment activities of their products in retailer locations.

Vendor Put Insurance: An insurance policy that mitigates suppliers' nonpayment risk.

References

Al-Shibeeb, D. (2024). Walmart Canada to break ground for huge distribution centre in Vaughan. *Vaughan Economic Development (Digital)*. https://bicersupplychain.short.gy/DjrXzx.

Anderson, C. (2004). The long tail. *The Wired Magazine, October Issue*, 86–103. www.wired.com/2004/10/tail.

Anderson, E. T., Fitzsimons, G. J., & Simester, D. (2006). Measuring and mitigating the costs of stockouts. *Management Science, 52*(11), 1751–1763. https://doi.org/10.1287/mnsc.1060.0577.

Andersson, K. (1992). Efficiency considerations in tax policy. In V. Tanzi (Ed.), *Fiscal Policies in Economies in Transition* (Ch. 5, pp. 101–119). Washington: International Monetary Fund. https://doi.org/10.5089/9781557751911.071.

Anzolin, E., & Aloisi, S. (2021). Focus: How global supply chains are falling out of fashion. *Reuters (Digital)*. https://bicersupplychain.short.gy/HlTJwU.

Aspromourgos, T. (2008). *The Science of Wealth: Adam Smith and the Framing of Political Economy*. London: Routledge. https://doi.org/10.4324/9780203889572.

Bailey, D. (2009). Half of U.S. auto suppliers face bankruptcy: Study. *Reuters (Digital)*. www.reuters.com/article/us-autos-study-sb-idUSTRE52I7GL20090319.

Bain, M. (2019). Richemont is destroying its expensive, unsold watches to save their brand value. *Quartz (Digital)*. https://bicersupplychain.short.gy/k7sV0n.

Basquill, J. (2022). Supplier demand for early payment has doubled over past five years, Taulia reveals. *Global Trade Review (Digital)*. https://bicersupplychain.short.gy/324M1Y.

Batra, I., Mathur, A., Zevin, M. et al. (2024). Apple in payments: Winning by influencing. *Boston Consulting Group White Paper*. https://media-publications.bcg.com/Apple-in-Payments.pdf.

Bellamy, W. (2020). How the aerospace industry is finding new 3D-printing use cases for old aircraft parts. *Aviation Today (Digital)*. https://bicersupplychain.short.gy/prINRd.

Benetton Group S.r.l. (n.d.). Profile: Company vision. *Benetton Company Report*. www.benettongroup.com/en/the-group/profile/company-vision.

Berger, P. (2023). How digital freight darling convoy ran off the road. *The Wall Street Journal (Digital)*. https://bicersupplychain.short.gy/hxiwnU.

Berger, P., & Paris, C. (2024). Importers face surging shipping costs, delays as Red Sea diversions pile up. *The Wall Street Journal (Digital)*. https://bicersupplychain.short.gy/y9oYPN.

Berthelsen, C., & Baer, J. (2015). Goldman tries a new commodities play. *The Wall Street Journal (Digital)*. https://bicersupplychain.short.gy/9JKbvw.

Besler, C. (2023). 5 types of watches define the market. *The New York Times (Digital)*. www.nytimes.com/2023/04/03/fashion/watches-collection-categories.html.

Bhalla, H. (2023). The Hershey company announces organizations changes to its international business to accelerate growth in key markets. *Business Wire (Digital)*. https://bicersupplychain.short.gy/TA6Zgr.

Bhatia, G., Lane, C., & Wain, A. (2013). Building resilience in supply chains: An initiative of the risk response network. *World Economic Forum Industry Agenda*, Product ID: REF150113. www.weforum.org/publications/building-resilience-supply-chains/.

Biçer, I. (2022). Securing the upside of digital transformation before implementation. *California Management Review (Digital)*. https://bicersupplychain.short.gy/FVk78h.

Biçer, I. (2023). *Supply Chain Analytics: An Uncertainty Modeling Approach*. Cham: Springer Nature. https://doi.org/10.1007/978-3-031-30347-0.

Biçer, I., Hagspiel, V., & De Treville, S. (2018). Valuing supply-chain responsiveness under demand jumps. *Journal of Operations Management*, 61, 46–67. https://doi.org/10.1016/j.jom.2018.06.002.

Biçer, I., Lücker, F., & Boyacı, T. (2022b). Beyond retail stores: Managing product proliferation along the supply chain. *Production and Operations Management*, 31(3), 1135–1156. https://doi.org/10.1111/poms.13598.

Biçer, I., Tarakci, M., & Kuzu, A. (2022). Using uncertainty modeling to better predict demand. *Harvard Business Review (Digital)*. https://hbr.org/2022/01/using-uncertainty-modeling-to-better-predict-demand.

Binkley, C. (2001). Starwood implements Six Sigma plan to enhance quality, boost cash flow. *The Wall Street Journal (Digital)*. www.wsj.com/articles/SB981328940993772263.

Blair, A. (2023). IHL study: Inventory distortion will cost retailers $1.77 trillion in 2023. *The Retail Touch Points Network (Digital)*. https://bicersupplychain.short.gy/EmpUvG.

Boffey, D. (2021). Dutch couple become Europe's first inhabitants of a 3D-printed house. *The Guardian (Digital)*. https://bicersupplychain.short.gy/XGITkY.

Bohn, R. E. (1994). Measuring and managing technological knowledge. *Sloan Management Review, Fall Issue*, 61–74. https://bicersupplychain.short.gy/Kf7lUA.

Boohoo Group PLC (n.d.). Our locations. *Boohoo Company Report*. https://careers.boohoogroup.com/our-locations.

Boston, W. (2020). Chip shortage slows global auto recovery. *The Wall Street Journal (Digital)*. www.wsj.com/articles/chip-shortage-slows-global-auto-recovery-11608320026.

Bray, R. L. (2023). Operational transparency: Showing when work gets done. *Manufacturing & Service Operations Management*, 25(3), 812–826. https://doi.org/10.1287/msom.2020.0899.

Briginshaw, D. (2022). SBB cuts losses by half in 2021. *International Railway Journal (Digital)*. www.railjournal.com/financial/sbb-cuts-losses-by-half-in-2021.

Broughton, K. (2020). Cash crunch at retailers stings suppliers during pandemic. *The Wall Street Journal (Digital)*. https://bicersupplychain.short.gy/U2Zj72.

Broughton, K. (2022). Jeans maker Kontoor Brands wants employee to focus on generating cash. *The Wall Street Journal (Digital)*. https://bicersupplychain.short.gy/pYTwRi.

Broughton, K. (2022b). Companies offer supply-chain financing to vendors as they bulk up on inventory, push out payment terms. *The Wall Street Journal (Digital)*. https://bicersupplychain.short.gy/plEVb5.

Brown, P. (2019, November 19). To truly delight customers, you need aesthetic intelligence. *Harvard Business Review Podcast* (Episode 710). https://bicersupplychain.short.gy/GlpS1W.

Brown, M., Phung, T., & Gentry, B. (2015). Palm oil in Indonesia: Environmental and social impacts. *Yale University Case Study*, Center for Business and Environment Case ID: 001. https://bicersupplychain.short.gy/lcvFjq.

Browning, T. R., & de Treville, S. (2021). A lean view of lean. *Journal of Operations Management*, 67(5), 640–652. https://doi.org/10.1002/joom.1153.

Brynjolfsson, E., Hu, Y., & Simester, D. (2011). Goodbye pareto principle, hello long tail: The effect of search costs on the concentration of product sales. *Management Science*, 57(8), 1373–1386. https://doi.org/10.1287/mnsc.1110.1371.

Bucy, M., Schaninger, B., Van Akin, K., & Weddle, B. (2021). Losing from day one: Why even successful transformations fall short. *McKinsey Insights*. https://bicersupplychain.short.gy/RX7mMO.

Byford, S. (2021). Samsung's profits rose in 2020 despite the pandemic. *The Verge (Digital)*. www.theverge.com/2021/1/28/22253844.

Callioni, G., de Montgros, X., Slagmulder, R., Van Wassenhove, L., & Wright, L. (2005). Inventory-driven costs. *Harvard Business Review, March Issue*, 135–141. https://hbr.org/2005/03/inventory-driven-costs.

Camuffo, A., Romano, P., & Vinelli, A. (2001). Back to the future: Benetton transforms its global network. *MIT Sloan Management Review, Fall Issue*, 46–52. https://bicersupplychain.short.gy/FmHWuW.

Canyon Bicycles GmbH (n.d.). How Canyon began. *Canyon Bicycles Company Report*. www.canyon.com/en-ca/jobs-bike-industry/how-canyon-began.html.

Carlson, N. (2009). In 2000, BusinessWeek wondered: "How will Google ever make money?" *Business Insider (Digital)*. https://bicersupplychain.short.gy/DqWXNj.

Cattani, K. D., Dahan, E., & Schmidt, G. M. (2010). Lowest cost may not lower total cost: Using "spackling" to smooth mass-customized production. *Production and Operations Management*, 19(5), 531–545. https://doi.org/10.1111/j.1937-5956.2009.01113.x.

Cherney, M. A. (2024). Exclusive: Intel manufacturing business suffers setback as Broadcom tests disappoint. *Reuters (Digital)*. https://bicersupplychain.short.gy/JemDwl.

China Export & Credit Insurance Corporation (n.d.). Corporate profile. *SINOSURE Company Report*. www.sinosure.com.cn/en/Sinosure/Profile/index.shtml.

Chod, J., Trichakis, N., Tsoukalas, G., Aspegren, H., & Weber, M. (2020). On the financing benefits of supply chain transparency and blockchain adoption. *Management Science*, 66(10), 4378–4396. https://doi.org/10.1287/mnsc.2019.3434.

Chopra, S. (2005). Seven-Eleven Japan Co. *Kellogg School of Management Case Study*, Product ID: KEL026-PDF-ENG. https://hbsp.harvard.edu/product/KEL026-PDF-ENG.

Cisco Systems (2014). How Cisco transformed its supply chain. *Cisco Case Study*, Product ID: 1488422208912825. https://bicersupplychain.short.gy/PLbm0i.

Cisco Systems (2022). Cisco reports fourth quarter and fiscal year 2022 earnings. *Cisco Investor Relations*. https://bicersupplychain.short.gy/FIhn3H.

Cisco Systems (2024). Acquisitions by year. *Cisco Company Report*. https://bicersupplychain.short.gy/1pNB86.

Citibank (2019). How treasury used a massive supplier chain finance programme to deliver huge free cash flow and productivity improvements. *Citigroup 2019 Adam Smith Awards*. www.citibank.com/tts/case-studies/procter-gamble.html.

Coase, R. H. (1937). The nature of the firm. *Economica*, 4(16), 386–405. https://doi.org/10.2307/2626876.

Cohen, B. (2022). Hershey's turnaround story isn't sweet. It's salty. *The Wall Street Journal (Digital)*. www.wsj.com/articles/halloween-hershey-stock-chocolate-candy-11666831636.

Cohen, B. (2024). The man in Silicon Valley who's completely obsessed with failure. *The Wall Street Journal (Digital)*. https://bicersupplychain.short.gy/fQw5yt.

Cohen, P. (2024b). Can Europe save forests without killing jobs in Malaysia? *The New York Times (Digital)*. https://bicersupplychain.short.gy/v0RHUP.

Connors, W., & Terlep, S. (2013). BlackBerry stuck with $1 billion in unsold phones. *The Wall Street Journal (Digital)*. www.wsj.com/articles/SB10001424127887323308504579087471781835480.

Cordon, M. (2023). Alibaba logistics unit Cainiao files for HK listing. *Tech in Asia (Digital)*. www.techinasia.com/alibaba-logistics-unit-cainiao-files-hk-listing.

Correll, J., & Palmatier, G. (2014). How good is your sales and operations planning/ integrated business planning process? *Oliver Wight Paper Series*. https://bicersupplychain.short.gy/skliRg.

Craig, N., DeHoratius, N., & Raman, A. (2016). The impact of supplier inventory service level on retailer demand. *Manufacturing & Service Operations Management*, 18(4), 461–474. https://doi.org/10.1287/msom.2016.0582.

Cusumano, M. A., Holweg, M., Howell, J. et al. (2021). Commentaries on "The lenses of lean". *Journal of Operations Management*, 67(5), 627–639. https://doi.org/10.1002/joom.1138.

C2FO (2023). C2FO, Starbucks CEO's foundation partner on $100M diversity business loan fund. *C2FO Company Announcement*. https://bicersupplychain.short.gy/m5qJmG.

Danaher, P. J., & van Heerde, H. J. (2018). Delusion in attribution: Caveats in using attribution for multimedia budget allocation. *Journal of Marketing Research*, 55(5), 667–685. https://doi.org/10.1177/0022243718802845.

Das, S. (2022). Paperchase has been rescued but greetings card artists are losing thousands. *The Guardian (Digital)*. https://bicersupplychain.short.gy/zGTyh4.

Davis, S. (2021). Tennis legend Andre Agassi once learned how to beat a rival by watching his tongue and then spilled the beans years later at Oktoberfest. *Business Insider (Digital)*. https://bicersupplychain.short.gy/F3mypx.

De Treville, S., Bicer, I., Chavez-Demoulin, V. et al. (2014). Valuing lead time. *Journal of Operations Management*, 32(6), 337–346. https://doi.org/10.1016/j.jom.2014.06.002.

Descalsota, M., & Duffy, K. (2023). A Patek Philippe watch just sold for $5.8 million, making it the most expensive watch ever sold at an online auction. *Business Insider (Digital)*. https://bicersupplychain.short.gy/4Xxdx0.

Diermann, C., & Huchzermeier, A. (2017). Case – canyon bicycles: Judgmental demand forecasting in direct sales. *INFORMS Transactions on Education*, 17(2), 63–74. https://doi.org/10.1287/ited.2016.0165ca.

Dooley, B., & Ueno, H. (2019). A 7-Eleven in Japan might close for a day. Yes, that's a big deal. *The New York Times (Digital)*. www.nytimes.com/2019/12/30/business/7-eleven-japan-work.html.

Dunbar, N. (2018). Supply chain finance yields $5 billion for P&G. *Euro Finance (Digital)*. www.eurofinance.com/news/supply-chain-finance-yields-5-billion-for-pg.

Eaglesham, J. (2020). Supply-chain finance is new risk in crisis. *The Wall Street Journal (Digital)*. www.wsj.com/articles/supply-chain-finance-is-new-risk-in-crisis-11585992601.

Eckert, N., & Felton, R. (2023). Fard stalls production of F-150 Lightning EV for additional week. *The Wall Street Journal (Digital)*. https://bicersupplychain.short.gy/fiKCi8.

Editorial Staff (2022). The British government made mistakes when sourcing protective gear. *The Economist (Digital)*. https://bicersupplychain.short.gy/7Q8sV3.

El-Naggar, M. (2013). In lieu of money, Toyota donates efficiency to New York Charity. *The New York Times (Digital)*. https://bicersupplychain.short.gy/omFe6t.

Erlenkotter, D. (1990). Ford Whitman Harris and the economic order quantity model. *Operations Research*, 38(6), 937–946. https://doi.org/10.1287/opre.38.6.937.

Erman, M. (2024). RSV vaccine makers vying for market share in second year of shots. *Reuters (Digital)*. https://bicersupplychain.short.gy/ukRrvv.

Esty, B. C., Mayfield, E. S., & Lane, D. (2016). Supply chain finance at Procter & Gamble. *Harvard Business School Case Study*, Product ID: 216039-PDF-ENG. https://hbsp.harvard.edu/product/216039-PDF-ENG.

Evans, P. (2023). What a blow! Kleenex pulling out of Canadian consumer market. *CBC News (Digital)*. www.cbc.ca/news/business/kleenex-canada-1.6947410.

Evans, P. (2023b). Bank of Canada holds interest rate steady at 5%. *CBC News (Digital)*. www.cbc.ca/news/business/bank-of-canada-rates-sept-6-1.6957903.

FDA (2024). Current good manufacturing practices (CGMPs) for food and dietary supplements. *U.S. Food & Drug Administration Regulation Report*. https://bicersupplychain.short.gy/QFWU78.

Feitzinger, E., & Lee, H. L. (1997). Mass customization at Hewlett Packard: The power of postponement. *Harvard Business Review, January–February Issue*, 116–122. https://bicersupplychain.short.gy/iYAy6m.

Ferreira, K., & Jagabathula, S. (2020). JOANN: Joannalytics inventory allocation tool. *Harvard Business School Case Study*, Product ID: 621055-PDF-ENG. https://hbsp.harvard.edu/product/621055-PDF-ENG.

Financial Post Staff (2020). Food suppliers feeling pinched as grocers hike fees. *Financial Post (Digital)*. https://bicersupplychain.short.gy/9PVs3N.

Fisher, M. L. (1997). What is the right supply chain for your product? *Harvard Business Review, March–April Issue*, 105–117. https://hbr.org/1997/03/what-is-the-right-supply-chain-for-your-product.

Fisher, M., Gaur, V., & Kleinberger, H. (2017). Curing the addiction to growth. *Harvard Business Review, January–February Issue*, 66–74. https://hbr.org/2017/01/curing-the-addiction-to-growth.

Fonrouge, G. (2023). Bed Bath & Beyond files for bankruptcy protection after failed turnaround efforts. *CNBC News (Digital)*. www.cnbc.com/2023/04/23/bed-bath-beyond-files-for-bankruptcy-protection.html.

Ford Motor Company (n.d.). The moving assembly line and the five-dollar workday. *Ford Corporation History*. https://corporate.ford.com/articles/history/moving-assembly-line.html.

Fowlie, M. L. (2009). Incomplete environmental regulation, imperfect competition, and emissions leakage. *American Economic Journal: Economic Policy*, 1(2), 72–112. https://doi.org/10.1257/pol.1.2.72.

Frank, R. (2023). LVMH buys eyewear brand Barton Perreira as it looks to rebound from luxury slowdown. *CNBC News (Digital)*. www.cnbc.com/2023/11/06/lvmh-buys-eyewear-brand-barton-perreira.html.

Friedman, M. (1970, September 13). A Friedman doctrine – the social responsibility of business is to increase profits. *The New York Times*, 32. https://timesmachine.nytimes.com/timesmachine/1970/09/13/issue.html.

Fung, E. (2023). FedEx restructures to combine ground and express delivery networks. *The Wall Street Journal (Digital)*. https://bicersupplychain.short.gy/358qSZ.

Fung, E. (2024). FedEx stocks jumps after company snaps streak of revenue declines. *The Wall Street Journal (Digital)*. https://bicersupplychain.short.gy/4sSdU4.

Gallagher, D. (2024). Mark Zuckerberg's AI vision makes metaverse a slightly easier to sell. *The Wall Street Journal (Digital)*. https://bicersupplychain.short.gy/p9mzmv.

Gartman, D. (n.d.). General Motors style overtakes Ford efficiency. *University of Michigan Case Study, Dearborn and Benson Ford Research Center*. www.autolife.umd.umich.edu/Design/Gartman/D_Casestudy/D_Casestudy3.htm.

Ge, J. (2024, April 19). Value of exclusive doorstep delivery in the last-100-meter distribution. Research Seminar, *Schulich School of Business, York University*. https://colab.ws/articles/10.2139%2Fssrn.4352455.

Gelderman, C. (n.d.). Later years of Henry Ford. *Encyclopedia Britannica*. www.britannica.com/money/Henry-Ford/Later-years.

Geraldo, R. (2022). Starbucks sales beat expectations, but profit dips. *The Seattle Times (Digital)*. https://bicersupplychain.short.gy/JNz9Cp.

Glusac, E. (2024). Standby cruising: A new option for bargain seekers. *The New York Times (Digital)*. www.nytimes.com/2024/04/05/travel/standby-cruising.html.

Goel, G., & Wohl, J. (2013). P&G taking longer to pay suppliers, offers financing. *Reuters (Digital)*. www.reuters.com/article/us-procter-suppliers-idUSBRE93G14Z20130417.

Gomelsky, V. (2023). Soon you may know exactly where your diamond was mined. *The New York Times (Digital)*. www.nytimes.com/2023/11/20/fashion/jewelry-diamond-origin-tracing-de-beers.html.

Goode, L., & Calore, M. (2023). Walmart and Amazon's race to rule shopping. *The Wired Magazine (Digital)*. www.wired.com/story/gadget-lab-podcast-602/.

Goswami, R. (2023). Cisco makes largest ever acquisition, buying cybersecurity company Splunk for $28 billion in cash. *CNBC News (Digital)*. www.cnbc.com/2023/09/21/cisco-acquiring-splunk-for-157-a-share-in-cash.html.

Govindarajan, A., Kohls, S., Liu, L. et al. (2022). Planning for 2023: How US-based businesses can succeed when capital and talent are constrained. *McKinsey Insights*. https://bicersupplychain.short.gy/7edW0R.

Grieder, D. (2023). Letter to shareholders. *Hugo Boss 2023 Annual Report*. https://bicersupplychain.short.gy/bAPsgP.

Griffith, K. (2023). Convoy trucking startup – hailed as "Uber for freight" and backed by Bill Gates and Jeff Bezos – shutters due to "massive freight recession." *Daily Mail (Digital)*. https://bicersupplychain.short.gy/jLMXri.

Grimson, J. A., & Pyke, D. F. (2007). Sales and operations planning: An exploratory study and framework. *The International Journal of Logistics Management*, *18*(3), 322–346. https://doi.org/10.1108/09574090710835093.

Guardian Cairo Staff (2021). Ever Given impounded as Suez Canal Authority pursues salvage costs. *The Guardian (Digital)*. https://bicersupplychain.short.gy/e6YL8D.

Hack, S. (2024). A day in the life of a Walmart fleet driver. *Walmart Canada Company Announcement*. https://bicersupplychain.short.gy/VaC6dK.

Haddon, H., Stefanescu, V., & Lin, L. (2024). What is wrong with Starbucks? *The Wall Street Journal (Digital)*. www.wsj.com/business/hospitality/whats-wrong-with-starbucks-de367a66.

Haden, J. (2020). 64 years ago, Ray Kroc made a decision that completely transformed McDonald's. *Inc. Magazine (Digital)*. https://bicersupplychain.short.gy/hEqQjV.

Haggin, P. (2017). Database provider Redis Labs raises $44 million led by Goldman. *The Wall Street Journal (Digital)*. https://bicersupplychain.short.gy/teXdDZ.

Hancock, B. (2012). Failure is not an option. *Inbound Logistics (Digital)*. https://bicersupplychain.short.gy/0c5EL0.

Harrison, K. (2024). Uber Eats announces exclusive delivery partnership with Domino's in Canada. *Canada Newswire (Digital)*. https://bicersupplychain.short.gy/9s8ORx.

Hausman, W. H., & Thorbeck, J. S. (2010). Fast fashion: Quantifying the benefits. In E. Chang & T. M. Choi (Eds.), *Innovative Quick Response Programs in Logistics and Supply Chain Management* (pp. 315–329). Heidelberg: Springer Nature. https://doi.org/10.1007/978-3-642-04313-0.

Hayashi, Y. (2022). Ukraine War creates worst global food crisis since 2008, IMF says. *The Wall Street Journal (Digital)*. https://bicersupplychain.short.gy/2qth5o.

Helft, M., & Bunkley, N. (2011). Disaster in Japan batters suppliers. *The New York Times (Digital)*. www.nytimes.com/2011/03/15/business/global/15supply.html.

Hernandez, A. (2020). Learning from Adidas' Speedfactory blunder. *Supply Chain Dive (Digital)*. https://bicersupplychain.short.gy/ZLof0f.

Hoffman, A. (2023). Rolex accelerates Swiss production boost to meet rising demand. *Bloomberg News (Digital)*. https://bicersupplychain.short.gy/ELlmLP.

Hoppe, J., & Petroni, G. (2024). Cocoa and coffee prices have surged. Climate change will only take them higher. *The Wall Street Journal (Digital)*. https://bicersupplychain.short.gy/QUpSwS.

Hu, K. (2023). ChatGPT sets record for fastest-growing user base. *Reuters (Digital)*. https://bicersupplychain.short.gy/4v50IH.

Hunter, E., Marchessou, S., & Schmidt, J. (2018). The need for speed: Capturing today's fashion customer. *McKinsey Insights*. https://bicersupplychain.short.gy/4eyGrK.

IISD (n.d.). Overseas investment insurance. *International Institute for Sustainable Development Report*. www.iisd.org/credit-enhancement-instruments/institution/sinosure.

Ikenson, D. (2022). The e-commerce revolution is transforming global trade and benefiting the U.S. economy. *Forbes (Digital)*. https://bicersupplychain.short.gy/0g8re0.

Intel Corporation (n.d.). Global manufacturing facts. *Intel Company Report*. https://bicersupplychain.short.gy/b1rkEZ.

Jack, L., & Frei, R. (2021). Fashion retailer Primark is refusing to sell online – here's why it is right to do so. *The Conversation (Digital)*. https://bicersupplychain.short.gy/BJbAg5.

Jackson, N. (2011). Infographic: How much does each piece of Apple's iPhone cost? *The Atlantic (Digital)*. https://bicersupplychain.short.gy/gZ9Skl.

Jargon, J. (2015). Starbucks teams up with Lyft to boost loyalty program. *The Wall Street Journal (Digital)*. www.wsj.com/articles/DJFVW00120150723eb7nmj0x7.

Jie, Y. (2022). China's Covid lockdown hits supplies to companies like Apple and Tesla. *The Wall Street Journal (Digital)*. https://bicersupplychain.short.gy/CoWG0D.

Jin, H. (2022). Explainer: How Tesla weathered global supply chain issues that knocked rivals. *Reuters (Digital)*. https://bicersupplychain.short.gy/ZdR9wA.

John, D. (2023). Tesla's giga Berlin faces production challenges amidst staff shortages: Report. *Drive Tesla Canada (Digital)*. https://bicersupplychain.short.gy/oS0n3g.

Johnson, L. (2012). Making it in the new industrial revolution. *Financial Times (Digital)*. www.ft.com/content/881de032-ee07-11e1-b0e4-00144feab49a.

Kadakia, P. M. (2020). Inside view: What happened when Jeff Bezos met Rukh Khan, Zoya Akhtar. *Forbes India (Digital)*. https://bicersupplychain.short.gy/aexL8k.

Kadet, A. (2013). Feeding New Yorkers with maximum efficiency. *The Wall Street Journal (Digital)*. www.wsj.com/articles/SB10001424052702303293604579256373952717120.

Kaplan, R. S., & Anderson, S. R. (2004). Time-driven activity-based costing. *Harvard Business Review, November Issue*, 131–150. https://hbr.org/2004/11/time-driven-activity-based-costing.

Kapner, S. (2022). Retailers' inventories pile up as lead times grow. *The Wall Street Journal (Digital)*. https://bicersupplychain.short.gy/DROuin.

Kapner, S. (2023). Retailers clamp down on returns. *The Wall Street Journal (Digital)*. https://bicersupplychain.short.gy/JeP8wA.

Katz, M. L., & Shapiro, C. (1985). Network externalities, competition, and compatibility. *The American Economic Review*, 75(3), 424–440. www.jstor.org/stable/1814809.

Keilman, J. (2023). America is back in the Factory business. *The Wall Street Journal (Digital)*. www.wsj.com/articles/american-manufacturing-factory-jobs-comeback-3ce0c52c.

Kell, J. (2024). A consumer-packaged goods giant is harnessing AI to produce more toothpaste and dog food in less time. *Business Insider (Digital)*. https://bicersupplychain.short.gy/gPrlXK.

Khalaf, R. (2020). Companies should shift from "just in time" to "just in case." *Financial Times (Digital)*. www.ft.com/content/606d1460-83c6-11ea-b555-37a289098206.

Khurana, A. (2020). Freightcom is an official shipping partner for the Walmart Canada Marketplace. *Freightcom Company Announcement*. https://bicersupplychain.short.gy/Ky0AJz.

Kim, E. (2019). FedEx will no longer provide express shipping for Amazon in the US. *CNBC News (Digital)*. www.cnbc.com/2019/06/07/amazon-fedex-end-shipping-contract-in-us.html.

Kim, W. (2023). The surprising reason luxury goods are booming. *Vox (Digital)*. https://bicersupplychain.short.gy/hLzTS9.

Kline, D. (2022). Apple has a $6 billion supply chain problem (that may get worse). *The Street (Digital)*. https://bicersupplychain.short.gy/04gCfQ.

Knaflic, C. N. (2015). *Storytelling with Data: A Data Visualization Guide for Business Professionals*. New Jersey: John Wiley & Sons. https://doi.org/10.1002/9781119055259.

Knight, F. H. (1921). *Risk, Uncertainty and Profit*. Boston: Houghton Mifflin. www.econlib.org/library/Knight/knRUP.html.

Kök, A. G., & Fisher, M. L. (2007). Demand estimation and assortment optimization under substitution: Methodology and application. *Operations Research*, 55(6), 1001–1021. DOI: https://doi.org/10.1287/opre.1070.0409.

Koltrowitz, S. (2017). Grey market has become a necessary evil for luxury watchmakers. *Reuters (Digital)*. https://bicersupplychain.short.gy/XZgWtx.

Lancaster, H. (1999). This kind of black belt can help you score points. *The Wall Street Journal (Digital)*. www.wsj.com/articles/SB936053823614583738.

LaRocco, L. A. (2023). West Coast port labor issues continue as some Los Angeles, Long Beach rail shipments get temporarily paused. *CNBC News (Digital)*. https://bicersupplychain.short.gy/76HZBZ.

LaRocco, L. A. (2023b). Vessel buildup grows at West Coast ports as maritime supply chain begins to break, echoing Covid chaos. *CNBC News (Digital)*. https://bicersupplychain.short.gy/dNyo5N.

Latour, A. (2001). A fire in Albuquerque sparks crisis for European cellphone giants. *The Wall Street Journal (Digital)*. www.wsj.com/articles/SB980720939804883010.

Lavelle, J., & Ruane, B. (2023, July 20). Gartner Survey shows just 27% of chief supply chain officers plan to implement a digital twin of the customer. *Gartner Press Release*. https://bicersupplychain.short.gy/0TxxbC.

Ledbetter, P. (2020). Why do so many lean efforts fail? *Industry Week (Digital)*. https://bicersupplychain.short.gy/2gE8mT.

Lee, H. L., Padmanabhan, V., & Whang, S. (1997). Information distortion in a supply chain: The bullwhip effect. *Management Science*, 43(4), 546–558. https://doi.org/10.1287/mnsc.43.4.546.

Lee, H., & Shao, M. (2009). Cisco Systems, Inc.: Collaborating on new product introduction. *Stanford Graduate School of Business Case Study*, Product ID: GS66-PDF-ENG. https://hbsp.harvard.edu/product/GS66-PDF-ENG.

Lego Group (n.d.). The Lego Group history. *Lego Company Report*. www.lego.com/en-us/aboutus/lego-group/the-lego-group-history.

Lindert, M. (2022). Picnic and Tony's Chocolonely: Innovating the supply chain for commercial success. *Supply Chain Movement (Digital)*. https://bicersupplychain.short.gy/cNGILE.

Loblaw Companies Limited (2023). 2022 fourth quarter results and fiscal year ended December 31, 2022 results. *Loblaw Company Report*. https://bicersupplychain.short.gy/wpP0ji.

Lohr, S. (2011). Stress test for the global supply chain. *The New York Times (Digital)*. www.nytimes.com/2011/03/20/business/20supply.html.

Loten, A. (2021). Global IT spending expected to rise 8.4% to $4.1 trillion this year. *The Wall Street Journal (Digital)*. https://bicersupplychain.short.gy/jLOBmu.

Loten, A. (2022). "Predictive-maintenance" tech is taking off as manufacturers seek more efficiency. *The Wall Street Journal (Digital)*. https://bicersupplychain.short.gy/nzfXTe.

Lozinski, L. (2016). How Ringpop from Uber Engineering helps distribute your application. *Uber Engineering Report*. www.uber.com/en-CA/blog/ringpop-open-source-nodejs-library.

Magretta, J. (1998). Fast, global, and entrepreneurial: Supply chain management, Hong Kong style. *Harvard Business Review*, September Issue, 102–114. https://bicersupplychain.short.gy/LpBPlD.

Mallon, R. (2022). Giant postpones payments to suppliers due to falling demand, rising inventory levels, and market "headwinds." *Road.cc News (Digital)*. https://road.cc/content/news/giant-postpones-payments-suppliers-298285.

Manik, J. A., & Yardley, J. (2013). Building collapse in Bangladesh leaves scores dead. *The New York Times (Digital)*. www.nytimes.com/2013/04/25/world/asia/bangladesh-building-collapse.html.

Manners, D. (2023). Lead times head on down except for power. *Electronics Weekly (Digital)*. www.electronicsweekly.com/news/business/818216-2023-04/.

McAfee, A., McFarlan, F. W., & Berkley-Wagonfeld, A. (2004). Enterprise IT at Cisco. Harvard Business School Case Study, Product ID: 605015-PDF-ENG. https://hbsp.harvard.edu/product/605015-PDF-ENG.

McCann, M. H. (2023). Food Bank of New York City and subsidiary: Consolidated financial statements. *Independent Auditors' Report*. https://bicersupplychain.short.gy/u9ET1M.

McDonald, W. M. (2022). The problem with Maslow's Hammer. *The American Journal of Geriatric Psychiatry*, 30(12), 1324–1326. https://doi.org/10.1016/j.jagp.2022.06.002.

Meijer, B. H. (2023). Philips to cut 13% of jobs in safety and profitability drive. *Reuters (Digital)*. https://bicersupplychain.short.gy/TCfsoD.

Merchant, B. (2017). Life and death in Apple's forbidden city. *The Guardian (Digital)*. https://bicersupplychain.short.gy/c7zxvc.

Miller, R. (2022). BlackBerry phones once ruled the world, then the world changed. *Tech Crunch (Digital)*. https://bicersupplychain.short.gy/oad8PT.

Mitchell, D. (2019). E2Open forecasting and inventory benchmark study finds demand sensing and multi-echelon inventory optimization combinations reduces safety stock by more than 30%. *Business Wire (Digital)*. https://bicersupplychain.short.gy/MAnfW9.

Mocker, M., & Ross, J. W. (2017). The problem with product proliferation. *Harvard Business Review*, May–June Issue, 104–110. https://hbr.org/2017/05/the-problem-with-product-proliferation.

Monroe, R. (2021). Ultra-fast fashion is eating the world. *The Atlantic (Digital)*. https://bicersupplychain.short.gy/Q5Hjhs.

Moses, C. (2023). Why is Switzerland – of all places – importing so much cheese? *The New York Times (Digital)*. www.nytimes.com/2023/07/21/business/swiss-cheese-import-export.html.

Mozur, P. (2017). Galaxy Note 7 fires caused by battery and design flaws, Samsung says. *The New York Times (Digital)*. https://bicersupplychain.short.gy/zmJFkN.

Nassauer, S. (2023, November 22). How Walmart is leveraging automation and AI to deliver faster. *The Wall Street Journal, Video Series* (Shipping Wars). https://bicersupplychain.short.gy/jiP0jK.

National Geographic Society (2011). Mar 11, 2011 CE: Tohoku Earthquake and Tsunami. *National Geographic Education (Digital)*. https://bicersupplychain.short.gy/s0j0CT.

Neil, D. (2000, April 16). A color only a fan could love. *The New York Times, Automobiles*, 1. https://timesmachine.nytimes.com/timesmachine/2000/04/16/787531.html.

Nelson, E., Ewing, J., & Alderman, L. (2021). The swift collapse of a company built on debt. *The New York Times (Digital)*. www.nytimes.com/2021/03/28/business/greensill-capital-collapse.html.

NetJets Inc (2018). The NetJets story: Our journey to the pinnacle. *NetJets Company Report*. www.netjets.com/en-gb/the-netjets-story.

NetJets Inc (2024). NetJets programmes. *NetJets Company Report*. www.netjets.com/en-gb/private-jet-programmes.

Neuman, J. (2022). Bed Bath & Beyond suppliers halt shipments despite new financing. *Bloomberg (Digital)*. https://bicersupplychain.short.gy/ohEBfC.

Nobel, C. (2017). A luxury industry veteran teaches the importance of aesthetics to budding business leaders. *Harvard Business School Working Knowledge*. https://bicersupplychain.short.gy/nGEEmS.

Norem, J. (2023). Intel to drop $14 billion on TSMC 3nm wafers in 2024 and 2025. *Extreme Tech (Digital)*. https://bicersupplychain.short.gy/1SqlJV.

Novet, J. (2023). Amazon says it will cut over 18,000 jobs, more than initially planned. *CNBC News (Digital)*. https://bicersupplychain.short.gy/wdUmhz.

Pallot, R. (2021). ITV News reveals scale of Amazon's waste across UK as footage shows unused returned food thrown away. *ITV News (Digital)*. https://bicersupplychain.short.gy/UsJH9P.

Parkes, D. (2021). 7 of the best Lunar New Year special-edition bottles. *South China Morning Post (Digital)*. https://bicersupplychain.short.gy/dGP8b8.

Parkes, J. (2021b). Joris Laarman's 3D-printed stainless steel bridge finally opens in Amsterdam. *Dezeen Magazine (Digital)*. www.dezeen.com/2021/07/19/mx3d-3d-printed-bridge-stainless-steel-amsterdam.

Pasquini, L., & Reid, H. (2023). Hugo Boss stays strong amid tough China, U.S. markets. *Reuters (Digital)*. https://bicersupplychain.short.gy/9cyRCG.

Paton, E. (2018). H&M, a fashion giant, has a problem: $4.3 billion in unsold clothes. *The New York Times (Digital)*. www.nytimes.com/2018/03/27/business/hm-clothes-stock-sales.html.

Paton, E. (2020). After factory disaster, Bangladesh made big safety strides. Are the bad days coming back? *The New York Times (Digital)*. https://bicersupplychain.short.gy/Ge7OVo.

Paton, E. (2021). LVMH, Richemont and Prada unite behind a blockchain consortium. *The New York Times (Digital)*. https://bicersupplychain.short.gy/jhiOqO.

Patton, L. (2022). Starbucks' $181 million in unused gift cards spurs labor group complaint. *Bloomberg (Digital)*. https://bicersupplychain.short.gy/q8E9M1.

Perez, I. G. (2022). LeBron James invests in Canyon Bikes to help fund US expansion. *Bloomberg (Digital)*. https://bicersupplychain.short.gy/gkXZfA.

Perrigo, B. (2023). The story of one iPhone factory powering Apple's pivot to India. *Time Magazine (Digital)*. https://time.com/6318369/apple-iphone-factory-india/.

Petrova, M. (2018). A look at the complex, global supply chain and dozens of minerals needed to build an iPhone. *CNBC News (Digital)*. https://bicersupplychain.short.gy/owPbGS.

Phillips, E. E., & Morris, B. (2015). Food companies scramble to cut palm oil from supply chains. *The Wall Street Journal (Digital)*. https://bicersupplychain.short.gy/ShsXGG.

Plumer, B. (2023). Climate change is speeding toward catastrophe. The next decade is crucial, U.N. Panel says. *The New York Times (Digital)*. www.nytimes.com/2023/03/20/climate/global-warming-ipcc-earth.html.

Popomaronis, T. (2020). Jeff Bezos: Amazon turned into "the everything store" thanks to an email to 1000 random people. *CNBC News (Digital)*. https://bicersupplychain.short.gy/uspRlR.

Porter, J. (2023). ChatGPT continues to be one of the fastest-growing services ever. *The Verge (Digital)*. www.theverge.com/2023/11/6/23948386/.

Pringle, D. (2002). Samsung, Nokia gain market share in hardest year ever for cellphones. *The Wall Street Journal (Digital)*. www.wsj.com/articles/SB1013467238915375200.

Procter & Gamble Co. (n.d.). Supply chain financing. *Procter & Gamble Company Report*. https://pgsupplier.com/supplychainfinancing.

Purdy, C. (2017). McDonald's isn't just a fast-food chain – it's a brilliant $30 billion real-estate company. *Quartz (Digital)*. https://bicersupplychain.short.gy/aOh2cF.

Qu, T. (2023). Alibaba logistics arm Cainiao rolls out half-day express delivery service in 8 major cities, as firm seeks to help stimulate consumption. *South China Morning Post (Digital)*. https://bicersupplychain.short.gy/6UPmER.

Rahman, S., & Yadlapalli, A. (2013). Years after the Rana Plaza tragedy, Bangladesh's garment workers are still bottom of the pile. *The Conversation (Digital)*. https://bicersupplychain.short.gy/4tdSqj.

Raimondi, M. (2023). SBB Cargo is all back in the hands of the Swiss government. *Rail Freight (Digital)*. https://bicersupplychain.short.gy/9FgOie.

Raman, A., Gaur, V., & Kesavan, S. (2005). David Berman. *Harvard Business School Case Study*, Product ID: 605081-PDF-ENG. https://hbsp.harvard.edu/product/605081-PDF-ENG.

Rana, P., & Haddon, H. (2023). Who should eat the cost of pricier delivery menus? *The Wall Street Journal (Digital)*. https://bicersupplychain.short.gy/M1clqu.

Reiff, N., Rasure, E., & Schmitt, K. R. (2024). 10 biggest restaurant companies. *Investopedia*. https://bicersupplychain.short.gy/BRzXaC.

Reiss, D. (2019). The CEO of Canada Goose on creating a homegrown luxury brand. *Harvard Business Review*, September–October Issue, 37–41. https://bicersupplychain.short.gy/YUa0Gy.

Repko, M. (2022). Target expects squeezed profits from aggressive plan to get rid of unwanted inventory. *CNBC News (Digital)*. www.cnbc.com/2022/06/07/target-markdowns-plan-to-cut-inventory.html.

Richardson, K. (2007). The "Six Sigma" factor for Home Depot. *The Wall Street Journal (Digital)*. URL: www.wsj.com/articles/SB116787666577566679.

Richter, F. (2024). Amazon: Not just an online store. *Statistica*. www.statista.com/chart/15917/amazon-revenue-by-segment.

Ridley, C., & Talukdar, L. (2024). Moderna reports fourth quarter and fiscal year 2023 financial results. *Moderna Inc. Company Report*. https://bicersupplychain.short.gy/or5YAX.

Roberts, S. (2020). Embracing the uncertainties. *The New York Times (Digital)*. https://bicersupplychain.short.gy/aIH2fS.

Roland, D. (2021). Philips recalls millions of CPAP, ventilator machines over potential health risks. *The Wall Street Journal (Digital)*. https://bicersupplychain.short.gy/MlsY2Q.

Rome, D. (2023). Canyon eyes future growth as annual sales top EUR 400 million. *Velo News (Digital)*. https://bicersupplychain.short.gy/8bBZ98.

Rosendaal, F. D., & Wetendorf, B. (1981). Corporate and tax law in the Netherlands: A review of a modern common market law system (Part II). *International Lawyer*, 15(1), 105–129. https://www.jstor.org/stable/40706253.

Rosoff, M. (2012). Former Microsoft Zune boss explains why it flopped. *Business Insider (Digital)*. https://bicersupplychain.short.gy/6b0U7W.

Rossetti, C., & Choi, T. Y. (2005). On the dark side of strategic sourcing: Experiences from the aerospace industry. *Academy of Management Perspectives*, 19(1), 46–60. https://doi.org/10.5465/ame.2005.15841951.

Roy, R., Kubota, Y., & Wen, P. (2023). Top Apple supplier Foxconn plans major India expansion. *The Wall Street Journal (Digital)*. www.wsj.com/articles/top-apple-supplier-plans-major-india-expansion-f2908b88.

RTP Editorial Staff (2016). How many products does Amazon carry? *The Retail Touch Points Network (Digital)*. www.retailtouchpoints.com/resources/how-many-products-does-amazon-carry.

Ryan, C. (2023). Hermes shines in a scruffy luxury market. *The Wall Street Journal (Digital)*. www.wsj.com/business/retail/hermes-shines-in-a-scruffy-luxury-market-e12981bf.

Sarin, N., Summers, L., Zidar, O., & Zwick, E. (2022). Rethinking how we score capital gains tax reform. *Tax Policy and the Economy*, 36(1), 1–33. https://doi.org/10.1086/718949.

Schneider, P. J., & Biçer, I. (2024). Securing payment from a financially distressed buyer. *Schulich School of Business, York University, Working Paper*.

Seifert, R. W. (2002). "Mi Adidas" mass customization initiative. *IMD Case Study*, Product ID: IMD159-PDF-ENG. www.imd.org/case-study/mi-adidas-mass-customization-initiative.

Seifert, R. W., Kayyali-Elalem, Y., & Biçer, I. (2022). Take the circular route to curbing over-production. *I by IMD*. www.imd.org/ibyimd/magazine/take-the-circular-route-to-curbing-over-production.

Seifert, R. W., Tancrez, J. S., & Biçer, I. (2016). Dynamic product portfolio management with life cycle considerations. *International Journal of Production Economics*, 171, 71–83. https://doi.org/10.1016/j.ijpe.2015.10.017.

Shapiro, C., & Varian, H. R. (1999). *Information Rules: A Strategic Guide to the Network Economy*. Boston: Harvard Business School Press. https://hbsp.harvard.edu/product/863X-HBK-ENG.

Shenstone, L., & Hyndman, R. J. (2005). Stochastic models underlying Croston's method for intermittent demand forecasting. *Journal of Forecasting, 24*(6), 389–402. https://doi.org/10.1002/for.963.

Shiller, R. J. (2016). *Irrational Exuberance: Revised and Expanded* (3rd ed.). Princeton: Princeton University Press. https://doi.org/10.1515/9781400865536.

Shin, J., Sudhir, K., & Yoon, D. H. (2012). When to "fire" customers: Customer cost-based pricing. *Management Science, 58*(5), 932–947. https://doi.org/10.1287/mnsc.1110.1453.

Silcoff, S., McNish, J., & Ladurantaye, S. (2013). How BlackBerry blew it: The inside story. *The Globe and Mail (Digital)*. https://bicersupplychain.short.gy/rCBapg.

Slagmulder, R., & Van Wassenhove, L. N. (2004). Hewlett Packard: Performance measurement in the supply chain. *INSEAD Case Study*, Product ID: INS530-PDF-ENG. https://hbsp.harvard.edu/product/INS530-PDF-ENG.

Sloan, A. P. (1964, January 19). In these years the company went into high gear. *The New York Times*, 34. https://timesmachine.nytimes.com/timesmachine/1964/01/19/118651080.html.

Smith, S. (2022). Boohoo revenue drops as inflation challenges continue. *The Industry Fashion (Digital)*. www.theindustry.fashion/boohoo-revenue-drops-as-inflation-challenges-continue.

Sorkin, A. R., & Petersen, M. (2000, January 17). Glaxo and SmithKline agree to form largest drugmaker. *The New York Times*, 1, 10. https://timesmachine.nytimes.com/timesmachine/2000/01/17/388904.html.

Souza, K. (2024). The supply side: Walmart marks 30 years in Canada. *Talk Business & Politics*. https://bicersupplychain.short.gy/Czy71W.

Sozzi, B. (2022). Tesla's new Gigafactory is its biggest strategic endeavor in a decade. *Yahoo News*. https://bicersupplychain.short.gy/eZ1CwP.

Steinberg, J., & Wallace, J. (2020). Insurance freeze snarls U.S. supply chains. *The Wall Street Journal (Digital)*. www.wsj.com/articles/insurance-freeze-snarls-u-s-supply-chains-11600772974.

Sterlink, T. (2024). Intel is taking another of ASML's high NA tools, says CEO. *Reuters (Digital)*. https://bicersupplychain.short.gy/xvUkbn.

Stevens, P. (2021). The ship that blocked the Suez Canal may be free, but experts warn the supply chain impact could last months. *CNBC News (Digital)*. https://bicersupplychain.short.gy/WBfHPR.

Stohr, C., & Westermann, C. (2021, August 4). Hugo Boss presents new growth strategy "Claim 5" aimed at doubling sales to EUR 4 billion by 2025. *Hugo Boss Press Release*. https://bicersupplychain.short.gy/PWevPq.

Storbeck, O. (2023). Roman Arnold: The German entrepreneur who bet big on bikes and won. *Financial Times (Digital)*. www.ft.com/content/4b036dbb-f2f1-4c46-b51b-aa82bfaa587a.

Stroh, K. (2024). Wendy's co-op aims to integrate supply chain network. *Supply Chain Dive (Digital)*. www.supplychaindive.com/news/wendys-AI-integrate-supply-chain-palantir/723842/.

Tabuchi, H., & Wassener, B. (2011). Earthquake and aftermath push Japan into a recession. *The New York Times (Digital)*. www.nytimes.com/2011/05/19/business/global/19yen.html.

Talukder, H. (2024). Trial drags on as all accused except Sohel Rana out on bail. *Views Bangladesh (Digital)*. https://bicersupplychain.short.gy/Lxe73W.

Tarasov, K. (2022). Inside ASML, the wildly successful company that every advanced chipmaker relies on. *CNBC News (Digital)*. https://bicersupplychain.short.gy/Mly9mR.

Timbuk2 Company (n.d.). Frequently asked questions: How long will it take for my order to ship? *Timbuk2*. https://www.timbuk2.com/pages/faqs.

Toh, M. (2021). Nike is scrambling to fix supply chain problems as holiday shopping looms. *CNN News (Digital)*. www.cnn.com/2021/09/24/business/nike-stock-earnings-supply-chains-intl-hnk.

Tomlin, B. (2006). On the value of mitigation and contingency strategies for managing supply chain disruption risks. *Management Science*, 52(5), 639–657. https://doi.org/10.1287/mnsc.1060.0515.

Toneguzzi, M. (2022). Walmart invests further in Canadian operations with opening of state-of-the-art west coast distribution centre. *Retail Insider (Digital)*. https://bicersupplychain.short.gy/JETDJ6.

Uberti, D. (2020). How BMW used pandemic plant stoppages to boost artificial intelligence. *The Wall Street Journal (Digital)*. https://bicersupplychain.short.gy/9nzW8R.

Van Campenhout, C. (2024). Dutch online grocer Picnic raises $388 mln from investors, Gates Foundation. *Reuters (Digital)*. https://bicersupplychain.short.gy/HDvprX.

Varian, H. R. (2007). Kaizen, that continuous improvement strategy, finds its ideal environment. *The New York Times (Digital)*. www.nytimes.com/2007/02/08/business/08scene.html.

Vega, N. (2023). Big Mac prices are up: Here's how much you'll pay for McDonald's signature sandwich state by state. *CNBC News (Digital)*. www.cnbc.com/2023/03/20/mcdonalds-big-mac-prices-state-by-state.html.

Vizard, S. (2019). Adidas: We over-invested in digital advertising. *Marketing Week (Digital)*. www.marketingweek.com/adidas-marketing-effectiveness.

Volkswagen Group (2021). Production and locations. *Volkswagen Newsroom.* www.volkswagen-newsroom.com/en/production-and-locations-3695.

Wainwright, J. (2014, September 9). How to get luxury items for less. *The Wall Street Journal (Online Video).* https://bicersupplychain.short.gy/9IO3nj.

Wallace, J., & Steinberg, J. (2020). Your holiday present's arrival could depend on these fund managers. *The Wall Street Journal (Digital).* https://bicersupplychain.short.gy/fE4uoP.

Walmart Canada (2020). Walmart Canada announces major $3.5 billion investment for growth and customer experience transformation. *Walmart Canada News.* https://bicersupplychain.short.gy/GCSccJ.

Weissman, R. (2018). Nestlé, Starbucks deal will shift the coffee supply chain. *Supply Chain Dive (Digital).* https://bicersupplychain.short.gy/IX9N3u.

Westermann, C. (2022, April 21). Hugo Boss to launch resale platform "Hugo Boss Pre-loved" as part of commitment to circularity. *Hugo Boss Press Release.* https://bicersupplychain.short.gy/S1TNGG.

Westermann, C. (2024, May 22). Hugo Boss launches innovative customer loyalty program and introduces a new world of engagement. *Hugo Boss Press Release.* https://bicersupplychain.short.gy/3I4cFN.

Westermeyer, P. (2020). Dutch unicorn Picnic has designs on revolutionizing grocery shopping. *Online Marketing Rockstars (Digital).* https://bicersupplychain.short.gy/V0rpwx.

Wheeler, A. (2022). Can Hugo Boss actually be cool? *The New York Times (Digital).* www.nytimes.com/2022/01/26/style/hugo-boss-rebrand.html.

Wheelwright, S. C., Bowen, H. K., & Elliott, B. (1992). Process control at Polaroid. Harvard Business School Case Study, Product ID: 693047-PDF-ENG. https://hbsp.harvard.edu/product/693047-PDF-ENG.

Whiting, K. (2023). 3 new and emerging jobs you can get hired for this year. *World Economic Forum Report.* www.weforum.org/stories/2023/03/new-emerging-jobs-work-skills.

Williams-Alvarez, J. (2023). CFOs focus on building resilient supply chains, even as pandemic disruptions fade. *The Wall Street Journal (Digital).* https://bicersupplychain.short.gy/rxUHWs.

Womack, J. P., Jones, D. T., & Roos, D. (2007). *The Machine that Changed the World.* New York: Free Press. https://bicersupplychain.short.gy/tFMsh0.

Wong, J. (2023). Samsung is a case study in how manufacturers leave China. *The Wall Street Journal (Digital).* https://bicersupplychain.short.gy/lxOrq6.

Yardley, J. (2013). Report on deadly factory collapse in Bangladesh finds widespread blame. *The New York Times (Digital)*. https://bicersupplychain.short.gy/FhB4Oq.

Yardley, J. (2013b). The most hated Bangladeshi, toppled from a shady empire. *The New York Times (Digital)*. https://bicersupplychain.short.gy/eXQpIX.

Young, L. (2023). Retailers are turning to AI to get smarter about inventory. *The Wall Street Journal (Digital)*. https://bicersupplychain.short.gy/eaLB8H.

Index

aesthetic intelligence, 121, 135, 145
Airbus, 16, 57
Amazon, 19–20, 24, 60, 91, 218
  fulfillment, 32, 134
  network externalities, 17
  product variety, 82, 134, 135
  risk management, 70–72
annual operating plan, 195
Apple, 10
  competition with Samsung, 17
  fulfillment, 85
  procurement strategy, 13

Bank of Canada, 18–19
Bill of Material (BoM), 200
blockchain, 35, 43, 123, 128–131, 138, 140
Boeing, 16, 57
Brown, Pauline, see aesthetic intelligence
buffering
  capacity, 30, 34, 150
  inventory, 34, 45, 79, 144, 150, 158, 219
business cycle, 24

capacity management, 37–38, 87–90, 97–98
ChatGPT, 175–176
circular operations, 134, 140, see also corporate social responsibility
Cisco Systems, 11, 78–80, 85
consignment inventory, 27, 34
corporate social responsibility, 221–224
  palm oil deforestation, 223
  Rana Plaza disaster, 221–222
cost accounting, 34–35
cost efficiency, 9, 12, 43, 87, 95–96, 99, 158

cross docking, 26
customization, 21, 65, 82–83, 88, see also long tail operations

delayed differentiation, 93–95, 97–98, 99
demand management, 124–128, 140
  demand sensing, 208, 213
  demand shaping, 208, 213
demand uncertainty, see risks and uncertainties
descriptive analytics, 35, 174–177, 212
digital transformation, 55, 131, 138, 219, see also Chapters 8 and 9
  autonomous vehicles, 189
  big data analytics, 189
  data lake, 171–172
  data types, 168–169
  database management systems, 169–170
  digital twins, 138, 190–191, 203, 219
  hybrid databases, see database management systems
  in-memory databases, see database management systems
  on-disk databases, see database management systems
  primary data, see data types
  secondary data, see data types
direct shipping, 27
disintermediation, 16–17, 58, 77

e-commerce, 135, 167, 180, 207–209, see also Amazon
economic perspectives
  Adam Smith, 4–6, 215
  division of labor, 4–6, 44, 142, 215
  factor of production, 7–9, 11–12, 142, 216, 221, 224
  market efficiency, 4–6, 215, 221

Index

Ronald Coase, 4, 7–9, 11
scale economies, 9–10
environmental sustainablity. *See* circular operations

fast fashion retailing, 37, 65, 77–78
FedEx, 17
firing customers, 33–34
Food Bank of New York City, 158–159
Ford Motor Company, 9–10, 13, 44, 53
Friedman, Milton, 222–223

General Motors, 44, 52
Generative AI, 175, 188, *see also* ChatGPT
GlaxoSmithKline, 92, 97–98
Google
  early years, 12
  OR-Tools, 183
  Vision AI, 176

Hal Varian, *see* Google: early years
Hershey Company, 217–218
Hewlett Packard, 14–15, 95
Hugo Boss, 124, 137–140, 141

innovative business development, 40–42, *see also* supply chain finance
interest rates and inflation, 22, *see also* monetary policy
International Motor Vehicle Program, 144
inventory optimization, 201–204, 211, *see also* prescriptive analytics
  base stock model, 202
  economic order quantity (EOQ) model, 203
  newsvendor model, 202
  reorder model, 203
inventory turnover, 41–42, 46, 49, 92, 144, 196, 224
irrational exuberance, 54

Kimberly-Clark, 15
Knight, Frank, 53
Kordsa Inc., 191–193

lead time reduction, 90–92, 96, 97–98, 99
lead times, 60–70, 87

cash conversion cycle, 66–67, 70, 72, 100–102, 103, 105, 119
customer waiting time, 68
days of payables, 66
days of receivables, 66
decision lead time, 65
delivery lead time, 63
demand lead time, 65, 68
operating cycle, 66
operating lead time, 64, 70
procurement lead time, 61–63
production lead time, 63
resource acquisition time, 68
resource idle time, 68
resource utilization time, 70
supply lead time, 61–63
lean manufacturing, 43–45, *see also* Chapter 7
  aggressive selling, 45, 153–155, 160
  categories of waste, 145–147
  Heijunka, 149–150, 160
  just in time, 44, 143–144, 152–153, 160
  Kaizen, 148–149, 160
  Kanban, *see* just in time
  Six Sigma, 150–151, 160
  statistical process control, 156, 160
  value stream mapping, 160–161
long tail operations, 134–137, 141
luxury operations management, *see* premium business

market analysis, 19–21, *see also* economic perspectives: market efficiency
McDonald's, 104–105, 112
  franchising, 29, 101
  logistics outsourcing, 27
modularization, 93–95
monetary policy, 17–19

network externalities, 15–17

omnichannel retailing, 27, 47–48
ontological uncertainty, 55
operational complexity, 40, 81–87
operational due diligence, 165–167

Philips, 23, 24
  plant fire, 51

Philips (cont.)
  product recall, 53
  product variety, 83–84
Picnic Online Supermarket, 218–219
predictive analytics, 35, 177–181, 198–200, 212
premium business, 42–43, 49, *see also* Chapter 6
prescriptive analytics, 35, 181–188, 212
  deterministic optimization, 183–184
  dynamic optimization, 186–187
  objective function, 183
  set of constraints, 183
  set of variables, 182
  stochastic optimization, 184–186
price uncertainty, *see* risk and uncertainties
process innovation, 23
product innovation, 23
product variety, 81–85, 93–95

reverse factoring, 41
risk and uncertainties
  price uncertainty, 22, 54, 217, *see also* monetary policy
  demand uncertainty, 53, 54, 65, 123, 124–128, 142, 143, 177–181, 184–188, 191–192, 201, 202, 217, 226, *see also* supply chain trade-offs: excess inventory vs. product shortages, *and* supply chain integration
  epistemological uncertainty, 55, 56–59, 60, 72
  ontological uncertainty, 59–60, 71, 73
  operational risk, 54, 55–56, 60, 72
  quality problems, 52–53
  supply disruptions, 51, 61

sales and operations execution, 195, 197–210
  demand forecasting, 198–200
  demand fulfillment, 207–210
  inventory management, 201–204
  order management, 207
  supply management, 200–201
sales and operations planning, 194, 195–197
  demand planning, 197

profit & loss (P&L) statements, 197
supply planning, 197
Samsung, 3, *see also* Apple: competition with Samsung
setup times, 39, 64
Seven Eleven Japan, 48–50
Slimstock, 198, 212
Starbucks, 31, 118
  collaboration with Nestle, 20
supply chain finance, 40–42, *see also* Chapter 5
  dynamic discounting, 41, 115, 118, 119
  inventory financing, 106–110, 113, 119
  inventory securitization, 107
  letter of credit, 113, 119
  reverse factoring, 119
supply chain integration, 22, 36–40, 217–219, *see also* Chapter 4
supply chain investments, 13–15, 224–227
  capacity expansion, *see* network externalities
  capital markets, 224
  Convoy failure, 225–226
  offshore vs. domestic production, 22, 37, 61–63, 77, 91, 95, 102–103, 121, 134
supply chain networks, 3–4, 9, 10, 13, 22, 37, 77, 78, 85–87, 94, 98, 147
supply chain trade-offs, 27–32, *see also* Chapter 2
  amortization vs. inventory costs, 29–30, 46, 145, 220
  excess inventory vs. product shortages, 30–31, 47, 160, 202, 214
  in-house production vs. outsourcing, 27–29, 46, 80
  revenue growth vs. mismatch costs, 31–32, 47, 124
  utilization vs. lead times, 30, 37–38, 46, 68, 145
supply chain transparency, 43, 128–131, 140, 161, 194, 222, 223
Switzerland, 21–23

tax policy, 219–221
  capital gains tax, 220

Index

goods and services tax, 220
value added tax, 220
Tesla
  capacity management, 88
  capital expenditure, 13
  innovative business development, 100
Toyota Production System, *see* lean manufacturing

Uber, 7–8, 68–70
  capacity management, 37
  comparison with Convoy, 225
  network externalities, 16
unsupervised learning, 174–177

k-means clustering, 174–175
principal component analysis, 175–176
prompt engineering, 176

vendor put insurance, 41, 111, 119
vendor-managed inventory, 27

Walmart Inc., 29, 40, 82
  Canada operations, 45–48, 86
  comparison with Primark, 87
  comparison with Seven Eleven Japan, 48–50
  predictive analytics, 178
Womack, James, 144

For EU product safety concerns, contact us at Calle de José Abascal, 56–1°, 28003 Madrid, Spain or eugpsr@cambridge.org.

www.ingramcontent.com/pod-product-compliance
Ingram Content Group UK Ltd.
Pitfield, Milton Keynes, MK11 3LW, UK
UKHW020854071025
463690UK00022B/1024